5000
YEARS
OF
POPULAR
CULTURE

5000
YEARS
OF
POPULAR
CULTURE

POPULAR
CULTURE
BEFORE
PRINTING

*Edited
by
Fred
E.H.
Schroeder*

Bowling Green University Popular Press
Bowling Green, Ohio
1980

LC No.: 79-92474
ISBN.: 0-87972-147-2 Cloth
        0-87972-148-0 Paper

Acknowledgements

Essays by Fred E.H. Schroeder, Darrel W. Amundsen, Gerald Erickson,
Steve Overhelman, Pierre Boglioni, Klaus P. Jankofsky, Joseph J.
Hayes, Frederick O. Waage, and John Frye were originally published in
Journal of Popular Culture, Volume XI:3, Winter 1977. Reprinted with
the permission of the authors and the editor.

To my father, Alfred W. Shroeder,
at whose table all the world's history was popular entertainment

CONTENTS

Foreword

This collection of articles has been developed to fulfill four purposes. First, it was conceived as a method of broadening the study of popular culture which is too often regarded in the academic world as restricted to the mass culture of twentieth century America. Second, it gives recognition to the fact that a number of disciplines have been investigating popular phenomena on different fronts, and it is designed to bring examples of these studies together under the common rubric of "popular culture." Related to this is a third purpose of providing instances of original and innovative interdisciplinary approaches. Finally, the collection should be a worthwhile contribution to the body of knowledge not only in popular culture but in the component disciplines represented.

The history of this collection began with the 1976 Chicago Conference of the Popular Culture Association where the editor organized several sectional meetings on "Popular Culture Before 1776" in which a dozen papers were presented. Seven of these papers, plus additional articles by Darrel Amundsen and the editor were gathered together in the Winter 1977 *Journal of Popular Culture* (XI:3) as an "In-Depth" special section on "Popular Culture Before Printing." At the same time, the editors of the Popular Press of Bowling Green University proposed an enlarged book edition of which this volume is the result. Eight new articles have been added and all the articles which appeared in the *Journal of Popular Culture* have undergone revisions.

In the original version of the introductory essay, Fred Schroeder stated that "With more space and time, I would have sought additional representative studies that employed archaeological methods, and I would have included studies outside the European tradition." This goal has been well satisfied. Archaeologists are represented by Denise Schmandt-Besserat, Ronald Marchese and David Gerald Orr, while Wilson Strand's examination of Assyrian humor and Doran Ross' article on the Fante Asafo of Africa go well beyond Europe and the classical world. The theme of the city which was an undercurrent in the earlier collection is more thoroughly grounded in Marchese's article, and the theme of the "religious life of the people" which Pierre Boglioni so clearly introduced is further explored in the articles by Oberhelman, Orr, Benko and Klassen.

1

The general literary approach of the first collection is balanced by the two art historians, Ross and Schmandt-Besserat, and Tim Lally's speculative essay on synchronism and diachronism adds an extra dimension to literary studies. A few words of explanation about the title and the subtitle of this collection may be in order. The title, *500 Years of Popular Culture,* should be regarded as emblematic rather than as limiting; it is intended to signal the time scope of the popular culture phenomenon which has most commonly been associated solely with recent history. The subtitle, *Popular Culture Before Printing,* is somewhat more definitive, reflecting the view that the introduction of mass-distributed printing into a society marks a watershed in social and cultural history. There is considerable validity to this view, yet, as this collection unfolds, the arbitrariness of the designation "before printing" will become apparent. There are cultures today in which the direct effects of print are still remote from the people in general, although the metropolitan cultures of the past possessed means of mass replication and dissemination of non-literary materials that are analogous to print. Furthermore, print is irrelevant to many aspects of popular culture today as in the past: circuses, religious rituals, politcal and military pageantry and news-broadcasting have never been wholly dependent upon either literacy or print. Nevertheless, the use of printing as a divider has seemed to many of us a handy tool, affording a sliding scale for different cultures that is less arbitrary than chronologies, geographic borders, ideologies or formal structures of society or expression. It is arbitrary, in other words, but it is an arbitration that points up the relationship between technology and culture, which is an undercurrent theme throughout this book.

Acknowledgements of advice and assistance are noted in the individual articles, but the editor wishes to thank Ronald Marchese and Robin Poynor for their assistance in locating some new contributors. Ray and Pat Browne of the Popular Press of Bowling Green University have been infinitely encouraging and helpful at every stage in the development of this book.

I
Introduction:
The Discovery of Popular Culture Before Printing

This introductory essay argues for a long history of popular culture in opposition to the more usual conception of popular culture as a product ofd the nineteenth and twentieth centuries. Fred E. H. Schroeder relates the popular culture study movement to interdisciplinary scholarship and takes note of several specialized fields that are particularly sympathetic to non-elite subject matter. Maintaining that historical perspective is not only useful to students and scholars, Schroeder provides a broad definition that helps one to recognize early popular culture and to identify points of intersection where study will be most fruitful.

Fred E.H. Schroeder teaches humanities at the University of Minnesota, Duluth. He is past-president of the Midwest Popular Culture Association, Vice-President of the Popular Culture Association, and has been a contributor to the Journal of Popular Culture, *to* Icons of Popular Culture *and to* Popular Culture and Curricula. *His book on popular arts,* Outlaw Aesthetics, *was a recent publication of the Bowling Green University Popular Press, and he is currently editing a collection of articles on twentieth-century popular culture in museums and libraries.*

The Discovery of
Popular Culture Before Printing

Fred E.H. Schroeder

My discovery of early popular culture occurred at the Chicago Museum of Natural History. Like many students of popular culture, I had come into this field of study by way of twentieth-century American mass-distributed media entertainment, and I was tantalized by the problem of how far back into history one could extend the mass production of cultural artifacts, which at the time I believed to be the essential distinguishing characteristic of what we might rightly call popular culture. And, like many visitors to the Field Museum, I had come into the basement gallery to look at the remote and the exotic culture of ancient history, archaeology and Egyptology. What I discovered, though, was a clay mold from which small ushabti figurines were mass-produced for funerals and for popular religious worship. On the same visit, I later observed similar molds from Tibet, and it became clear to me that I had found a technological connecting link to Sony radios, Coke bottles, penny-dreadfuls, the Bay Psalm Book and the Gutenberg Bible. I had discovered ancient popular culture.

More importantly, my discovery freed me. In the pages that follow, I invite the reader to share in the freedom that comes with the discovery of early popular culture. This discovery is of two kinds. First is the uncovering of the past for those who have presumed that popular culture is a modern phenomenon. As with all discoverings of the past this is an act that provides useful perspectives. To the student or scholar, such perspectives are useful because they open new channels of precedence, influence and evolution that always serve to illuminate contemporary phenomena; but the usefulness of long perspectives is not limited to academic persons. There is equally important value for many other people in the world today.

We now live in a world that is dominated by a doomsday psychology fostered by unending lamentation about the uniqueness of the modern situation. "Complexity of modern life," "technological revolution," "alienation," "impersonal forces," "deteriorating morals," "slipping standards," and the "mass mind"

4

are all viewed in popular journalism and discourse as unprecedented phenomena with which we are unable to cope. Even those who respect the past and appreciate the perspective that its study affords us must find the traditional "high culture anthology" of history, literature and the arts somewhat remote and inapplicable to a world society whose elite leisure class has declined in numbers and in purity, and whose leaders no longer retain exclusive access to knowledge. That traditional cultural "anthology" is made up of the works and lives of men and women of power, prestige, genius and sophisticated expression, but we now recognize that the perspective of the past must also draw attention to the people, to the popular mind, and to the resiliency and adaptability of the mass of human beings in times of change, crisis, confusion and despair. There are no specific lessons of history; this we all know. On the other hand, there are probably no unique situations in the modern world, at least none for which there is not a precedent, parallel or analog from the past, and this includes popular culture.

The second kind of discovery is similar in that it is of value both to academics and to the wider public. This is the discovery of a common concern among specialists from different disciplines. Popular culture studies are not new by any means, but ordinarily students of popular cuture have pursued their investigations within the borders of their home disciplines, with little opportunity for exchange among students from other disciplines. This is true not only for the traditional "single" disciplines, such as English, history and sociology, but also for the established interdisciplines, such as classics, medieval studies, comparative literature and archeology. The collection of articles that follows provides a setting in which we can observe recent studies from a variety of disciplines, encompassing a wide range of periods of history, all held together by one common thread, that of popular culture. The result of this should at least be the multiplication of perspectives, but it is not unlikely that some valuable cross-fertilization might occur as well. The general application of this discovery of a common concern among several disciplines is once more related to issues of the contemporary world. We are told that we are now in the midst of a "knowledge explosion." It is not the first in history, certainly: fifteenth-century Europe and nineteenth-century Japan are but two historical parallels. We are also said to be in the midst of an "age of specialization." Together, the knowledge explosion and extreme specialization combine to produce among intellectuals a posture of hopelessness at our ever being able to communicate again, and even more, they have resulted in the habit of surrendering decision-making to an oligarchy of specialists. Paradoxically, this surrender is occurring at a time when literacy and education have become almost universal, when the technology of communication spans all parts of the world, and when the acceptance of common symbols among all humans verges on that achieved in the Roman empire and in medieval Christian Europe. In short, when one might hope that world-wide the human access to knowledge could be approaching a zenith, it appears to be declining toward its nadir. It is not merely a matter of C.P. Snow's "two cultures"; even among humanists there is far too little meeting of minds. Classicists do not look into medievalists' research; neither inquires into American studies; it is all one big round-robin of non-communication.

Mine is not a plea that we abandon our specialties. Nor am I denying the existence of many syntheses. I am simply asking that we search for means of communicating with one another about common concerns that bridge different areas of study. And it is my faith that wherever we find a common research concern, it is quite likely that we will also find a common human concern. The relevance of our studies is to be found in the connections, not in the specialties.

Thus, although the articles that follow this essay are specialized studies, they also suggest points of connection with contemporary popular culture and with continuing humanistic concerns. In addition, they represent a variety of methods of examining popular culture before the development or introduction of modern mass media. It is interesting to observe the various ways in which specialists from different disciplines have been drawn into popular cultural study. For example, although it is probably still the dream of every archaeologist to find a cache of those prized relics of the past that we name masterworks, there are two forces that hold archaeology close to popular culture. The first is the anthropologist's scientific method which has replaced the grave-robber selectivity of earlier centuries. The second force is practical: there is more popular residue available than masterworks. Specialist-scholars who work in nations that are influenced by marxist thought, as Pierre Boglioni indicates in his article in this collection, have for ideological reasons replaced the traditionally elitist, establishment and art history topics with inquiries into the popular mind and mass movements. But as in the case of archaeology, some fields of study are edging toward popular culture without marxist influences. History of medicine, for example, has recently shown a shift in emphasis from "great leaders" toward questions of behavioral science, including normal health care and provincial practices. Several articles by classicists included here reflect similar interests. History of technology is another field of material culture that is inherently related to popular culture, and Denise Schmandt-Besserat's article might well be read in that light. The upsurge of concern about urban history in recent decades has opened new avenues of study about the popular mind in early cities, as we see in Ronald Marchese's contribution to this collection. In the study of literature, various influences including such disparate things as Jungian archetypes and minority studies have increased the attention paid to the audience for literature. A concomitant influence in literature as in other fields has been that of the well running dry for original scholarship on major figures and established art works. There is no doubt about it: the study of popular culture is a significant movement in many, many academic disciplines.

At this point, one may begin to ask whether there are any limits to popular culture: Did my "discovery" in the Field Museum not only set me free, but make me run berserk? What sort of definition of popular culture could admit such a gamut of disciplines, arts and histories?

Definitions of popular culture abound, and to those who have arrived at a satisfactory working definition, the subject is wearisome. Certainly there is common-sense agreement among active students of popular culture that they know what they are talking about. Or more likely, they know what they are *not* talking about, which is the elite, cultivated tradition of arts, thought, discourse and life styles. Underlying the cultivated tradition, I would venture, is leisure, but it is leisure that is tied to a class system. What comes first, we may never know, but when wealth falls to a leisure class, there is time to select the best, to explore refinements of thought, expression, action and object. Leisure, refinement, contemplation, cultivation, patronage: all are intertwined into that which we all polished; civilized; urbane.

At the other end of the cultural spectrum is the folk tradition, and this also is what is *not* meant by popular culture, regardless of how much folk culture is a culture of the people. The folk tradition is a local phenomenon, and in its purest form, it is mainly governed by personal, one-to-one relationships. Parents, grandparents, wise ones of the tribe are the transmitters of the culture; learning is effected by means of direct demonstrations by immediate persons. Contact with other cultures is restricted or almost non-existent. Authority is not remote, and, except for supernatural forces, it is visibly embodied in real persons. Above all, pure folk cultures are illiterate.

In simple terms, then, we know that we will not find popular culture among the isolated mountain tribes of New Guinea, nor are we to look for it in the court of Renaissance Urbino, where Castiglione set standards for conscious, literate, cosmopolitan civilization. Aside from the extremes, however, clear definitions are impossible, and the cultures of both extremes feed into the popular tradition, and we are left with a network of nagging questions. Is popular culture a reflection of the palace culture? Or is popular culture a development of folk cultures as they are increasingly influenced by outside cultures? Or is popular culture a third entity, an independent outgrowth of economic, political and technological factors?

The truth, I think, lies in the combination of all three, but I tend to believe the last named factors are most important. In other words, I have not abandoned my original belief that mass production, mass distribution and mass communication are the primary distinguishing features of popular culture. Indeed, if we focus on this definition, a surprising similarity between the elite and folk traditions is brought to light. They are both characterized by immediate personal relationships. Among the elite, the artists, the tastemakers, the leaders and thinkers are known directly rather than by media and middlemen. The courtiers in Urbino did not look at copies of Raphael's paintings; they walked up and talked with Raphael. The "Beautiful People" and "jet setters" did not read of Jacqueline Bouvier Kennedy Onassis and of Henry Kissinger in *Newsweek;* they travelled and partied with them. The *salons* of Gertrude Stein and Madame du Pompadour, the coffee houses of Dr. Johnson, David Garrick and Sir Joshua Reynolds, the intriguing palaces of Elizabeth I, Haroun-al-Raschid, Montezuma and the Ptolemies, the discussion clubs associated with Confucius, Petronius and Socrates are not second-hand cultures. They are immediate and personal, just as immediate and personal as cultures of the campfire and the kiva. Lest I be misunderstood, let me reiterate the immense differences. The elite cultures are literate, rich and above all, cosmopolitan. The folk cultures are illiterate, merely subsistent and local. But neither receives the bulk of its culture second-hand.

Popular culture emerges along with taxes, most of all. Taxation implies a political structure, an economic system and an ideology that transcends the natural units of family, tribe and clan. It also implies extended lines of communication (and with them, non-local authority, maintenance and policing). And it implies the metropolis. This does not mean that popular culture is itself an urban culture. The farmer in the wheatfields of Saskatchewan who reads the

Sunday paper, the cotter of medieval Northumbria who attends his parish church, the carpenter of Nazareth who returns to his birthplace for the imperial census are all participating in popular culture; not to the same degree as a Toronto teenybopper, a Canterbury pilgrim or a Roman bathhouse entertainer, surely, but it is popular culture just the same. Nonetheless, it does seem inconceivable to have popular culture emerging directly from a rural economy. The dependence of rural life styles on the natural cycles builds in a resistance to the arbitrary and necessary imposition of consistent schedules from the metropolis. The word *metropolis*, we should note, means "mother city." The metropolis does not necessarily require large size to produce its spawn or to exercise its influence over its subject hinterlands and colonies. It requires means of imposing consistency. Three means have already been mentioned: taxation, efficient communication and some sort of mass production technology. But what lies behind the concept of metropolis and its need for imposing consistency upon subjects and offspring? The answer is to be found in conquest and in public works. Frequently these are coexistent and large public works projects follow military conquest, as in the cases of the Hellenistic and Roman worlds. Sometimes conquest appears to operate without major public works projects, as in the Spanish conquests of Mexico and Peru. But even there where we tend to see only the destruction of cities, temples, highways, canals and records by the Spanish, there is a phoenix-like raising of missions, forts, docks and mines. In other places, it is reasonable to suppose that public works extended the influence of the metropolis without what we ordinarily regard as conquest. Irrigation and drainage projects in particular are peaceful means of extending the culture into previously uninhabited regions, but even mercantilistic colonial enterprises are not always warlike. Mesopotamia and Egypt provide examples of the former, Greece and Phoenecia suggest examples of the latter. The significance of these factors in the development of popular culture may yet seem remote, especially as we look forward to the articles in this collection. But if we recognize that the factors of conquest and public works projects produce masses of people who are beyond immediate authority, and that they also produce economic structures that cannot tolerate non-conformist individual actions, it should be clear that conquest and public works projects must produce mediate or surrogate authority, and machinery to guarantee conformity in behavior. For these reasons, it would be quite shortsighted and provincial for us to regard the popular culture phenomenon as a modern invention.

Nevertheless, there are decided differences between modern and older popular culture. The invention of movable type printing in 1450 (and the development of cheap papers) spurred the protestant reformation, and along with it, popular literacy. The span of time between Gutenburg and a genuinely modern popular literature varies from place to place but it would be safest to think in terms of one or two centuries. Luther's popular influence begins a good seventy-five years after Gutenburg, and the Italian inventions of italic type, pocket editions and printing of music are parallel in time with the Reformation. Popular, mass-produced *visual* arts, however, are Northern European occurrences that antedate the printing of books, primarily in the forms of playing cards and religious souvenirs.

Religion is the common ground, or the pivot between popular culture before and after printing. Religious cultural materials and practices were mass-produced or mass-disseminated at an early time in history, because of the desirability of consistent value and conforming behavior among constituent, colonial or subservient peoples. Hence my discoveries of mass-production molds for religious artifacts in ancient Egypt. Following the Gutenburg revolution, however, the almost exclusive religious, political, economic and military dimensions of popular culture have given room to entertainment popular culture. This is worth emphasizing, because it will help to focus the articles in this collection. If you mention "popular culture" to a typical person today, the immediate associations are with mass entertainment: comic books, television comedies, movie westerns, paperback mysteries, junk foods and the like. In large part, this is due to the popular definition of *culture,* which does not include such anthropologically significant elements as banks, supermarkets, schools, churches and the army. But even more sophisticated academics will forget their anthropological and sociological training when confronted with the term "popular culture," and make the narrower, and therefore easier, association with entertainment. The reason, I suspect, is to be found in the new preponderance of secular, recreational mass production. New, that is, in preponderance, for the increase has accelerated exponentially world-wide, and it becomes an insoluble puzzle to many persons when they are asked what the populace did for entertainment before television, movies, radio, vaudeville and newspapers. The answers are partly given by folk studies: even today we continue to have self-generated traditional uses of leisure time, such as are provided in street games, traditional rhymes and melodies. But folk studies have not addressed mass entertainments, institutionalized activities, or written popularizations of either elite or folk cultures. Ordinarily, non-folk cultural historians have concerned themselves with the other end of the spectrum, singling out the masterpiece for study. Thus, although we know a good deal about the audiences of Elizabethan England, it is primarily because of interest in Shakespeare rather than in the mass audience and their popular entertainments. Most of the articles in this collection are directed toward that vast middle-ground of entertainment between the folk and the masterpiece.

Such remarks about approaches to scholarship and study in early popular culture are called for, not only for persons who would like to consider investigating this immense untilled field, but for all readers who wish to know how to approach this highly eclectic selection of specific studies. As I mentioned earlier, all cultural syntheses (and antitheses, for that matter) ultimately must rest upon specific studies. The broad generalizations of this introductory essay are themselves informed speculations that should invite more rigorous testing in specific studies. The field of investigation is wide open, despite the fact that various specialties have shown interest in aspects of popular culture. These, as was pointed out earlier, are relatively new interests, and there has been far too little cross-referencing under the interdisciplinary and intercultural heading of popular culture, and too little "practical" application by means of comparison with twentieth-century mass culture.

The extended definition of popular culture that I have proposed, and the examples of early popular culture here and in articles following will suggest the scope and the longevity of popular culture. The places in which to look for stimulating topics for investigation are at the points of intersection. One of the most frequent points of intersection is that at which the traditional, non-metropolitan culture is asked to assume the dominant metropolitan culture. Here there is always stress, resistance and subversion, as well as displacement, reinterpretation and amalgamation. One of the best-documented of these intersections relates to the superimposition of Christian culture upon pagan folk cultures. The resultant festival practices, for example, are no longer pagan, but neither are they consistent with elite theological principles. A related point of intersection is linguistic. From Gaul before Caesar, to Imperial Gaul, to France is a transition of less than ten centuries in which the entire populace changed its grammar and vocabulary twice. When, how, over what time-span were these changes effected? How did linguistic art-forms change? A similar linguistic intersection occurred in Mesoamerica; many others in the Near East and North Africa. Another point of intersection is where literature touches (and often fixes) oral traditions. Two of our articles inquire into that intersection. Klaus Jankofsky's study of the thirteenth-century *South English Legendary* is in part a look into a literary document that was read aloud to illiterate and semiliterate persons, and Frederick Waage's study of seventeenth-century broadside ballads suggests similar uses, in spite of the ballads' being printed.

One of the most significant points of intersection for popular culture is that at which manufactory technology meets the creative process. I mean these terms in their broadest senses. For some persons, this will necessitate a certain readjustment of definitions, because for the past two centuries, manufactory technology has come to refer to automated machine production powered by remote energy sources, while creative process has come to be associated with romantic, intuitive, mystically inspired artistic expression. In broader understanding, however, the former term refers to how things are made, while the latter refers to how things are conceived mentally, along with strategies for converting the conception into objective reality. Bearing in mind these broader definitions, then, we should accustom ourselves to looking for the existence of molds, patterns and formulas.

Molds are the most obvious and least ambiguous of mass-production techniques. They are indicators of the alienation of creator from the product, and producer from consumer, and they are indicators of a metropolitan (i.e. "mother-city") value system. There are ambiguities in molds, though. The lost-wax process of sculpture, for example, is an ancient mold process, but hardly suitable for extensive mass-production. Signature seals and stamps, such as those with which Mesopotamian merchants and bureaucrats signed clay tablets are, of course, individual. These instances are not exceptions to the general statement that molds are indicators of popular culture; rather, they are cautions to be precise in our understanding of the functions of molds in the cultural setting.

Patterns and formulas extend the scope of popular culture beyond material artifacts, but they also increase the ambiguities and the necessity of precision in our studies. As any folklorist would know, the creative process in a non-literate, local culture is in large part a manipulation of memorized formulas. This is true not only for the refrains and phrases in ballads, but for the conventions of the oral traditions that underlie the great literary epics such as *Beowulf* and *The Iliad*. The decorative arts of folk cultures are also the products of patterns; one thinks immediately of pottery and cloth designs. These patterns, however, are usually executed freehand, and thus, although the folk artist may lack originality, or even "creativity," his product is not a mass-duplication to the same degree as it would have been had he used a template or a pattern-book, or had he learned his song from a broadside sheet. Pattern-books and broadsides, of course, connote printing and literacy. But the very existence of any written patterns and formulas are indicators of popular, rather than folk, culture. One thinks, for example, of the vast number of ancient Egyptian memorials (e.g. *The Book of the Dead*) in which the only individuation is in the fill-in-the-blank spaces for such things as the names of the dead person, donors or places. Or one might think of the grid-pattern papyri according to which parts of Egyptian stone and wood sculpture might be carved by different artisans at different locations. Similarly, from classical Rome, we have Vitruvius' *Ten Books on Architecture,* which, it is true, were addressed to the imperial court, but which are certainly based on Greek and Roman technical manuals and patterns. Written patterns and formulas, in other words, do not require mass distribution or universal literacy to become instruments of popular culture and consistent metropolitan styles.

There are also agents of intersection in popular culture who are neither elite trendsetters nor immobile agricultural folk. These range from counter-cultural lower classes such as are described in Joseph J. Hayes' article on Gothic Paris and in John Frye's article on colonial Massachusetts, to other highly mobile agents such as freemasons, merchants, students and soldiers. None of these is tied to the natural cycles, and all the latter are communicants with the elite culture. The powerful effect of military conscription on individuals toward indoctrinating popular, mass life styles must have been as great in the days of Alexander, Cyrus and Caesar, as it was in World War II America, when poor blacks, whites and Indians became like the great middle-class in literacy and aspirations. The point of intersection for all these is the city, about which we know very little, at least concerning the life styles of the populace. Written documentary evidence is slight, because there are very few commentators who looked among them. Beyond Aristophanes, Apuleius, Juvenal, Chaucer and Sebastian Brant, we nonspecialists are hard pressed to discover perceptive, comprehensive observers of the urban animal until eighteenth-century comedy and nineteenth-century novels, and, except for Jacques Callot and William Hogarth, the visual illustrations of people in urban settings are rarer still. We might also note how heavy our reliance is on satirists, whose perception should always be slightly suspect. Urban popular culture has always been unpopular among the elite, and their distorted views are compounded if the elite observations are made by religious reformers. From the prophets of the Old Testament, through the apostles, church fathers like Jerome and Augustine, and the many medieval polemicists, the city of man is a harlot and a fleshpot of temptation.

As a last recommendation of points of intersection to which we can look for significant studies in popular culture before printing, I suggest the two great levellers, death and taxes. The one implies religion, but death's secular dimensions are examined by both Jankofsky and Hayes. Death also implies illness, trauma and medicine, and the articles by Darrel Amundsen, Gerald Erickson and Steve Oberhelman are all concerned with health care. Taxes and money also imply government and the judicial system, and John Frye thereby discovered an otherwise voiceless subculture in court records of New England.

The territory for further and highly original research lies open and inviting, and yet it can hardly but be intimidating. In this small collection alone, we have reference to previously untranslated works in Sumerian, in classical and medieval Latin, in Byzantine Greek, in Middle English and Old French. Clearly, all of us must lean heavily on the experts, and cultivate alliances with specialists in many fields. Certainly one of the most important requisites of interdisciplinary studies is to develop the ability to make a hard-headed estimation of how much knowledge is needed to solve a particular problem, or to place it into a larger perspective, but oftentimes this can be satisfied by consulting references, bibliographies and secondary works outside our own disciplines. Other times, we will see that another lifetime is called for to acquire the appropriate tools for authoritative study. But as a modest proposal, I urge that this collection be used as a caution against cultural provincialism, timid scholarship and what we might call twentieth-centrism. The problems that we face today in our world of potentially volatile mass culture are too important to approach without the tempering perspectives of history. In discovering the popular culture of the remote past, we may come closer to discovering ourselves.

Bibliographical Note

The only collections similar to this are Norman F. Cantor and Michael S. Wertham's *The History of Popular Culture to 1815* (New York: Macmillan, 1968), which is primarily drawn from selected chapters of standard historical works, and Stanley Chodorow and Peter N. Stearns' *The Other Side of Western Civilization* (New York: Harcourt, Brace, Jovanovich, 1975). Many of these overlap with topics in our collection and these anthologies are highly recommended. Both have fine bibliographies. Aside from these collections, studies in popular culture before printing are scattered among general social, cultural and technological histories, monographs on specific historical periods, and articles that do not have any common place for indexing, or even any common terminology for index words.

For current articles on early popular culture, a good starting point is the *Humanities Index* (superseding the *Social Sciences and Humanities Index)* which indexes periodical literature in major journals of history, religion, literature, archaeology and allied areas, including the *Journal of Popular Culture.* These are largely English-language sources from the United States; the *British Humanities Index* will extend these references. Two immensely detailed international bibliographies of scholarly studies will give access to almost any current studies in classics, medieval studies and folklore. These are *L'Anee Philologique,* which includes anything relating to Greek, Hellenistic, Roman, Byzantine and Latin culture, and the Modern Language Association's annual *MLA International Bibliography,* which includes medieval Latin and European literatures (and all literatures following to the present day), as well as folklore, including rituals, festivals, games, medicine, architecture and more. Except for folklore, however, the *MLA International Bibliography* is literary and linguistic, and it will be necessary to consult more restricted indexes, such as *Art Index, Index to Religious Periodical Literature* and *Index Medicus* for non-literary subject matter.

The bibliographies for each of the articles in this collection will be useful, too. The introductory essay is not based on specific sources, but readers may be interested in consulting Gosta E. Sandstrom, *Man the Builder* (New York: McGraw-Hill, 1970), John Pfeiffer, *The Emergence of Society* (New York: McGraw-Hill, 1977), Erwin Panofsky, "The History of the Theory of Human Proportions as a Reflection of the History of Styles" in *Meaning in the Visual Arts* (New York: Doubleday, 1955), and Gillo Dorfles, "The Man-Made Object" in *The Man-Made Object,* ed. Gyorgy Kepes (New York: Braziller, 1966) for some perspectives on early technology and on the development of the metropolis.

II

An Archaic Recording System Prior to Writing

Popular culture is "throwaway" culture. The commonplace abundance of any popular artifact or phenomenon during its time ordinarily leads to extreme devaluation in ensuing generations. A resulting paradox is that although individual masterworks survive horrendous natural and historical catastrophes, the popular object often becomes a rare commodity because of an inexorable force—neglect.

This article by Denise Schmandt-Besserat is a story of twofold neglect.The tiny clay objects that she argues are the earliest precursors of writing lost all value when writing evolved, and were for years subject to further neglect in museum collections, where nobler objects received attention rivaled only by that most humble currency of archaeology, the potsherd. Schmandt-Besserat's article unfolds like a detective story. Beginning with the puzzle of the ubiquitousness of these neglected bits of clay and of strange clay envelopes called bullae, she builds a case which places the invention of abstract symbolism in communication nearly three thousand years earlier than the usual date for the invention of writing around 3100 B.C. At the same time, she suggests that picture-writing may be a secondary invention to accommodate the addition of technological advances and of things not included within the cultural range of these commercial precursors of writing. The article is an appropriate opening to this collection not only because its chronology reaches back ten thousand years, but because it incorporates three aspects of popular culture that remain throughout history: consistent replication, mediated communication and close ties to the commercial sector of human affairs.

Denise Schmandt-Besserat was educated at the Ecole du Louvre in Paris with further work at Harvard and Radcliffe. She is currently Assistant Professor of Art and Assistant Director of the Center for Middle Eastern Studies at the University of Texas at Austin. Her research has been supported by the Wenner-Gren

*Foundation and the University of Texas Research Institute and has
taken her to museums and archaeological sites in a dozen countries.
Other published reports of her research have appeared in* Syro-
Mesopotamian Studies *and in* Scientific American.

An Archaic Recording System Prior to Writing

Denise Schmandt-Besserat

Writing has been invented independently several times in various parts of the world, in particular in China around 1300 B.C., in Mesoamerica ca. 600 B.C., and in the Easter Islands during the Christian era. The Sumerians, who inhabited Mesopotamia (present day Iraq), are generally credited for the first invention of writing around 3100 B.C. This assumption is based on the recovery of a body of approximately 4000 texts found in the Sumerian city of Uruk.

The archaic texts of Uruk have a number of peculiar characteristics. For instance, they are written on cushion-shaped lumps of clay called tablets. The choice of clay impresses one as being quite impractical as it is a soft material which smears easily and requires a time consuming drying or firing process before handling. Also, the strikingly convex shape of the tablets surprised A. Falkenstein, the German scholar who first studied the early texts. The other early scribes selected hard and flat materials, such as bone and shell in China, stone in Mesoamerica and wood in the Easter Islands, which seem more advantageous. The choice of clay in Mesopotamia is usually explained by the fact that few other raw materials were available in the alluvial plain. But bones and pebbles were certainly abundant, and this explanation may therefore be insufficient. The characters written upon the Sumerian tablets were inscribed in the soft clay by means of a stylus made of wood, bone or ivory and which had one blunt and one pointed extremity. There were basically two types of characters: the numerical signs were impressed with the blunt end of the stylus (fig. 1), while the remaining signs, representing goods and commodities, were incised with the pointed end (fig. 2).

The current theory on the origins of writing states that the characters evolved from a pictographic stage, where each item was represented by its small picture and that, in the course of time, the signs became, by the carelessness of the scribes, more and more abstract until they evolved into the cuneiform writing of the IIIrd Mill B.C. This hypothesis, however, is not confirmed by the early Uruk tablets where characters in the form of small pictures are

19

Fig.1 Numerical Clay Tablet. Susa, Iran. Courtesy Département des Antiquités Orientales, Musée du Louvre, Paris, France

Fig. 2 Uruk tablets with impressed and incised signs. Courtesy Pergamon Museum, Berlin, DDR.

rarities and reserved only for unusual words such as those for wild animals (fox, wolf, etc.), and advanced technology (chariot, sledge, etc.). The majority of the signs is totally abstract and cannot be readily understood by the uninitiated. In fact, the Uruk tablets are mostly undeciphered and remain enigmatic to epigraphists. The few signs identified are those whose evolution can be traced back through several stages from the cuneiform characters of the IInd Mill B.C. to their archaic prototypes. It is of importance to note here that the repertory of signs used by the Uruk scribes was extensive, and included probably no fewer than 1500 signs. From the glimpse we have of the content of the tablets, they are mostly economic texts dealing with such matters as business transactions, land sales and remuneration of workmen for services. Some of the most frequently used terms are food rations, beer, garments, sheep, cattle, women and so forth.

Since the first discovery of the archaic tablets at Uruk by a German team directed by Julius Jordan in 1929-1930, similar texts have been found in various other Mesopotamian sites such as Kish and Ubaid. In recent years archaeologists have been startled by the fact that similar tablets were recovered in excavations outside Mesopotamia and as far as Godin Tepe in Iran and Hababu Kabira and Jebel Aruda in Syria. Except for Uruk, where the tablets were found in a temple complex, the usual context in which the documents are found is private houses, where seals and jar sealings indicate business activities.

Because of the great number of signs represented on the tablets, and their abstract shape, and because of the wide geographical distribution of the tablets, a growing feeling arose among epigraphists that the archaic texts of Uruk might not represent the first beginnings of writing after all, but rather an already advanced stage. It was hypothesized that a truly pictographic stage of writing might have existed earlier covering an unknown period of time during which the characters would have multiplied and evolved to the abstract stage of Uruk. However, as nothing of the kind had ever been found in excavation, it was suggested that this earliest stage might have developed on a perishable material such as wood, parchment or papyrus, which would not have survived to us. On the contrary, my present research leads me to believe that the peculiarities of the tablets underlined above (the choice of clay, the convex face of the tablets and the shape of the characters) may be precious leads to what preceded the Uruk tablets.

In 1958 the late A. Leo Oppenheim of the Oriental Institute, the University of Chicago, disclosed the existence of a recording system based on tokens in the ancient Middle East. From the translation of short economic notes found in the archives of the palace of Nuzi (Iraq) which mentioned "counters" (akkadian abnu, pl. abnati) that were "deposited"/"transferred"/"removed," Oppenheim was able to conceive that, parallel to the elaborate system of cuneiform writing used by the scribes of Nuzi about 1500 B.C., the administration of the palace relied upon a convenient accounting system based on tokens. This was used in particular to keep track of the numerous animals of the herds. Each animal was represented by one token in the administrative office. When animals were born, the appropriate number of tokens were added, when some were transferred from one shepherd to another, or from one pasture to another, were shorn, and so forth, the relevant number of tokens were placed in appropriate containers; when they were butchered or sacrificed, the tokens were removed. The system allowed easy checking at any time from the administration building and was certainly advantageous in dealing with illiterate shepherds. A peculiar "egg-shaped" tablet found in the same levels at Nuzi which bore the inscription of a detailed list of 48 animals on its face, and contained 48 tokens inside, came to verify Oppenheim's hypothesis (fig. 3). It probably represented a transfer of tokens from one service of the palace to another as indicated in the administrative notes. The hollow tablet of Nuzi was found intact in excavation and was carefully opened at one extremity by the excavators to check the content. Unfortunately the tokens have subsequently been lost and we have no accurate description of them.

Oppenheim's study permitted Pierre Amiet to confirm in 1964 the existence of a similar counting system discovered at Susa and which is characterized by a series of hollow clay balls called "bullae" (sing. "bulla") containing series of tokens. Pierre Amiet's discovery was of great importance because the Susa bullae dated to about 3100 B.C. and it therefore extended the existence of the recording system back two thousand years, to a time either contemporary with or slightly preceding writing. Furthermore, Amiet's study described the nature of the tokens. They were small clay artifacts of various geometric shapes, including spheres, discs, cones, tetrahedrons, cylinders, as well as other odd shapes (fig. 4).

In 1969 I started a research project on the beginnings of the use of clay in the Middle East which prompted me to visit most collections of excavated clay artifacts dating from the IX-VIIth Mill B.C. in museums of the Middle East, Europe and the U.S. Along with the clay beads, figurines, bricks and pieces of mortar I had expected to find, I discovered an unexpected category of objects. They were small tokens of various shapes. The most frequent forms were spheres, discs, cones and tetrahedrons, but there were also ovoids,

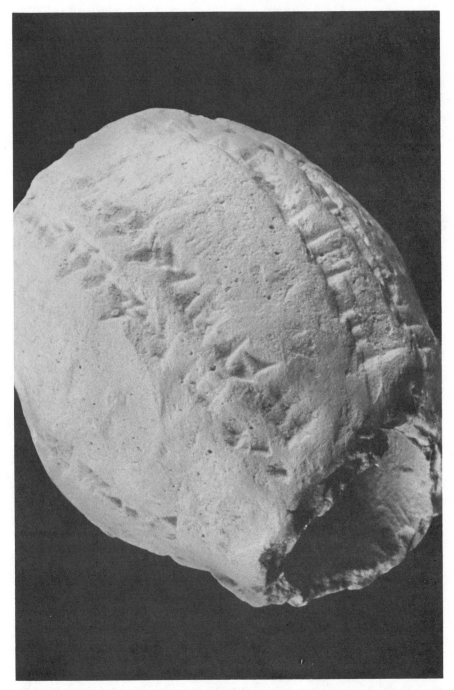

Fig. 3 "Egg-shaped tablet" from Nuzi. Courtesy Ernest R. Lacheman.

Fig. 4 Bulla from Susa (Iran) with the tokens contained inside. Courtesy Département des Antiquités Orientales, Musée du Louvre, Paris, France.

triangles or crescents, biconoids, rectangles and odd shapes difficult to describe (fig. 5). The tokens are of small size and vary between 3 mm. to 5 mm. with an average of 1-2 cm. Most of the types occur in various sizes; and there are in particular small cones (c. 1 cm.) and large cones (c. 3-4 cm.); small spheres (c. 1 cm.) and large spheres (c. 3 cm.) (fig. 5). The spheres come in various fractions including 3/4, 1/2 and 1/4. Some tokens bear specific markings such as deep incised lines, shallow circular impressions or appliqué pellets and coils, all of which seem to confer a special meaning. All the shapes are simple geometric forms which arise quite naturally when one fiddles with clay. Their manufacture is achieved by simple hand modelling, either rolling a small lump of clay between the palms of the hand or pinching it between the fingertips. The clay chosen for their manufacture is fine and does not show any particular preparation such as levigation or tempering. The tokens vary in color from buff to red, with many gray and blackish examples, and consistently show traces of firing. The tokens are present in virtually all Neolithic assemblages and they sometimes occur in large quantity. For instance, Jarmo (Iraq), an early village dating c. 6500 B.C., produced 1153 spheres, 206 discs and 106 cones. The tokens are generally found in excavations lying on the floors of houses. If they were held in containers, these must have been baskets or leather pouches which would have disintegrated with time. The tokens are found scattered in various parts of the sites, but they may have a tendency to cluster in groups of 15 or more in the storage areas.

I became interested in the small objects because of their specific shapes, the care with which they were made and their quantity suggested a function of some importance. The feature which puzzled

Fig. 5 Tokens from Jarmo (Iraq), ca. 6500 B.C.: cones, discs, and tetrahedrons. Courtesy the Prehistoric Project, the Oriental Institute, the University of Chicago.

me most was their seeming ubiquitousness. I found them in Iraq and Iran, but they were also present in Turkey, the Levant, and I have reasons to suspect that their distribution even extends to Egypt as far as Khartoum and in the Indus Valley (fig. 6). While collecting information on the tokens I did not miss an opportunity to ask their excavators about their possible function, but no one seemed to know. Often the tokens are not even mentioned in site reports and if they are, they usually appear under such headings as "objects of uncertain purposes" or "mystery objects." Carleton S. Coon, in his congenial jovial tone, probably expressed best in his report of Belt Cave the normal reaction of archaeologists when uncovering the small geometric objects: "From levels 11 and 12 come five mysterious unbaked conical clay objects, looking like nothing in the

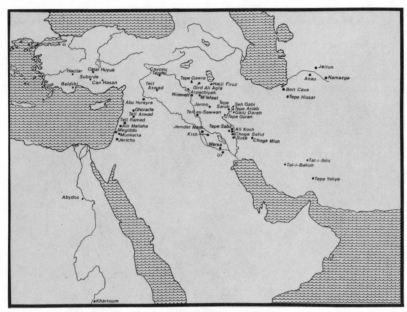

Fig. 6 Map of distribution of tokens. Drawn by Ellen Simmons.

world but suppositories. What they were used for is anyone's guess."
Some authors have ventured to assign various functions to some of
the tokens according to their shapes, and the cones, for instance, are
viewed by some as schematic female figurines but by others as
phallic symbols, as nails, game pieces or amulets. The spheres are
usually interpreted as marbles or sling shots, but Walter B. Emery
and Vivian Broman also suggested that they might be counters.
What may have prevented the identification of the tokens is that
they were usually separated into several headings in the site reports
according to their shapes and were never viewed as belonging
together. Long after having compiled information on hundreds of
tokens, I realized that they were identical to the counters found by
Pierre Amiet in the bullae from Susa. It seemed at first impossible
that they be related, as the tokens of the IXth-VIIth Mill in which I
was interested were separated from those of Susa by three
millennia. However, the investigation of clay assemblages of series
of sites of the VIIth-IVth Mill B.C. proved that such tokens
continued to be found without interruption during the entire period.
The combined results of these studies mentioned above therefore led
to the identification of a recording system based on tokens and
which was widely used in the ancient Middle East. This system of
accounting is in no way different from most archaic counting

systems. In classical times, the Romans used tokens called "calculi." From the XIIth century to the end of the XVIIIth century A.D. the British treasury used counters on the exchequer's table to calculate the amount of taxes to be paid by individuals. Today, Iraqi shepherds still keep account of the animals in their care by means of pebbles and the abacus is still a normal feature in the Middle Eastern bazaars.

The archaic Middle Eastern recording system seems, however, to have been more complex than its more modern counterparts. It consisted of 15 main types of tokens (fig. 7) which may be divided into about 200 subtypes according to size, fractions and markings. Obviously each particular shape must have conveyed a particular meaning and we may assume that some had a numerical value while others represented commodities.

The clue to the meaning of the various shapes of the tokens may lie in the signs of the archaic tablets of Uruk, which they reciprocally may elucidate. Indeed, a number of characters seem to

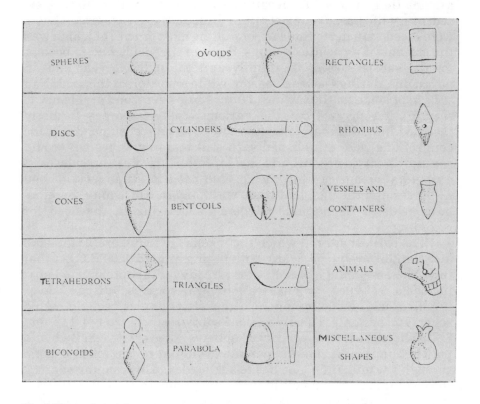

Fig. 7 Illustration of the 15 types of tokens and some subtypes. Drawn by Ellen Simmons.

represent exactly the shapes of the tokens. For instance, a disc with an incised cross is similar to the sign for sheep (a cross enclosed in a circle) and a disc with 4 parallel lines is similar to the sign for garment (4 parallel lines in a circle) (fig. 8). The sign for oil appears to be the image of the tokens in the shape of ovoids with a circular incision at the maximum diameter. All signs for numbers can also be matched with tokens, and in particular the small cone for one, the sphere for 10, the large cone for 60, and so forth. Many tokens, such as the biconoids, triangles, also find their counterpart among undeciphered signs. The evolution of the token system indicates that the relationship between tokens and signs is not fortuitous and that the tokens indeed led to writing.

The first tokens appear in the early Neolithic period, which was a time of profound changes in the human society. They seem to be part and parcel of the Neolithic phenomenon in which farming, with the domestication of plants and animals, slowly replaced the former economy based on hunting and gathering. One may therefore assume that the need for recording arose as a corollary to the new sedentary life based on agriculture. Indeed, the early agriculturists were faced with new problems, one of the most crucial of which was the storage of agricultural crops. Some of the yields had to be kept for the subsistence of the family unit through the year and, in particular, during the lean season, while a portion of the seeds had to be kept aside for the sowing of future crops. A second problem was securing resources from the various ecological areas formerly included in an annual nomadic route. One may assume that trade connections were established with still roaming tribes who could secure the exotic product and raw materials from distant places in exchange for agricultural yields. The need to keep track of food resources and the incipient trade with foreign tribes may therefore be considered as possible triggers in ushering in the need for recording.

The earliest sites in which the tokens are found are Tepe Asiab and Ganj-i-Dareh tepe (Iran), both dating around 8500 B.C. At that time, the assemblage of shapes is already quite sophisticated as it includes 9 types among which are spheres, discs, cones, tetrahedrons, ovoids, cylinders, bent coils, triangles, rectangles and schematic animals. Twenty various subtypes included 1/4, 1/2, and 3/4 spheres, as well as cones, spheres, discs with incised and punched marks. If one follows the evolution of the token system through the millennia, one has to acknowledge little change during the Neolithic and Chalcolithic period covering the VIIIth-IVth Mill B.C. This may be due to the fact that the system was well adapted to the needs of the household economy of the early farmers.

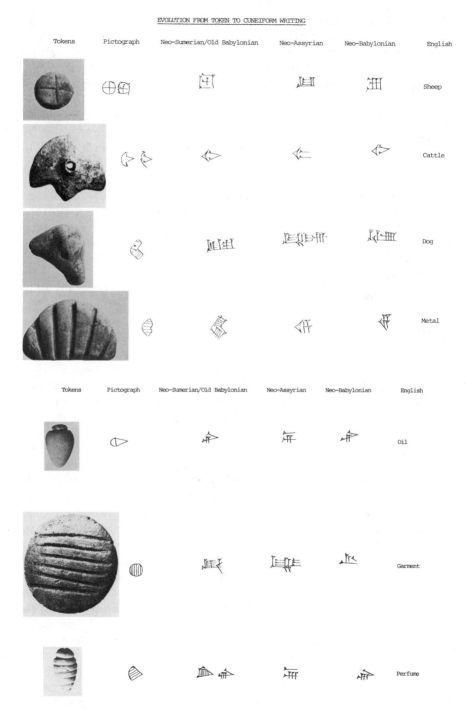

Fig. 8 Chart of evolution of tokens to cuneiform writing.

The token assemblage of Tepe Sarab (Iran) c. 6500 B.C. features 28 subtypes among which all basic shapes (spheres, discs, cones, tetrahedrons, triangles, rectangles, animals, etc.) are represented with the usual size differences and markings. Among the new subtypes are pyramids (4 sides) and the stylized representation of the bull as a bucranium.

It may be that during the course of the Chalcolithic period surpluses of the communities began to be pooled in the temples by the means of taxes. Keeping track of individual contributions would certainly have necessitated recording, but this new need for accounting did not seem to usher in any modification of the system. Tokens in sites such as Tell Arpachyiah, Tell es-Sawwan, Chaga Sefid and Jaffarabad between 5500-4500 B.C. reflect only minor changes. One may acknowledge only the appearance of a new type in the shape of biconoids and also the fact that various markings may appear painted with black dots and lines instead of the usual impressed and incised techniques.

It is only in the Bronze Age, around 3500-3100 B.C. that remarkable changes occur in the recording system. This period is the frame of the second great cultural "revolution," namely the emergence of cities. The survey of ancient Mesopotamian and Iranian sites indicates a drastic increase of population followed by the appearance of urban centers constituting large concentration of people next to the traditional villages. Excavations of these various types of settlements indicate specialization of crafts and the beginning of mass production. The fabrication of raw materials such as bitumen or bronze and of finished products such as stone vessels and pottery seem to concentrate in specific places. The invention of the potter's wheel, for instance, allows the creation of industrial pottery workshops which distribute their goods in a wide radius and supersede the former home potters. Of course the specialization of crafts greatly fostered local and distant trade. The presence of exported goods such as obsidian and lapis lazuli in Bronze Age assemblages indicates that exchanges were frequently carried out with faraway countries. The new economic system based on intensified trade obviously increased the need for recording. Production, stored goods, shipments and payment of wages needed to be computed with accuracy. Records of transactions had to be kept in the merchant's archives for possible challenge. The pressure on the token system by the more complex business accounting needs are clearly visible, especially around 3100 B.C.

Before turning to the description of the major changes in the recording system, one should first emphasize that all early types of tokens such as spheres, discs, cylinders, cones, tetrahedrons, biconoids, rectangles, etc., are still present in sites of the IVth Mill B.C. such as Uruk, Tello, Fara (Mesopotamia), Susa, Chogha Mish (Iran), and Habuba Kabira (Syria). New types of tokens appear in the assemblages and, in particular, parabola, rhomboids and miniature replicas of containers. The most important change, however, seems to be the proliferation of markings. In a recent study based on 660 tokens dating about 3100 B.C. from the above mentioned sites, 55% bear incised markings (fig. 9). The incisions are mostly deep groves performed with a pointed stick or stylus. They are placed in the most conspicuous part of the objects and with a concern for symmetry so typical of the art of the period. On globular shapes such as spheres, cones, ovoids, cylinders, etc., the incisions usually run around the center of the object and can be viewed from all sides. On flat tokens such as discs, triangles, rectangles, etc., the markings are practiced on one face only. The patterns consist mostly of parallel lines, but there are also crosses and criss-cross lines. The number of lines does not seem to be applied at random and although all numbers from one to ten are represented, numbers such as 1, 2, 3 and 5 occur with conspicuous frequency. It is noteworthy that, except for number 2 the uneven numbers are more requently used. Circular impressions applied with the blunt end of a stick or stylus also occur on 4% of the specimens, distributed among all types of tokens (fig. 9). They occur mostly as a single punch mark or in a cluster of six arranged either in a single line or two rows of 3. Rare specimens have appliqué markings such as pellets or coils. The proliferation of markings seem to indicate that more pressure was exerted on the system to become more precise or to increase its vocabulary to a greater number of concepts.

Another remarkable feature is the greater care involved in the manufacture of the tokens. The clay chosen for their production is very fine and was obviously levigated to separate all inclusions. The various shapes are carefully made, the edges become very straight and sharp and one would be tempted to think that the tokens are made in a mold, but the lack of standarization in size contradicts this assumption. The great homogeneity of the appearance of series of tokens found in an area covering not only Mesopotamia, but also Syria and Iran, in the quality of the clay involved, their color, manufacture and surface treatment, would suggest that they were no longer the product of individual households, but were made in workshops. Other revealing changes in the token system include the appearance of perforations (fig. 9). Thirty percent of the tokens around 3100 B.C. have a small perforation throughout their thickness. The perforated specimens are found among the 15 types

Fig. 9 Incised, punched and perforated tokens from Susa (Iran) ca. 3100 B.C. Courtesy Département des Antiquités Orientales, Musée du Louvre, Paris, France.

and among plain, incised and punched subtypes. In other words, all types of tokens seemingly occur both in a perforated and an unperforated form. This indicates that there were two ways of handling them: by simple manipulation or strung. Several explanations come to mind: first the tokens could be worn as amulets around the neck; second the tokens could be mounted in the fashion of a present day abacus with rows of counters held in parallel rows on pliable rods. A last possibility was that the tokens of special transactions might have been strung together. This last hypothesis could be supported by the fact that the perforation was small and could allow only a small string to pass through. More important, I have not been able to notice any wear around the perforations I have checked, which suggests a single use or light handling, as would occur if a string of tokens were kept in archives.

It is also around 3100 B.C. that the clay envelopes called "bullae" made their appearance. They illustrate the need for securing together tokens representing a special transaction. The envelopes were manufactured very simply by pressing the fingers into a clay lump the size of a tennis ball to provide a cavity where the tokens were tucked. Subsequently, the bulla was totally closed with an additional patch of clay upon the opening. There is no doubt in my mind that the bullae were primarily invented to provide a smooth clay surface where, according to the Sumerian custom, all parties involved could impress their seal to validate the transaction. Indeed, most bullae bear the impressions of two seals (fig. 10). Pierre Amiet suggested that the bullae may have been used as a bill of change accompanying finished products such as textiles which were manufactured in the country and transferred to the redistribution center in the city. The producer consigned his goods to the care of a middle man together with a bulla containing a number of tokens corresponding to the load of goods. The bulla was duly sealed for authentication. The recipient of the load could check the accuracy of the shipment upon arrival by breaking the bulla. The bullae were therefore very convenient items. However, there was an important drawback in the innovation: the opacity of clay hid the number of tokens included in the envelopes, and any verification necessitated the breaking of the clay ball with the sealings. A solution was found to overcome this shortcoming. It consisted of reproducing on the surface of the balls the image of all tokens contained inside (fig. 4). In this fashion we find spherical marks standing for spheres or discs, and conical marks for cones, etc. The

Fig. 10 Bulla with seal impressions representing a line of prisoners from Susa (Iran)). Courtesy Département des Antiquités Orientales, Musée du Louvre, Paris, France.

most striking example comes from Habuba Kabira where a clay bulla was founding containing 6 tokens of ovoid shape with a deep groove on the maximum diameter. These tokens were obviously impressed upon the surface of the bulla before being enclosed in it, as they fit exactly in the imprint left. The ovoid depression shows a ring in relief in place of the groove of the token, and the resulting imprint is exactly in the shape of the early sign for "oil" on the Uruk tablets. These marks were certainly not meant by their inventors to supersede the token system, but they did. The innovation proved of great convenience as it allowed one to "read" at all times the amount and kind of tokens without breaking the bulla and its sealing. The use of the images of the tokens—signs—rather than the tokens themselves may be viewed as the crucial link between the archaic system of recording and writing. It provides the key to the similarity between the tokens and the early signs on the Uruk tablets. As soon as the system of marks on the exterior of the bullae was generaly adopted and understood, it obviously made the system of tokens inside the bulla superfluous and obsolete. Hollow clay balls filled with tokens—bullae—were in time replaced by solid clay balls— tablets—marked with signs (fig. 1). The token system ushered in a new phase: writing.

The signs on the bullae and possibly on the earliest tablets were crudely impressed by a variety of techniques including the imprint of the token themselves, or with a finger or a blunt tool. These signs did not allow much precision and in particular there was little difference possible between the representation of a sphere or a disc; between a cone and a tetrahedron. Later, signs incised with a specialized pointed tool or stylus were developed which could render the shapes of the tokens and their various markings with more accuracy. These signs can be called pictographs. However, they did not represent the shapes of the items themselves, but rather the tokens by which they were represented in the previous recording system. As writing evolved, new vocabulary expressing new inventions such as metal tools, the plow, chariot and so forth, which did not have tokens, were transliterated and their signs constitute the few true pictographs, i.e. signs, drawn according to the objects themselves.

Writing may not have been a sudden invention, as previously assumed, but may represent a new step in the evolution of a system of recording which was indigenous to the Middle East since the IXth Mill B.C. This first accounting system was based on tokens of various geometric and odd shapes. It was used without apparent modifications until the IVth Mill B.C., when the development of trade ushered the system in a drastically new course. The use of clay envelopes—or bullae—to secure the tokens of particular transactions for the use of merchants received marks on their surface in order to repeat for convenience the number of tokens inside. The system of using the images of the tokens or signs proved effective and soon supplanted the old system of recording. If this hypothesis is correct it would explain some of the characteristic features of the archaic tablets and, in particular, the material in which they were made, clay, and their convex form, both of which were inherited from their progenitor—the bullae. It would explain the abstract shapes of some of the early signs which perpetuated the shapes of the tokens, and finally, it would explain the rapid adoption of writing in a wide geographical area: it relied upon well-known shapes borrowed from the previous recording system, which had been in use for five millennia in the entire Middle East.

Bibliography

Schmandt-Besserat, D., "The Earliest Precursor of Writing," *Scientific American,* Vol. 238, No. 6, pp. 50-59 (June 1978).

Schmandt-Besserat, D., "An Archaic Recording System and the Origin of Writing," *Syro-Mesopotamian Studies,* Vol. 1, No. 2 (July 1977).

Oppenheim, A. Leo, "An Operational Device in Mesopotamian Bureaucracy," *Journal of Near Eastern Studies,* Vol. 17 (1958), pp. 121-28.

Amiet, Pierre, "Glyptique Susienne," *Mémoires de la Délégation Archéologique en Iran* Vol. XLIII, Paris: Paul Geuthner (1972), Vol. I, p. 60 ff., Vol II, p. 61 ff.

Pullan, J.M. *The History of the Abacus*, 2nd. ed., New York: Praeger (1970).

Clairborne, Robert, *The Birth of Writing,* New York: Time Life Books, The Emergence of Man Series (1974).

III

In Search of an Assyrian Sense of Humor

For most people today, the image of life in the ancient Near East is derived from biblical sources, either directly or through the popular media of epic movies, historical novels, Sunday-school readers and Bible comics. The image is one of millenia of unsmiling, humorless good guys and bad guys whose only laughter is in mirthless roars of uncharitable conquest, and whose only mirth exists in short-lived illicit orgies. As Wilson E. Strand demonstrates in this essay "In Search of an Assyrian Sense of Humor," many historians and Assyriologists have reinforced the popular image. Strand, however, argues persuasively that the humanizing characteristic of a sense of humor is not to be denied even in this warlike, bureaucratic nation of the eighteenth to the seventh centuries before Christ. Warning us of the hazards of judging humor from ethnocentric and twentieth-century perspectives, he is yet able to present an array of illustrations that appear to indicate not only a sense of the comic among the Assyrians, but a sense of humor regarding sexes, the generation gap, the officious fool and the "ethnic" alien. This is not easily done. Not only are we reminded of theories of the comic that find the origins of smiles in tooth-baring snarls, and of laughter in degrading ridicule, but we are left unsure as to whether ancient proverbs that we can regard as witty irony may have once been profound expressions of wisdom, or whether the startling juxtapositions in graphic art of trivial details in solemn ritual contexts may contain deeply significant mythic referents.

Strand's essay points to a potentially rich area of study in popular culture. Humor, play and the comic rarely make their way into cultural history; by and large, history is told the way the establishments have wanted it to be told, wherein the value of existence is displayed in having fought well and thought well, with unrelenting single-mindedness and rigorous avoidance of the recognition that our ambitions, rewards and glories are vulnerable to laughter from the people and from the gods.

Wilson E. Strand teaches history at Hope College in Holland, Michigan. The research for this essay was initiated at a National Endowment for Humanities post-graduate seminar at the University of Chicago's Oriental Institute.

In Search of an Assyrian Sense of Humor

Wilson E. Strand

Gilgamesh, having failed in his quest for everlasting life, is consoled with the lot of mankind:

> Make thou merry by day and by night
> Of each day make thou a feast of rejoicing.[1]

When Ashurbanipal (in whose library the epic of Gilgamesh was found) becomes king, a letter to the new monarch assures him that his subjects in happy anticipation are doing just that: "Old men dance, young men sing happy songs, women and young girls happily learn to do what women do." i.e. to bear babies.[2] Later in his reign when faced with a difficult battle against Elam Ashurbanipal is calmed in a dream by the goddess Ishtar, who tells him, "Eat, drink wine, make merry."[3] The goddess would take care of the enemy.

From such evidence the student with no familiarity with the Assyrians might conclude quite reasonably that the Assyrians were a fun-loving people who, as their gods had intended, sought and found happiness and a good life. Every day for these people must have been a "feast of rejoicing," filled with music, dance and amusement.

Indeed there is considerable evidence that music, musical instruments and musicians, especially in accompaniment to religious and royal events, were not wanting in Assyrian life.[4] Sennacherib and Ashurbanipal were among the kings who enjoyed music within their palaces.[5] Festivals seem to have been common. Royal feasts, accompanied by beer and wine, appear to have been most bountiful and such kings as Ashurnasirpal II bragged with obvious pleasure of the lavish hospitality he provided his 69,574 guests during ten days of revelling and feasting.[6]

Did the Assyrians also have a sense of humor? If humor is defined as that which evokes amusement, it would seem to follow that any people full of the joy of life must have had a well-developed sense of humor.

Yet even the possibility of humor among the Assyrians is usually ignored, as if to say that their lasting image as the "scourge of the East" precluded such consideration, as if to say that if any people ever—an unlikely proposition, considering human nature—lacked a sense of humor, it was surely the Assyrians. That the Assyrian king was also a spectacular builder, a pious individual and a patron and preserver of literature does not really alter that image, for the Assyrian was, above all, a man of war. According to one writer, the Assyrians were bloodthirsty and inhuman, frightful and wicked. For them war was often an end in itself, an exercise of the violence inherent in their nature while victory provided them with enjoyable opportunities for torturing others. A glimpse of "their garden of torments," according to this author, best enables moderns to understand the ancient Assyrians.[7]

The cause of so sober and violent a character is variously explained. It might be due, suggests Jacobsen, to the violent and unpredictable forces of nature in Mesopotamia.[8] It might be the only nature possible for people in such a rich valley setting, surrounded as they were on almost all sides by envious neighbors. It might have been a cause, or result, of their religion. "Their life was stifled beneath the dogmas of what was surely one of the harshest religions ever practiced by man," declares Contenau, and their daily lives were entangled "in a web of pitiless obligations" in which one with any accidental step might unwittingly commit a sin of ritual and bring down upon himself the wrath of heaven in the form of all types of earthly misfortunes. Even the afterlife cut them off from the lifegiving sun and half-engulfed them in the clinging, inescapable dust of the violent sand storms of ancient and modern Mesopotamia. The Assyrians were "prisoners in unrelievable misery." The Assyrian was, he concludes definitively, "a stranger to laughter."[9] Perhaps a stronger, more depressing statement on Assyrian character has never been made. Yet, without debating the nature of man, this essay proposes to demonstrate, despite the scarcity of explicit evidence, that the Assyrian was not without a sense of humor.

Modern humor is of almost endless variety and frequently, even when separated from the reader by only a few decades or a few thousand miles, not understood or if understood, unappreciated. Thus the cartoons in the British magazine *Punch* are seldom appreciated by Americans who have not come to know the British. Humor often relies upon specific contemporary references, word meanings, contrasts or social understandings which are easily missed by outsiders. For example, Mesopotamians in general enjoyed puns but these are missed completely by all moderns save the Assyriologists and by them sometimes recognized only with difficulty. Humor can be one of the most sophisticated and esoteric means of human expression and, try as we moderns will, we can but glimpse a small part of whatever humor has survived.

Everyday humor among any largely illiterate people is presumably overwhelmingly oral. The only known Mesopotamian drinking song, for example, is Sumerian and it presumably survived not because it celebrated the "blissful mood," the "happy liver" and the wonderful mood it says beer produces, but because it was, as a hymn to the beer goddess Ninkasi, a form of religious literature.[10] Since there continued to be beer, wine and song, however, it must be assumed that drinking songs continued and existed among the Assyrians as well.

It may also be that they were no longer written down because of a change of values. Thus proverbs, though plentiful in Mesopotamia before Kassite times, all but disappear thereafter from formal literature in Mesopotamia, apparently because the scribes no longer considered them worth recording. Yet they are known to have existed orally because they were inserted into Neo-Assyrian and Neo-Babylonian letters.

Humor is present, but only rarely, in correspondence. In a Babylonian letter from an official to his superior the official complains that where he is there is neither doctor nor mason, but that the wall is crumbling. Unless the wall is soon repaired a falling stone may soon injure someone. Won't your lordship be so kind therefore as to send a mason—or at least a doctor?[11]

The two major sources to be examined for recorded humor must of necessity be literature and perhaps art. Yet humor in art is conspicuously absent, with a few possible exceptions. In one bas-relief in the British Museum two barefoot comics in lion masks cavort while a man beside them strums a guitar.[12] This scene is part of a larger relief of a military camp and is dated to the reign of Ashurnasirpal II, generally considered the most violent and cruel of Assyrian kings. Another presumably joyful scene on a relief from Nineveh shows a band of men playing musical instruments on the march, followed by women or children clapping their hands,[13] but the occasion is the celebration of their king's victory over King Teumman of Elam.

Other works may well have been considered humorous to the artist, the viewer or both but it is difficult to be certain: an animal orchestra which may have recalled a specific humorous folktale;[14] two dromedaries more interested in kissing than in eating;[15] the stag (fig. 1) that looks back wistfully at its frightened hunter;[16] the smiling monkey which climbs over the immaculate coiffure of the grim-faced tribute bearer;[17] Ashurnasirpal II gazing greedily with anticipated pleasure at a bowl of wine.[18]

Fig. 1 The shooting of a stag. The craning back of the stag's head, the eyes and the whole composition suggest a mood other than serious. Courtesy Alleppo National Museum.

It seems unlikely, however, that royal artists would ever make fun of royalty. What appears humorous to moderns may not have been so for ancients. Ashurnasirpal, for example, is seen leading his soldiers, elaborately protected with a sort of armor from their necks to their chins in the difficult siege of Amedi. From the top of the fortress three hundred feet above them the enemy rains down missiles upon their attackers yet the Assyrian king's only protection is a parasol![19]

The flight of Kudurru and his son downstream on blown-up goatskins,[20] on the other hand, may have been shown deliberately to touch the pride of the victorious Assyrians and to amuse them at the comically helpless plight of their enemies. Perhaps even the notorious relief (fig. 2) of Ashurbanipal and his queen enjoying palace life while on a tree nearby is stuck like the star of Bethlehem on a modern Christmas tree the gruesome head of Teumman, king of Elam,[21] may have evoked laughter at the contrast or at the futility of opposition to the Assyrians, just as it still does when noticed by today's undergraduates. Yet Assyrian art invariably stressed Assyrian military accomplishments, whether for calculated frightfulness or religious fulfillment. Thus the joyful scenes so cherished from Egyptian daily life are simply ignored by Assyrian artists as irrelevant and contrary to the wishes of its monarchs.

Fig. 2 The famous relief of an Assyrian king and queen enjoying the good life is traditional and quite serious—until one notices the Christmas-like ornament, the head of an enemy, adorning one tree. Was the macabre detail added for laughs? Courtesy British Museum, London.

Humor in Assyrian literature is more frequent but not always more evident. The idea of a worm begging the god of justice for food and being assigned human teeth may appear humorous to moderns but was not a laughing matter to the ancient Mesopotamian with a toothache who considered the literary work a religious incantation which would hopefully exorcize the worm and relieve his pain.[22]

When humor appears most clearly it does so in what modern scholars have labeled "wisdom literature," especially within the following categories: 1) proverbs and riddles, 2) scribal literature, 3) contest literature, 4) epic literature and 5) folk literature.

Proverbs more frequently evoke a smile at the wit's recognition of a truism than an outright laugh: "If I save, I shall be robbed. If I squander who will provide for me?"[23] Several are sayings among men: "A house without an owner (is like) a woman without a husband."[24] "Has she become fat without eating?"[25] which may refer not to weight but to pregnancy without a husband. About a woman: "Like an old oven, it is hard to replace you."[26]

One about a fisherman and his friends' trick on him seems most serious until the second sentence: "They pushed me under the water and endangered my life. I caught no fish and lost my clothes."[27] Merchant humor: "Friendship lasts but a day, business connections for ever."[28] All these are Assyrian but may well have been older in origin. Short and pithy, all were no doubt told orally before being written down. In all cases the degree of humor or wit is difficult to determine.

Yet few if any topics were safe from such attack. One comments ironically on the military campaign of a king or noble: "You went and plundered enemy territory. The enemy came and plundered your territory."[29] A Neo-Babylonian proverb, quite likely shared with the Assyrians, suggests that they may have laughed even at death: "Don't say to Ningishzida (a god of the underworld) 'Let me live!' "[30] But such a saying could also have applied to numerous situations. Perhaps it only meant, as a modern might say, "Don't say to the tax collector, 'Make me a loan!' "

A damaged Middle Assyrian collection of proverbs, if Landsberger is right, is really a unique dialogue between an Amorite and his wife with a clever, if not somewhat perverted, humorous twist. The couple dress up in each other's clothes, then proceed to woo each other with proverbs, e.g., the "man" (really the wife) reminds the "wife" (the man) "Whom you love—you bear (his) yoke." As such it is a contest of wits with still recognizable humor, as when the "wife" describes "her" physical charms, "My figure is a protecting angel, my hips are absolute charm.Who will be my voluptuous spouse?"[31] The possibilities are endless.

Riddles were clearly meant to puzzle, challenge and amuse, but are frequently no longer comprehensible. One of the simplest ends:

> One whose eyes are not open enters it,
> One whose eyes have been opened comes out of it.[32]

It refers, of course, to the scribal school.

The respect for these types of wisdom may be seen from the fact that after the time of Tiglath-pileser III the god mentioned most frequently on Assyrian tables is not Ashur or Ishtar but Nabu, the god of scribal wisdom, even though as a god he lacks a mythological background such as the other important gods have and is the god of Borsippa, a relatively unimportant city.[33] Though primarily the patron of scribes Nabu is credited in several tablets in Ashurbanipal's library with making the king learned.[34]

The King Esarhaddon, in writing to the leaders of the non-Babylonian element in Babylon cites two proverbs to explain why he is returning their letters without opening them. "The potter's dog, once he crawls into the (warm) potter's shop, barks at the potter" is utilized to ask why they have "barked" at the king and behaved as if they were Babylonian. "What the adulteress says at the door of the judge's house carries more weight than the words of her husband (from afar)" asks them to bring their message in person.[35] Humor is thus utilized to lighten the royal remonstrance and to encourage compliance.

Humor in scribal literature, frequently a sort of "in-humor," is the most obvious, very likely because it was used pedagogically and because students must have enjoyed copying those narratives or dialogues which contained humor. Several Mesopotamian proverbs are of this type. "A chattering scribe—his guilt is great"[36] suggests that the proper role of the scribe was to hear rather than to be heard but that it was sometimes, if not often, otherwise. Elsewhere the wise man, most often the scribe, is told not to waste his time chattering with the gossip or the ignorant idler, for they will divert him from his proper tasks and steal his ideas.[37]

An Old Babylonian composition entitled "Schooldays" tells with an air of burlesque of the subtle but timeless relationship which may exist between students and teachers. All went well, the student tells his parents after his first day at school, but in pungent contrast all goes wrong after he arrives late for his second day. He is criticized and beaten by one school official after another. The head of the school beats him "for wasting his time in the street on the way to school and for not dressing properly," his teacher for his mistakes of the first day, and so on throughout the day. After such a miserable experience he plots with his father to try a different educational approach, its first known use but far from its last. The teacher is invited to the student's home where he is wined and flattered and given gifts until he praises the student, who presumably thereafter has no more difficulties in scribal school.[38] Scribal life quite naturally is often a target for scribal humor. The self-image of the scribe, suggests Landsberger, referring specifically to "Schooldays," reflects a sense of humor.[39]

Dialogues or verbal contests must have amused countless generations of students. As a genre of Mesopotamian literature they represent a literary genre well known to the Babylonians and Assyrians. As the date palm and the tamarisk sit side by side in the royal garden the two debate rhetorically over which is of superior value to man. The tamarisk at first addresses its opponent in mock respect as "O father of the wise" but the date palm soon rages back, "Pay attention, lunatic!"[40] Since a judgment by a god or king usually ended the composition, readers or listeners here, as in many earlier contests, e.g. in the courtship of Inanna by a farmer and a shepherd,[41] probably participated vicariously, chuckling at each telling point as scored by the side they favored.

One such contest, obviously very popular from the many copies found,[42] pitted the presumptive freshman against the arrogant upperclassman. The first year student shocks his "big brother" student assistant, who no doubt has very specific directions from the teacher as to how he should direct the freshman, with the playful but unorthodox suggestion, probably to see how much he can get away with, that it's time he wrote something of his own. The assistant, perhaps a sophomore, is not only scornful of the ignorant naivete of the younger student but perhaps also afraid of losing his position as assistant, for he asks the student, "If you decide what's to be done then what am I for?" He decides nevertheless to handle the situation diplomatically if he can, addressing the younger student, "O intellect of weighty mind" before pointing out quite specifically why the student is not yet a scribe. He writes up an account but forgets to total it. He writes a letter but uses a wrong address. He divides up property so that brother contends against brother. Then the assistant attempts to squelch him completely, "O man without praise among the scribes, what are you good for?"

The student in turn attacks the assistant as incompetent. He can't handle his multiplication nor does he know how to write up a prayer. The assistant is a big mouth with an evil tongue. Back and forth it rages as the opponents become increasingly more angry. The assistant rages, "But you are a young dunce, a braggart....You cannot (even) write your own name."

From another tablet, discovered later, comes the ending. The headmaster arrives on the scene to find the two fighting, attempts briefly to reason with the younger student before threatening him with fearful punishments: a beating with a stick, a chain about his foot and two months' imprisonment in the schoolhouse. It then, surprisingly, ends happily as the teacher takes them both by the hand.[43] With the problem solved, perhaps the antagonists shake hands as friends (or some such equivalent) or perhaps all three then went off hand-in-hand for a beer and reconciliation. The whole composition, suggests Kramer, has an air of burlesque to it.[44]

In an exam text, one of several, a teacher asks his "son," a perpetual student it would seem, if he has learned the scribal art. After the student assures him confidently that he has, the teacher proceeds to demolish his student's arrogance with difficult questions which he cannot answer, then reproaches him, "What have you done, what good came of all your sitting here? You are already a mature man and close to being aged! Like an old ass, you are not teachable any more.... How long will you play around?" The teacher then, however, assures him that it is not yet too late; he can still become a scribe if he but applies himself night and day and listens humbly to his colleagues and teachers.[45] The student has failed his examination yet the humorous language keeps the text from appearing too serious or frightening.

The level and progress of literature in general depended to a large extent upon the intellectual level and curiosity of the scribes.

Though frequently "bookkeepers" in practice, the scribes nevertheless acquire for moderns some personality as a group through their scribal literature. In a highly disciplined, autocratic society one should not expect to find very much free expression, yet the humor present in such literature demonstrates that the Assyrians were, as Gadd believes, deeply interested in contemporary life and "had a keen appreciation of the human comedy."[46] Very likely they were the liveliest, if not the most liberal, minds around.

The well-known "A Pessimistic Dialogue between Master and Servant," probably Assyrian,[47] is the masterpiece in this genre but may well not have been intended to have been pessimistic at all. Rather than an all-out verbal contest as in the previous examples, this dialogue is a polite conversation between a bored aristocrat who can't decide how to while away his time and a "yes man," his servant, who loyally seconds each suggestion. In each case, after the servant has cited why his master should do as suggested, the master rejects his own suggestion, after which the servant just as ably and as agreeably gives reasons why the master should not. For example:

> Servant, agree with me.
>
> Yes, my lord, yes.
>
> I will love a woman!
>
> So love, my lord, so love!
> The man who loves a woman forgets want and misery!
>
> No, slave, I will not love a woman.
>
> Love not, my lord, love not!
> Woman is a snare, a trap, a pitfall;
> Woman is a sharpened iron sword
> Which will cut a young man's neck.

The answers, most likely stereotyped sayings, matter little, as long as they are witty and amusing. Thus the dialogue is a game for entertainment in which the master tests the wit of his servant until the servant wearies of such sport and rebels.

> Slave, agree with me!
>
> Yes, my lord, yes!

Now then, what is good?

To break my neck and thy neck,
To fall into the river—that is good.

From these lines some scholars evoke a nihilistic philosophy. But if
the master has demonstrated his authority, the wise servant has
demonstrated even better the aristocrat's lack of values. What is
good? Surely not the usual activities of the noble, neither piety nor
love nor charity nor patriotism. In the world of aristocrats, which
the servant gaily satirizes with his wit, all is vanity. The master, for
the first time offering his own wit, announces:

No, slave, I will kill only thee and let thee precede me!

The servant, still playing the game but now more seriously, gets the
last word:

And would my lord want to live (even) three days (without) me? [48]

He realizes that the only good for such a bored individual, or idle
class, is the amusement it can extract from clever servants.

Interpretations of the dialogue differ widely but that implied by
the title should be seriously questioned. Speiser sees it as a burlesque
or a farce because if taken seriously it would be too blasphemous to
have survived.[49] Oppenheim believes it obviously comic, with its
major purpose laughter and entertainment. Though it can scarcely
be the battle of wits he sees, for the master has little if any, it may
have been intended as Oppenheim suggests to demonstrate that
proverbs—the answers of the servant—are a poor guide to life.[50] Its
intent to amuse and entertain is much easier to accept than its
interpretation as a serious philosophical tract.

Even such literature as the Babylonian Creation Epic may be
held suspect of humorous intent. Babylonians and Assyrians, if
only judged from the quantity of their omen literature, seem to have
taken their religion most seriously, but were some intellectuals and
scribes skeptical of it all? The behavior of the gods in the Creation
Epic might suggest so. Apsu, after all, seeks to destroy the noisy,
unruly gods—why?—so that he may get some sleep in quiet.[51]
Tiamat has Mother Hubur making roaring dragons, each of which
is crowned with a halo as if they were gods. Upon facing Tiamat and
her forces the gods are frightened and cowardly. "They yelp like
dogs." When the mighty Anshar is asked to go into battle against
Tiamat,

> Speechless is Anshar, as he stared at the ground,
> Hair on edge, shaking his head at Ea.

In the flood episode the gods harangue each other most vituperatively. When they discover that one man has been saved and is offering sacrifice they greedily gather about him "like flies" for their share. Ishtar, however, blames Enlil and tries to exclude him from the sacrifice. Enlil, for all his power, however, is ignorant of the fact that one man has escaped. When he rightfully accuses Ea of saving mankind, the god of wisdom can only stammer and lie like a foolish mortal, "I said nothing. It was the reeds."[52]

Was such ungodly behavior worshipped or laughed at? Are their antics to be taken as serious or merely amusing? Contenau seeks the explanation in the early origin of such stories among a primitive people and their retention for countless centuries without updating. Though he feels that some priests wanted to make the gods more lovable and adorable, such attempts had little success.[53] If so, no matter how serious such portrayals of the gods were originally they must have increasingly become, at least for the most critical minds, a parody of the gods, comical antics to be winked at.

Folk literature, along with the scribal literature already considered, includes the most easily recognizable humor. A fable of a fox was known to Esarhaddon as well as to Middle Assyrians. The fox, who apparently persuaded a wolf to steal for him, is brought to trial but defends himself with such great cleverness against the charges of the ever-watchful guardian of man, the dog, that neither Shamash nor Enlil have him punished despite all his trickery.[54] The character of Reynard the Fox is already well established. But since no moral is possible the only purpose of the fable can be amusement.

From Ahiqar, apparently a sage in the court of Sennacherib or Esarhaddon:

> A man one day said to the wild ass,
> "Let me ride upon thee, and I will maintain thee."
> But the wild ass said, "Keep thy maintenance and thy fodder
> And let me see thy riding."

Or, in other words, with wider application:

> Let not the rich man say, "In my riches I am glorious."[55]

At least one miniature essay, although incomplete, still maintains something of a punch line:

> The pig himself has no sense...

When at leisure...he mocked his master,
The master left him...the butcher slaughtered him.[56]

Collections of such popular sayings are best known from an
Assyrian tablet from the time of Sargon II and from two smaller
collections found in the library of Ashurbanipal.[57]

The following, paraphrased more smoothly in my own words,
was originally Akkadian but was probably known to the Assyrians
just as it was to be known later to the Greeks in the writings of
Aesop:

A gnat, as it sat on an elephant,
Politely said, "Blood-brother, do I bother you?
If so, I'll be off without further ado."

But the elephant answered, "I really won't know
If you're there at all or at what time you go."[58]

The best example of folk humor is "The Poor Man of Nippur,"
fragments of which have recently been found at Nineveh and
Nippur though the major text is a seventh century schooltext from
Sultantepe, east of Carchemish, at a time when the Assyrians
dominated the area. Gimil-Nunurta, the "hero," is neither king nor
god but merely "a man of Nippur, poor and humble." As everyman's
underdog, he possesses a likable combination of persistence and
ingenuity. Although almost completely destitute he decides to buy a
sheep, trading his dirty clothes for what turns out to be a scrawny
goat instead. Rather than share so little with all his relatives and
friends, he decides to present it as a gift to the mayor of Nippur with
the hope that the mayor will return hospitality for a gift by inviting
him to a feast.

The mayor, however, is insulted instead, thinks it a bribe, gives
him some bone and a swallow of cheap beer and has him sent away.
The mayor overhears the frustrated Gimil-Nunurta as he departs
swear to pay the mayor back three times for the insult, and laughs
about it all day. The rest of the tale concerns the three tricks played
on the mayor, each of which ends with the arrogant mayor being
fooled and beaten. On the first day the poor man, now nobly dressed,
arrives in a chariot, supposedly with a box of gold from the king for
the temple. When the nonexistent gold vanishes the mayor is held
responsible for its loss and is beaten. Gimil-Nunurta is given two
minas of gold (one more than he's paid rental for the chariot!) as
"hush money." Shaving off his beard so that he won't be recognized,
he appears the next day at the mayor's house as a doctor from Isin to

treat his bruises. He tells the mayor that he gives cures only in the privacy of darkness but, once away from the others, of course gives the mayor more bruises instead. The mayor no longer laughs but instead alerts his household to keep on the watch should "the madman" try to return the third time as promised. When they hear a man, hired by the poor man to shout that he is the man with the goat, they all rush out to seize him, leaving the mayor alone, who is subsequently beaten for the third time to settle the score.[59]

Such a story must have held great appeal and humor for any poor Assyrian who felt he had ever been mistreated by an official. Beating was no doubt considered a slapstick humor, not sadism. The popularity of the story has been demonstrated by the tracing of various humorous elements from the story to later folktales in Turkey, Hungary, Rumania, Crete, Sicily, Italy, France, Iceland, Spain, Germany and India, all the way down to the Brothers Grimm in modern Germany.[60]

Though frequently difficult to recognize or to appreciate fully, the Assyrian and the Mesopotamian in general, as most clearly seen in their literature, quite obviously did have a sense of humor. Although vicious in war, he was quite human when at peace. Olmstead, who considered the Assyrian a "normal, cheerful individual" in his daily life,[61] was one of the few authorities to recognize this. He declared decades ago, "We can no longer consider the Assyrian merely a brutal man of war; he stands forth in all his humanity as a man like unto ourselves."[62] While most authorities will never go that far—that the Assyrians were as normal as you or me—need we continue to deny them that humanizing characteristic which clearly they had—a sense of humor?

Notes

[1]J.Pritchard, ANET, 96—hereafter always referred to in the third edition (1969).
[2]A. Oppenheim, *Letters from Mesopotamia* (1967), No. 86, Cf. ANET, 626-27.
[3]ANET, 606.
[4]A. Olmstead, *History of Assyria* (1923), 83-84.
[5]A. Parrot, *Art of Assyria* (1961), 311-12.
[6]ANET, 559-60.
[7]H. Berr in introduction to L. Delaporte, *Mesopotamia* (1925).
[8]T. Jacobsen in *Before Philosophy* (1949), 138-40.
[9]C.Contenau, *Everyday Life in Babylon and Assyria* (1954), 301-2.
[10]M.Civil in *Studies Presented to A. Leo Oppenheim* (1964), 74.
[11]H.Saggs, *The Greatness that was Babylon* (1962), 444n.
[12]E. Budge, *Assyrian Sculptures in the British Museum* (1914), pl. xvi.
[13]Parrot, pl. 392.
[14]Parrot, pl. 100.
[15]C. Gadd in *Antiquity* 9 (1935), pl. 1, 216.

[16]Parrot, pl. 97C.
[17]Budge, p. xxviii.
[18]Olmstead, fig. 104.
[19]Olmstead, fig. 90.
[20]Olmstead, fig. 91. Cf. Contenau, pl. iii.
[21]Parrot, pl. 60.
[22]ANET, 160-61.
[23]W. Lambert, *Babylonian Wisdom Literature* (1960), 247.
[24]Lambert, 232.
[25]Lambert, 247.
[26]Lambert, 247.
[27]Lambert, 250.
[28]Lambert, 259.
[29]Lambert, 250.
[30]E. Gordon, *Sumerian Proverbs* (1959), 43.
[31]Lambert, 230.
[32]S. Kramer, *The Sumerians* (1963), 236.
[33]Olmstead, 617-18.
[34]Olmstead, 618.
[35]Oppenheim, No. 116.
[36]Gordon, 210.
[37]Lambert, 99.
[38]S. Kramer in JAOS LXIX (1949), 205-10.
[39]B. Landsberger in K. Kraeling, *City Invincible* (1960), 95.
[40]ANET, 410-11.
[41]ANET, 41-42.
[42]Kramer, 199, 213n.
[43]C. Gadd, "Teachers and Students in the Oldest Schools," (1956), 30-36.
[44]Cited in Gadd, "Teachers and Students," 36.
[45]Landsberger, 100-01; Kramer, 243-46.
[46]Gadd, "Teachers and Students," 38.
[47]Jacobsen, 231.
[48]Jacobsèn, 231-32.
[49]E. Speiser in JCS 8 (1954), 98-105.
[50]Oppenheim, *Ancient Mesopotamia*, 274.
[51]Cf. ANET 106, where Enlil can't sleep because of the noise of mankind.
[52]ANET, 64.
[53]Contenau, 226, 266.
[54]Lambert, 191-209.
[55]ANET, 430.
[56]Lambert, 219.
[57]Lambert 215.
[58]Saggs, 444.
[59]O. Gurney in *Anatolian Studies* VI (1956), 145-62. See also AS VII (1957), 135-36; AS XXII (1972), 149-58; and JCS XXVI (1974), 88-89.
[60]Gurney in AS XXII (1972), 149-58.
[61]Olmstead, 626.
[62]Olmstead, x.

IV

Urbanism in the Classical World: Some General Considerations and Remarks

During the late 1960s and early '70s two immensely popular television serial comedies contrasted ludicrously with political and social unrest in Viet Nam, civil disobedience, minority rights agitation and counter-cultural movements. In The Beverly Hillbillies *and* Green Acres, *oversophisticated rational urban life styles were pitted against the innocent commonsense of ignorant rural clowns. The rural cohorts always prevailed, but without any polishing of their rustic crudity. Such pairings of urban and rustic life styles have a long history in comedy, reaching back beyond Shakespeare's* A Midsummer Night's Dream *to Terence's* The Brothers. *This essay by Ronald T. Marchese explores the underlying factual distinction between these contrasting life styles, which he finds in the classical Greek city-state and in the Roman imperial structure. In both political structures, rights of citizenship could be equally extended to city-dweller and to country-man.*

In addition to the contrast between rustic and civilized images, Marchese contrasts modern and ancient definitions of the city. Modern definitions are related to size and to a complex of functions, while the ancient city is defined according to legal terms which may or may not relate to our modern concepts. But regardless of definitions, the city emerges as a center for cultivated arts and activities as well as a center for mass culture with physical places for economic exchange, for political convenings, for rituals and entertainments that touched and influenced all who lived in the classical world.

Ronald T. Marchese is an archaeologist as well as an Assistant Professor of History at the University of Minnesota, Duluth. Readers of this article will especially want to examine his photographic illustrations of archaeological sites along with their illuminating captions. These, along with Marchese's article provide an excellent material and institutional backdrop for the four articles that follow, all of which look into specific popular phenomena of the classical city, and for a later article in which Joseph J. Hayes notes a reversal in Gothic Europe, when civilization was associated with the countryside.

Urbanism in the Classical World: Some General Considerations and Remarks

Ronald T. Marchese

The quality and importance of life in antiquity can be expressed from two conflicting points which dominated the spiritual and mental fiber of man. Simply stated, these were defined in the terms *urbanitas* and *rusticitas*—the former emphasizing the cultured, refined and educated life of an urban elite; the latter a statement which expressed the rustic, perhaps rude, illiterate and simple virtues of the country folk. Though simple expressions, they were the embodiment of the pleasures, hopes, fears and sorrows of those who resided in the numerous communities of the ancient world. Perhaps the most noteworthy examples of these attitudes appear in the histories of Thucydides, Livy, Polybius and Plutarch; the political rhetoric of Plato, Aristotle, Theophrastus and Cicero; the geographies of Strabo, Pausanius and Ptolemy; and finally the poetry of Hesiod, Hipponax, Phocylides, Theognis and Menander. All provide the concrete statements which express the cultural ideals, beliefs and popular interpretations of daily life from the Archaic to Roman Imperial periods (c. 700 B.C.—150 A.D.). Though textual references abound, the following characterize life in the ancient world—a world which emphasized the attitudes and cultural definitions of the city-dweller in contrast to the rude, simple virtues of the country folk.

Perhaps the best expression which contrasts the lifestyles and attitudes of the ancient world appears in the following statement:

The story goes that on this occasion, while the votes were being written down, an illiterate and uncouth rustic handed his piece of earthenware [*ostrakon*] to Aristides and asked him to write the name of Aristides on it. The latter was astonished and asked the man what harm Aristides had ever done to him? 'None whatever' was the reply, 'I don't even know the fellow, but I am sick of hearing him called the Just everywhere.' When he heard this, Aristides said nothing but wrote his name on the *ostrakon* and handed it back (Plutarch: 7, 117).

This one statement captured an historical reality—a reality which indicated the dichotomy of life between the educated, cultured and wise exemplified by the noble character of the Athenian Aristides the Just and that of the illiterate and uncultured rustic who came to the city of Athens to exercise his political rights. However, the political freedom enjoyed by the rustic indicates a mean life filled with animosity and hatred for all things good and cultured. A statement of life is obvious —a statement which exemplifies a strong reaction against the character, principles and ideals of the cultured and intellectual capacity of the city-dweller.

Further support of the popular definitions of life can be seen in the philosophical characterizations of man. The following, a remark from the fourth century B.C. philosopher Theophrastus, illustrates the point:

Boorishness I would define as uncivilized ignorance. The boor is the sort of man who drinks barley-brew before going to the Assembly; who asserts that garlic smells as sweet as any perfume; wears shoes too big for his feet; and can't talk without bellowing. He won't trust his friends and relations but he'll retail all the affairs of the Assembly to the laborers he employs on his farm. He sits down with his clothes hitched above the knee exposing his private parts. In the streets, other sights arouse in him no interest or surprise whatsoever, but if he sees a cow or a donkey or a goat he stops and inspects it. He can't fetch a bit of food without nibbling at it on the way; he drinks his wine straight. He quietly tries to rumple the bakery-maid, after he's helped her to do the grinding for the whole household.... He feeds his horses while still eating his breakfast.... When he has been paid by someone with a silver coin, he rejects it, saying it is worn too smooth, and takes another instead. If he has lent his plough, or a basket, or a sickle, or a bag, he remembers it as he lies awake and goes to ask for it in the middle of the night. On his way down to the city he asks anyone he meets what price hides or bloaters were fetching in the market, or whether the new-moon festival is being celebrated today. And in the same breath he tells you he is going down to get his hair cut; and while he's passing that way he means to call at Archia's for some fish. He sings in the public bath; and he drives hobnails into his shoes (IV, 1-14., 48-51).

The Boor, in actuality a rustic, epitomized the uncultured buffoon who occasionally entered the city either for business, to exercise his political rights in the public Assembly or to enjoy an alternative lifestyle. However, he brought with him his peculiar way of life, his uneducated speech and rude dress and his popular culture which was in contrast to the refined expressions and manners of the city. Though the physical surroundings changed from the rustic village to the complexity of the city, the cultural heritage of the individual remained the same. Within the environs of the city he stood out. He became an object of scorn, cheapness, the embodiment of pettiness, and finally laughter and buffoonery. The latter can be seen in the following passage:

Put on, as I bid you, a soft coat and a tunic to the feet to shield your body—and you should weave thick woof on thin warp. In this clothe yourself so that your hair may keep still and not bristle and stand on end all over your body. Lace on your feet close-fitting boots of the hide of a slaughtered ox, thickly lined with felt inside. And when the season of frost comes on, stitch together skins of firstling kids with ox-sinew, to put over your back and to keep off the rains. Over your head above wear a shaped cap of felt to keep your ears from getting wet...(Hesiod: 535-550, 42-43).

To the city-dweller the rustic was a fool, but a fool who was at times admired for his common sense and straightforwardness. The brunt of laughter did appear in a different light:

I'm a rough countryman, I don't say otherwise. I don't know all the ins and outs of city ways. Still, I keep learning more and more as time goes on (Menander: 97. 338-339).

And

I'll tell you...who seems to me to have the happiest life; the man who takes a steady look at the majestic sights our world offers—the common sun, stars, water, clouds, fire, and having seem them, and lived free from pain, at once goes back to where he came from. The same sights will be, if you live to a hundred, always there, always the same; and equally if you die young; you will never see more majestic sights than these. Think of this time I speak of, as a people's festival, or as a visit to some city, where you stand and watch the crowds, the streets, the thieves, the gamblers, and the way people amuse themselves. If you go back early to your lodging, you'll have money in your pocket, and no enemies. The man who stays too long grows tired, loses what he once had, gets old, wretched, and poor, wanders about, makes enemies or falls prey to plotters, till at length...death sends him home (Menander: 481K. 1-15. 442-3).

The rustic virtues were simple. Happiness was expressed in the enjoyment and perfection of nature. This appears in contrast to the greed and mean life of the city. It is in the city that thieves and swindlers live and take advantage of those who periodically attend the public functions of the community.

The reaction against the city, however, appears in the minority. Those who resided in the city were aware of the drastic differences in lifestyles and thus spent much time and energy extolling the virtues of their own society. They were conscious of the fact that social upheaval could damage the quality of life expressed in the city and substitute the cultured exponents of the community for the rude rabble of the countryside.

Kyrnos, this city is still the same, but its people are different. Those who before knew nothing of lawsuits, nothing of laws, who went about in goatskins flapping over their shoulders, who lived on the ranges, far out from the town, like deer, these are now the Great Men, son of Polypas. Our former nobles are rabble now. Who could endure it when things are so? They swindle each other, they mock at one another, and meanwhile understand nothing at all of what good and bad men think. You must know that their purposes are unpleasant, and there is no trusting them in any matter at all, but treachery, and deception, and catch-as-catch-can is their nature (Theognis: 53-67. 27).

The final and certainly strongest statement which exemplifies the cultural ideals expressed in the ancient world appears in the philosophical exegesis of Aristotle. In one passage he captures the importance and significance of the cultured, good life which dominated the reality of the fourth century B.C.:

The partnership finally composed of several villages is the city-state.... It comes into existence for the sake of life, it exists for the good life. Again the object for which things exist, its end, is its chief good.... From these things therefore it is clear that the city-state is a natural growth, and that man is intended by nature to be an animal that lives in the city-state and a man who is by nature and nearly by fortune citiless is either low in the scale of humanity or above it... (I.i. 8-9, 8-9).

The cultured, good life was directly associated with the city-oriented state. Only one focus for human existence is evident—the city. Within its confines the popular expressions of daily life, cultural heritage and institutional complexity appear. Without the city cultured life was impossible. The alternative was the simple, rude qualities and expressions of the rustic. The complexity of life and its popular statements, thus, remained in the city.

In the preceding pages numerous contemporary elements have been stated. Some extol the virtues of the rustic—his definition of happiness and his hatred of city life. The opposite view is also evident—a reaction by the city-dweller to the uneducated, cultured buffoon of the country. Two worlds existed—worlds which were at opposite ends of the social and cultural spectrum. Both revolved around specific attitudes and beliefs which were at times hostile and pointed. Such expressions, however, were not isolated to the individual. They existed in a wealth of communities—some of which epitomized the city, others the countryside. All were centers of life—centers which varied in complexity and sophistication. As part of the urban scheme the city and its corresponding lifestyle stood out, but it was only one of many urban forms which existed in the ancient world.

In recent years much emphasis has been placed on the role and function of the city in the ancient as well as the modern world. As a distinct entity the city has been the focal point and definition of civilization and cultured life ever since its inception in the middle of the fourth millennium B.C.[1] Within the confines of the city the development of complex social, cultural and economic institutions, as well as the total organization of man's personal life, took form. Though cities existed at an early date in the ancient world, their greatest expansion and development appears in the Roman Imperial period of the first and second centuries A.D. However, the city was only one of many civic organizations which dominated the Roman world. A definite hierarchy existed—an arrangement of communities from the simple agricultural village to the most complex and privileged expression of urbanism in the ancient world, the city. It is within this broad context that the classical concept of the city and urbanism will be examined.

The typological classification and hierarchical arrangement of urban settlements—in a modern interpretation and definition of urbanism—revolves around popular numbers, density, areal size, specialized functions and finally organized services.[2] Such a classification categorizes settlements into separate and similar entities, for example, cities, towns, villages and hamlets. This hierarchical arrangement of communities defines the concept of urbanism. Settlements classified as cities by such criteria dominate the uppermost stratum of the urban hierarchy. They are the center of gravity politically, socially, culturally and above all economically. They rest on a broad-based economic foundation supported by complex commercial and industrial processes—that is, expressions of redistribution—rather than the limited production of agriculture. The city, in a modern interpretation, is a major point of consumption as well as a center of monumental production—production expressed in forms of specialized labor and complex social and political services. The lower levels of the urban hierarchy, that is towns, villages and hamlets, are less complex and usually associated with more rudimentary expressions of social, cultural and political life. Their economic base is less formalized in comparison to the city and is primarily involved in the production of basic raw materials—that is the exploitation of natural resources and the production of foodstuffs—which are needed to support city life and leisure. Thus, the modern world emphasizes a multi-level arrangement of communities which defines the concept of urbanism. Such an arrangement is based on a strict definition of size, categories of size (for example population numbers and area), and finally the level and type of complex services offered by the community in question.

In the ancient world, however, size was not a qualifying factor for the hierarchical arrangement of communities either in the real world or in philosophical exegesis. The desirable form, even for the major urban centers in the ancient world, was small both in the numerical population and the areal size of the community and its adjacent territory.[3] Such   limitations were determined by two important and integral processes: the idealized philosophical expressions which dominated man's political and social world (a narrow attitude which maintained that the attainment of the *good life* was associated with a direct personal interaction and recognition of all individuals who resided in the community as *city-dwellers*); and in the reality of a rudimentary and inadequate economic base associated with a primitive transport technology. A combination of an inefficient transport technology and rudimentary agricultural abilities had a profound effect on the growth and size of the ancient city. Simply stated, the city was effectively restricted to a predetermined size as based on the productive quality of its neighboring agrarian regions, their proximity to the city, the ability to transport basic foodstuffs to a point of consumption efficiently and finally the level of technology employed in agricultural pursuits.[4] Such factors placed severe limitations on the location, size and especially the number and type of services and opportunities offered to the individual by the community. As a center of life and innovation the city became the framework in which man functioned and eventually achieved complete social, cultural and political fulfillment. However, as a dynamic economic force based on a redistribution of wealth, the ancient city had a limited though constant impact on the surrounding countryside. The city was the center of a cultured personal life and thus the most important urban expression in a predominantly agrarian age.[5] The importance of the ancient world lies in the fact that it grew into a vast city-oriented entity based on rudimentary agricultural techniques. However, the majority of its people did not reside in the cities as townsfolk.[6] Perhaps no more than 5-10% of the ancient world's population lived in the cities as permanent residents engaged in non-agricultural pursuits.[7] For the majority of the population, in the city as well as in the surrounding subordinate districts, agriculture remained the essential occupation of life and in many respects the only socially acceptable form of free labor. When a village was transformed by political decree and necessity into a city it did not transform the villagers into townsfolk. They remained farmers and the community was as agrarian in nature and outlook as the village community had been. The ancient city, in many respects, became the center for an urban elite—an elite concerned with living the good life of a city-dweller. The cultured life expressed in the city was, however, in direct contrast to the simpler livelihood and attitude of the rural folk who occasionally attended the major religious festivals and social events in the city. Their life was one of the countryside—a countryside dotted with self-contained villages and small towns which enjoyed a rustic existence with distinct characteristics and beliefs. The rural folk had little in common with their city brethren. City life and size, thus, remained small and limited in scope for a minority of the urban population.[8]

Perhaps the greatest achievement of city life in the ancient world occurred during the Roman Imperial period. Though having a solid growth in the Archaic, Classical and Hellenistic periods in the East and West, city development reached its maximum expansion in the Mediterranean basin during the first and second centuries A.D. The importance of the Roman Imperial world lies in the fact that in the hierarchical arrangement of communities, it was a vast city-oriented entity enjoying peace and commercial prosperity in a predominantly agrarian age.[9] This was especially evident in the first half of the second century A.D. during the reigns of Hadrian (117-138) and Antoninus Pius (138-161). It is during this time-period when the sophist Aelius Aristides lived and wrote. His panegyric, *The Roman Oration,* perhaps best exemplifies the growth and material prosperity of city life in the Roman world.

For when were there so many cities both inland and on the coast, or when have they been so beautifully equipped with everything? Did ever a man of those who lived then travel across country as we do, counting the cities by days and sometimes riding on the same day through two or three cities as if passing through sections of merely one? Hence the inferiority of those who lived in former times...(99,990)

Cities gleam with radiance and charm, and the whole earth has been beautified like a garden. Smoke rising from the plains and fire signals for friend and foe have disappeared, as if a breath had blown them away, beyond land and sea. Every charming spectacle and an infinite number of festival games have been introduced. Thus, the celebration never ends...(99, 990)

The Empire in the second century A.D. was an unique organization based on a coherent and well-defined aggregate of autonomous and self-governing commonwealths and a highly centralized imperial administration. Indeed, Aristides and his contemporaries viewed the Empire as one vast world league comprised of two basic and integral parts: a federation of cities which possessed their own laws, customs, traditions and forms of government; and the concept of Rome as *hegemon* or leader over a unified world state. Rome was the common town and "...emporium where the commerce of all mankind [had] its common exchange and all the produce of the earth [had] its common market" (7, 982). However, the concept of Rome as the embodiment of city life and thus civilization was not new to Aristides and was often referred to by both earlier and contemporary authorities, particularly Strabo, Pliny, Pausanius and Ptolemy, who "habitually viewed the *orbis Romanus* as constituted by and summed up in a federation of municipalities"[10] scattered over the civilized world. At the center was Rome, the capital of a world league of cities. This point is excellently summarized by Aristides as he states

What another city is to its boundaries and territory, this city [Rome] is to the boundaries and territory of the entire civilized world, as if the latter were a country district and she had been appointed common town. It might be said that this one citadel is the refuge and assembly place of all who dwell in the outside demes (61, 987).

In this one statement Aristides captured the true essence of the Roman Imperial world of the second century A.D. It was one vast city-territory dominated by one central community. Thus, the Roman world was a mirror image, on a larger scale, of its basic component part—the individual provincial city and its sustaining territory. The provincial city stood in relation to its dependent towns, villages, hamlets and individual farmsteads in much the same way Rome stood to the cities; that is as the most important expression of political, social and finally cultural life.

The Roman world as defined by Aelius Aristides consisted of an aggregate of autonomous and self-governing communities joined in a legal federation under the ideal *hegemonia* of Rome. In this world state the city was the most privileged form of social, cultural and political organization. Basically, it was the independent cell from which the Roman state was formed. To Aristides and his generation the term city had a specific and distinct definition. A definite concept of the city existed—a term so strictly defined that confusion with any other form of urban life was impossible. Indeed, the entire world was both classified and categorized according to this strict definition which emphasized only the social, cultural and political aspects of the city-dweller. In the East a major difference existed between the *polis* and *kome* and, *demos* and *katoikia;* while in the West a distinction was made between *urbs, civitas, municipium, oppidum;* and *pagus vicus, form, conciliabulum* and *castellum.* All these were communities of some rank and status, but only those classified as cities enjoyed equality with Rome. The simpler expressions were subordinate and thus were not members of cultured life in the *orbis Romanus.* In many respects, they were irrelevant and insignificant urban expressions which could not be compared with true city life and organization.

Despite differences in size, population and wealth all

communities recognized as cities in the Roman world possessed basic and common features which distinguished them from all other forms of human organization. The most important element was the possession of either complete local autonomy or a substantial amount of self-government. Essentially, self-government was expressed in the rule of the limited territory of the community. This usually took the form of a deliberative council comparable to the Roman *senatus* or Greek *boule*. The total assembly of the citizen body, which possessed both legislative and elective functions, formed the *populus, ekklesia* or *demos*. Magistrates, elected annually by the citizen body and who conducted the specific business of the community, were also necessary. It was of prime importance that the community possess its own foundation legends as well as have a clear sense of its past history. The latter usually appeared in numerous decrees, dedications and donations by past citizens and foreign rulers granted to the community. Such material was highly visible on its major public monuments and structures and therefore a constant source of pride. The last necessary item a community had to possess was its own cult of the gods under whose protection the citizen body survived. Although their form and content varied from region to region, the community which did not possess these essential elements was not defined as a city.

However, the major factor in determining city status was in the official recognition by Rome. Recognition was not necessarily permanent and could be granted to or withdrawn from a community at will. Communities with a dwindling prosperity or which fell into disgrace (especially during times of conflict) could be and often were reduced to the status of village. Its recognized political life was lost. Even if the community continued to be heavily populated and maintained a high degree of material prosperity with marked expressions of specialization, functional activity and social and cultural life, it was no longer classified as a city. It became a subordinate community, that is an *attributum* of another.

In the East Rome inherited highly urbanized regions based on the Greek model of city organization, the *polis*. Rome continued the process of urbanization by encouraging and fostering city life on the Greek model.[11] This usually meant raising a pre-existing village to the rank and status of a city with newer rights and privileges. Communities which were already recognized centers of village commonwealths were raised to full city status. This process has an excellent illustration in Asia Minor where temple states, composed of villages under the administration of a priestly caste attached to a temple, were characteristic features of the land. These were easily transformed into new cities.[12] The seat of the temple became the city while the remainder of its former administrative area was converted into its territory.[13] Specific rights and privileges attested to the new status of the community, for example freedom (rarely) from imperial taxation (*immunitas a tributis*) and the right to issue currency. The latter usually publicized the recognition of a former village as a city and also served as an excellent vehicle for the community to boast of its newly acquired status. However, the community remained agricultural in scope with a narrow economic, social and cultural base. Thus, the legal fiction had a negligible impact on the lifestyle of the inhabitants.

In order to achieve the status of a city the community had to possess the following: a measure of self-government and local autonomy; a designated and well-defined territory which incorporated numerous subordinate communities; a deliberative council; an assembly of free citizens which was organized as a legislative and legal group; magistrates to administer the needs and guarantee the financial integrity of the community; and finally, a foundation legend, a sense of history, and organized religious cults. It was also essential that the community in question call itself and was called by others a city.[14] During the Principate this was required. Without such recognition a community existed as a subordinate element and was not considered an equal member of the Roman world. Social, cultural, political and economic relationships could not be conceived without the city. No region could call itself civilized or be civilized until it had within it a thriving, well-planned and well-equipped city.[15]

However, village communities also possessed a semblance of political life and organization. Evidence from western Anatolia and Syria[16] offers an interesting picture of the more loosely organized communities. It appears that the sovereign body in the village was the physical gathering of the villagers of *ochlos*. Though not constituting a formal *ekklesia* its function was no doubt similar to its more organized counterpart in the city. The *ochlos* passed decrees on all matters of local interest such as the use of village land, the organization of trust funds, the contribution of the magistrates to the village fund, and the annual election of the magistrates who carried out the business of the community.[17] There was also a council of elders or *gerousia* which functioned as a regulatory agency in the village. However, it lacked the constitutional prerogatives of the city *boule*. Thus, a similar, though less formalized expression of organization prevailed at the village level of the urban hierarchy. Such organization was based on the institutional life of the city. The impression is thus a mirror image of the city proper though on a smaller and less complex scale.

The importance of the villages, however, was monumental and must not be slighted. Within the confines of the city territory specific categories of villages existed. These categories were basically determined by land ownership: some were situated on the municipal lands of the city; some on lands privately owned by the citizens of the city; and others on land owned by citizen farming-communities.[18] The latter needs no clarification since it pertained to citizen communities which possessed equal rights and privileges and thus were exempt from villages situated on municipal lands. Both citizen and non-citizen villages were considered dependent communities of renters and were liable to a specific charge.[19] This basic tax was also extended to the individual farmstead and was applicable to both citizen and non-citizen alike. Functionally, the villages served the city in much the same way as the city served Rome; that is as smaller units of administration and, above all, as sources of limited production, and finally as sources of essential revenue (taxes). Thus, the revenues of the city were chiefly derived from its territory and the villages which were made up of agricultural peoples. These were regarded as "lessees in perpetuity of the land in which they worked."[20] The rent which the villagers paid not only contributed to the support of the city but also helped make the quota of Imperial taxes the city owed Rome.

To summarize, a dualistic harmony existed in the ancient world between the different levels of the urban hierarchy.[21] This harmonic expression was necessary to insure the stable growth and prosperity of the city. Two distinct levels were evident: the city or those entities which classified themselves as such; and the rural villages and town. Both maintained stratified centers of gravity based on common expressions of life exemplified in the attitudes of the city-dweller and country folk. However, the survival of the city and citylife was based on the ability of the subordinate forms of the urban hierarchy to generate the necessary surplus required and consumed by the city-dweller. In return the city provided the social and cultural expressions and broader world view of its realm to the rural folk.

In reality, the cultured life of the city dweller was secondary. Without a strong economic foundation based on substantial agricultural production and wealth, city life was impossible. The cultured life of the city was, thus, a luxury—a luxury supported by the majority of the urban hierarchy which was involved in narrow agrarian pursuits.

Urbanism in the classical world and especially the *orbis Romanus* emphasized basically one type of community. This was the city. It was the center of gravity and the focal point for the educated and well-born. Functionally, it was simply the governmental and social-cultural center of a limited territorial expression. In the city resided the wealthier local landowners, specialized laborers and artisans which supported their needs, municipal officials, educators, political theorists, commercial entrepreneurs and finally unskilled and semi-skilled non-agricultural workers. The city was also a market for its neighboring agrarian regions, buying and consuming the essential produce generated by the rural population and selling manufactured items which village artisans could not or would not produce. The city relied on the productive ability of its villages and towns to maintain its high standard of living as well as provide a limited market for its specialized production. In this respect the city became a dependent entity in relation to the near self-sufficiency expressed in lower urban forms. Towns, villages, hamlets and individual farmsteads were sources of essential production and centers of agricultural surplus. In reality it was the lower strata of the urban hierarchy which fostered the dynamic growth of city life and leisure in the ancient world. In many respects city life was an artificial luxury supported by narrow economic factors—factors which defined wealth in terms of agricultural production. Such wealth, personal as well as municipal, was accumulative and thus took generations to secure. Economically, the city absorbed much of the wealth generated by an agrarian society. In its place the city became the center for economic transaction and commercial enterprise—but enterprises which were luxury-oriented and which added little to the economic foundation of the society. In essence, the ancient city failed to diversify its economic base. It exploited a narrow agrarian economy without generating a new and stronger economic reality based on well-organized industrial and commercial processes.

In conclusion, a broad based foundation of urban life existed in the ancient world. At the top of the hierarchy was the city, the most important entity of urban life. This simple expression dominated the ancient world and especially the *orbis Romanus* of the first and second centuries A.D. Lower order settlements, which were far more numerous, were inferior expressions of social, cultural and political life and thus subordinant to the city. Economically they provided the essential elements for city life. Without them, the city could not exist as a distinct entity. Its survival depended on the strength and vitality of the numerous agrarian communities which dotted the countryside. As long as the towns, villages, hamlets and the individual farmsteads were able to create surplus and thus wealth, city life prospered. Once these sources of production failed to keep pace with the growing needs and demands of the city and the world state, city life stagnated, retracted and eventually declined. However, urban life continued. Hamlets, villages and small towns continued to exist and in some respects prospered. As a rudimentary expression of an urbanized society they became the supportive element and pride of the late classical world, especially in the East.

Notes

[1]A.J. Rose, *Patterns of Cities* (Australia: Thomas Nelson Ltd., 1976), p. 16; Mason Hammon, *The City in the Ancient World* (Cambridge: Harvard Univ. Press, 1972), pp. 33-47; Gideon Sjoberg, "The Origin and Evolution of Cities," *Scientific American,* 213 (Sept. 1965), p. 56; Robert M. Adams, "The Origin of Cities," *Old World Archaeology: Foundations of Civilization,* ed. C.C. Lamberg-Karlovsky (San Francisco: W.H. Freeman and Co., 1972), pp. 137-144.

[2]Sjoberg, pp. 55-56.

[3]John Scarborough, *Facets of Hellenic Life* (Boston: Houghton Mifflin Co., 1976), p. 1.

[4]D.H. Stott, "Cultural and Natural Checks on Population Growth," *Environment and Cultural Behavior,* ed. Andrew Vayda (New York: American Museum of Natural History, 1969), p. 91.

[5]Janet Roebuck, *The Shaping of Urban Society* (New York: Charles Scribner's Sons, 1974), p. 32; Gideon Sjobert, *The Preindustrial City Past and Present* (New York: Free Press, 1960), pp. 67-70.

[6]E. Jones, *Towns and Cities* (New York: Oxford Univ. Press, 1970), p. 81.

[7]John Sihamaki, *The Sociology of Cities* (New York: Random House, 1964), p. 52; Fritz Heichelheim, "Effects of Classical Antiquity on Land," *Man's Role in Changing the Face of the Earth,* ed. W.L. Thomas (Chicago: The University of Chicago Press, 1956), p. 172.

[8]Norman Pound, "The Urbanization of the Classical World," *Annals of the Association of American Geographers,* 59 (1969), pp. 135-36.

[9]J. Ward-Perkins, *Cities in Ancient Greece and Italy: Planning in Classical Antiquity* (New York: George Braziller, 1974), pp. 29-32.

[10]James Reid, *The Municipalities of the Roman Empire* (Cambridge: The University Press, 1913), p. 4.

[11]Hammond, pp. 288-289.

[12]A.H.M. Jones, *The Greek City* (Oxford: The Clarendon Press, 1940), p. 81.

[13]Allan C. Johnson, "Villages in the Orient," *Municipal Administration in the Roman Empire,* ed. Frank F. Abbott and Allan C. Johnson (Princeton: Princeton Univ. Press, 1926), pp. 23-24.

[14]C.B. Welles, "The Greek City," *Studi in Onore di Aristide Calderini e Roberto Paribeni,* I (Milan: A. Nicola & Co., 1956), p. 87.

[15]Roebuck, p. 33.

[16]A.H.M. Jones, pp. 367-378.

[17]A.H.M. Jones, p. 272.

[18]T.R.S. Broughton, "Roman Asia," *An Economic Survey of Ancient Rome,* ed. Tenny Frank (Patterson: Pageant Books, 1959), p. 637.

[19]Frank F. Abbott, "Municipal Finances," *Municipal Administration in the Roman Empire,* ed. Frank F. Abbott and Allan C. Johnson (Princeton: Princeton Univ. Press, 1926), p. 139.

[20]Johnson, p. 26.

[21]M. Diakonoff, "The Rural Community in the Ancient Near East," *Journal of the Economic and Social History of the Orient,* 18 (1975), p. 127.

Citations from primary classical sources are provided intertextually with reference to these editions.

Aelius Aristides. *The Roman Oration* (Greek Text and English translation), in James Oliver, *The Ruling Power: A Study of the Roman Empire in the Second Century after Christ Through the Roman Oration of Aelius Aristides, Transactions of the American Philosophical Society,* 43 n.s. (1953).

Aristotle. *Politics.* Greek Text and English Translation by H. Rackham. London: William Heinemann, Ltd., 1967.

Menander. *The Principal Fragments.* Greek Text and English Translation by Francis G. Allinson. London: William Heinemann., Ltd., 1959.

Paul. Acts. *New Testament.* Greek Texts and English translation by Alfred Marshall. London: Samuel Bagster and Sons, Ltd., 1958.

Pausanius. *Description of Greece.* Greek Text and English Translation by W.H.S. Jones. London: William Heinemann, Ltd., 1918-1935.

Plutarch. Aristides. *The Rise and Fall of Athens (Lives).* English Translation by Ian Scott-Kilvert. Baltimore: Penguin Books, 1964.

Theognis. Fragments. *Greek Lyrics.* English Translation by Richmond Lattimore. Chicago: The University of Chicago Press, 1967.

Theophrastus. *The Characters.* Greek Text and English Translation by J.M. Edmonds. London: William Heinemann, Ltd. 1946.

Thucydides. *The Peloponnesian War.* English Translation by Crawley. New York: The Modern Library, 1951.

Acknowledgments

I wish to thank Drs. F.E. Peters and Jill N. Claster for their critical evaluation of the manuscript. Their comments and suggestions were invaluable during the initial stages of research. Also, I wish to express my gratitude to my collegues Drs. W.P. Connor and Ronald Huch for their assistance. Finally, my appreciation to Ms. Vickie L. Mayberry and Jean N. Lindsey. They made me aware of additional shortcomings which were not ignored.

Special thanks is given to Dr. Kenan T. Erim, Director of the Aphrodisias Excavations, for allowing me to present the plates from the city site of Aphrodisias in Turkey. This is deeply appreciated.

Detail, head of Apollo from Olympia, fifth century B.C. Though numerous cults existed in the rural districts of the ancient world; it was in the city that the more formalized religious expressions and institutions appeared. The city survived under the protection of a supreme patron deity. It was in the city that the complex relationships between the guardian city god, the total cosmic order, and the earthly realm of man merged in a distinct statement of life. In this respect, the city, as the focal point between the gods and man, became a sacred entity.

Detail, head of a female deity, fourth century B.C. The delicate expression of beauty associated with the immortal gods of classical antiquity also personified the city. Harmony of form, beauty, and refinement as expressed in the idealization of the mind and spirit, had no equal and became the essential elements in city life.

Detail, Parthenon freize from the temple of Athena at Athens, fifth century B.C. The frieze captures part of the lavish celebration from the most important religious festival in the city-state of Athens—the Panathenaea. Every state had a major festival—an extremely complex religious celebration in which all elements of the society participated. It became a unifying factor of life. Such a festival captured the common heritage and citizenship enjoyed by all its participants irregardless of one's social standing and domicile. This section of the frieze captures only a small part of the Panathenaea—the nobility of man, heroic ideals, civic pride and patriotism of the citizen body.

Two-handled drinking vessel, or *kylix*, sixth century B.C. Two vessels are shown: a "round ship" or merchant vessel and a "long ship" or warship. Both epitomized the complexity of the city and city oriented life. Long distance trade brought in the luxury items and in certain cases the essential commodities of life which were consumed by the city-dweller. The embodiment of a well-organized military machine is expressed in the war vessel. It became the symbol of the power and prestige of the city in distant lands. To maintain economic control of specific markets and to guarantee the security of specific trade routes, vessels of this nature became a hallmark of numerous communities in the Classical Age. Whereas the countryside remained essentially self-sufficient, the city became the center for international organization and a hotbed for commercial enterprises. This is easily seen in Periclean Athens: "...the magnitude of our city draws the produce of the world into our harbour, so that to the Athenian the fruits of other countries are as familiar a luxury as those of his own" (Thucydides: II. 38. 104).

A large silver issue from Syracuse. Currency in the ancient world served numerous functions. An obvious function was in the highly formalized and complex expressions of intercity commerce. Municipal issues of this nature exemplified the harmony of form, the mind, spirit, and beauty of each city. It became a symbol of civic pride, prestige, and narrow civic traditions. The city was thus the only center of note for a cash economy, of formalized economic transactions, and finally of bankers and money changers.

Detail, storage vessel, mid-fourth century B.C. The rustic became a comical character and certainly a point of humor and ridicule. However, the rustic was the backbone of society. He was loyal, fiercely independent, and a stubborn patriot who preferred the simplicity of life and comradeship of his fellow farmers. The life of the farmer was a mean one, but individuals did achieve marked degrees of prosperity like the character Strepsiades in Aristophanes' *The Clouds*. However, his wealth was certainly negated by his mannerisms and traditions which were purely rustic. "The matchmaker ought to be cursed who got me to marry your mother. Me a happy clod, unwashed, unkempt, lying around teeming with honey and sheep and olive cake. And then a hayseed like me had to go and marry the niece of Megacles from the city, proud and luxury-loving like the rest of her family. We married and went to bed together, me stinking of wine, brine, and sheepdip, her all perfume and saffron and french kisses" (Frank J. Frost, *Greek Society*. London: D.C. Heath, 1971, p.88).

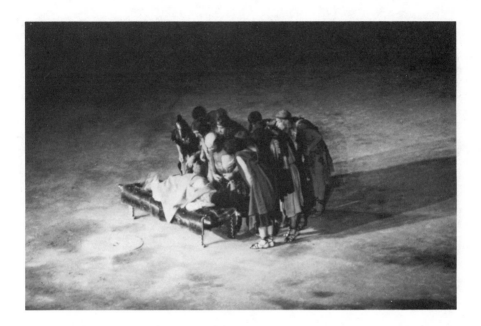

Detail, scene from Aristophanes' *The Clouds*. In this Socratic play numerous expressions of life are evident: philosphers, sophists, cultured individuals, rich students, aristocrats, and the rich farmer Strepsiades (lyiing on couch). All came together in the city—the focal point of two diverse worlds. The city was a source of education and virtue, two principles which dominated the utopian statements of Plato's *Republic*.

Theater complex, Ephesus. 1) Ancient Harbor 2) Arcadian Way 3) Intersecting Street 4) Harbor Gymnasium and Baths 5) *Skene* or Stage Building 6) Orchestra 7) *Cavea*. Hellenistic in date, the theater was enlarged during the Roman Imperial period as the community of Ephesus grew in size and prestige. Calling itself "the first city in the Roman province of Asia" Ephesus grew in size and complexity to rival the major cities in the roman Empire—cities such as Alexandria, Antioch-on-the Orantes, Corinth, and Carthage. The theater was only one of the many buildings associated with the city. It stood at the head of a vast complex of buildings, marble paved road ways, market-places, private houses, public baths, and exercise areas. As with all buildings in the ancient city, its function changed according to the needs of the society. The theater was the focal point of cultural and social life. It served as a place for public gathering—gatherings of citizens who performed political duties or the curious who came to listen to a noted speaker. The latter is well-stated in *Acts* as Paul delivered his sermon to the throng of Ephesians in the theater. "And when they heard these sayings, they were full of wrath, and cried out, saying, Great is Diana of the Ephesians. And the whole city was filled with confusion: and having caught Gaius and Aristarchus, men of Macedonia, Paul's companions in travel, they rushed with one accord into the theater" (28-29, 556).

The Odeion of Herodes Atticus, Athens, second century A.D. 1) Stage Backdrop 2) *Cavea*. Numerous structures appear in the city. All were formal architectural expressions which indicated a high technical and cultural quality as well as a vast expenditure of revenue. Some were paid out of the municipal treasury while others were financed by wealthy private citizens. The latter were usually dedicated to a past ancestor. The Odeion of Herodes Atticus, dedicated to the memory of his wife, had a seating capacity of 5,000. It was given to the citizens of Athens by the most noted Athenian of the time, Herodes Atticus. As an example of civic pride and patriotism, the Odeion was only one of many structures dedicated by wealthy citizens to cities with famous past heritages. The expenditure of private wealth enhanced the quality of life expressed in the city.

Temple of Hadrian, Ephesus, second century A.D. Dedicated to the Roman emperor Hadrian, the temple was a major attraction in the city. Financed by P. Quintilius, the temple was a small part of a larger complex of buildings. This was the second temple dedicated to a Roman emperor at Ephesus, and it was with much pride and honor that the Ephesians called themselves "Temple Wardens" of the deceased emperors.

The Scholastica Baths, Ephesus, first through fourth centuries A.D. 1) Temple of Hadrian 2) Scholastica Baths 3) Marble Way 4) Paved Road to the Theater 5) City *Agora* or Market-Place. The earthly pleasures of the city were not ignored. Clean living was important as was personal hygiene. Other pleasures were also associated with this large complex—a brothel which dates to the first and second centuries A.D. It appears to have been a major attraction for a seaport city like Ephesus and provided a comfortable outlet from the rigors of daily commercial life. The brothel was well situated to the major streets of Ephesus: the Marble Way which was dotted with numerous shopes, the major market of the city, and finally the theater which had a seating capacity of 27,000.

The Celsus Library, Ephesus, second through fifth centuries A.D. Knowlege was not slighted in the city. In fact, it was an integral part of city life. The library at Ephesus, situated next to the market and near the theater and Scholastica Baths, contained numerous manuscripts which were under the direct supervision of a librarian. The structure was three stories with a large enclosed central court. In the confines of the structure was a large statue of the goddess Athena, the patroness of wisdom and learning. Erected by Gaius Julius Aquila as a monument to his father Gaius Julius Celsus Polemaeanus, the family left 25,000 denarii for the purchase of manuscripts and the general upkeep of the structure and its staff. A private donation to the city, the structure became an integral part of the community. It served as a source of learning and a focal point for social gatherings.

Marble Way and the Monument of Memmius, Ephesus. 1) Monument of Memmius 2) Marble Way 3) Temple of Hadrian 4) Library of Celsus 5) Market. Crowded streets were a hallmark of city life. Public and private monuments abound in relation to the ebb and flow of city life. Streets of this nature were crowded with vendors plying their trade, shops, and outlet stores selling items of importance: perfumes, oils, wines, and honey from distant cities, individuals selling their personal favors, major colonnades and stoas which provided shelter from the mid-day sun and thus a setting for the cultured statements of the educated and profane alike. The Marble Way ran past the major market of the city as well as by the major and minor structures of the community. At places were private monuments donated by the city or by wealthy private citizens. The monument of Memmius, a grandson of the Roman dictator Sulla, was only one of many such structure which appeared at Ephesus. The cityscape became an accumulative expression of history and prestige.

Residential section, Ephesus. 1) Scholastica Baths 2) Temple of Hadrian 3) Private Houses. These multi-storied structures housed part of the urban elite. However, wealth was directly associated with cheap housing. Zoning regulations which designated areas according to wealth and class structure were absence as houses of the rich and poor alike dominated any one block. The houses of the wealthy had all the refinements of life: running water, sewage disposal, frescoed walls, mosaics of country scenes, covered walkways, fountains, and basins. Urban location is curious as these structures appeared near the major arteries of the community, the market-place, stoas, shops, temples, libraries, baths, and the brothel. City life was one of social commitments.

The city of Priene. 1) Temple of Athena 2) Stoa 3) *Agora* or Market-Place 4) Temple of Zeus 5) Theater 6) Gymnasium 7) Stadium 8) Private Houses 9) House-Shrine of Alexander the Great. City planning became an essential element of life during the Hellenistic and subsequent Roman Imperial periods. The well-ordered city provided all the qualities of the good and cultured life: running water, complex social and cultural institutions, architectural embellishment, an harmonious environment which satisfied the spirit and the mind of the city-dweller, and finally an ordered world expressed in intersecting streets and boulevards.

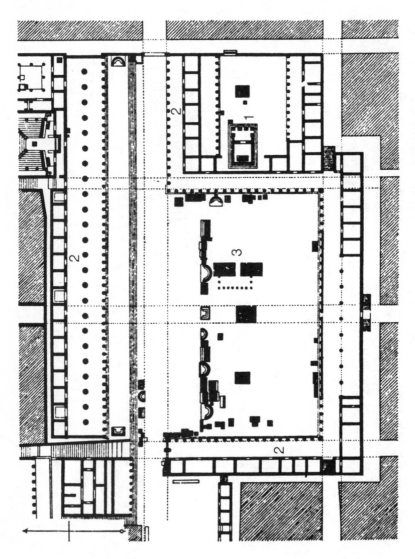

Detail, Priene, commercial district. 1) Temple of Zeus 2) Shops 3) Monuments. As with numerous cities Priene had a well-planned eommercial district. Numerous stoas or covered walkways were a hallmark of the *agora*. In the confines of the market individuals purchased the daily necessities of life. The market, however, served more than this simple economic function. It was a major center for social, cultural, and political life—essential elements in the definition of city life.

PRODUCT	ATHENIAN PRICE	MODERN US EQUIVALENT
food	(to be measured against a daily wage of one drachma a day)	(to be measured against $20 a day)

food

one quart figs or olives	1/3 obol	$ .40
five lbs. wheat	2 obols	6.67
a gallon of domestic wine	3 obols	10.00
a gallon of olive oil	3 drachmas	60.00
a loaf of bread	1 obol	3.33
one salted fish	1 obol	3.33
a small pig	3 drachmas	60.00

clothing

a woolen cloak	5-20 drachmas	100.00-400.00
a pair of shoes	6-8 drachmas	120.00-160.00

furniture

a stool	1 drachma 1 obol	23.33
a table	4-6 drachmas	80.00-120.00
an imported bed	8 drachmas	160.00

livestock

a cow or ox	about 50 drachmas	1,000.00
sheep or goat	10-15 drachmas	200.00-300.00

slaves

a Carian goldsmith	360 drachmas	7,200.00
a Macedonian woman	310 drachmas	6,200.00
Syrians	240-300 drachmas	4,800.00-6,000.00
Thracians and Illyrians	about 150 drachmas	3,000.00
a donkey driver	140 drachmas	2,800.00

miscellaneous

a ring, proof against snakebite	1 drachma	20.00
lady's cosmetics	2 obols	6.67
a small jug for oil	1 obol	3.33
to have a dream interpreted	2 obols	6.67
to sleep with a prostitute	about 4 drachmas av.	80.00

Reprinted by permission of the publisher, from Frank J. Frost: *Greek Society* (Lexington, Mass: D.C. Heath and Company, 1971).

The basic commodities of life. the *agora* became the center for economic life in the ancient city. Numerous items appeared on the open market of the city: food, furniture, clothing, livestock, slaves, cosmetics, and prostitutes. All had a price—a price based on a cash economy. Merchandise from all parts of the known world found their outlet in the city. Organized commercial enterprises became the prerogative of the city-dweller and his community in relation to the self-sufficient production and consumption of the countryside.

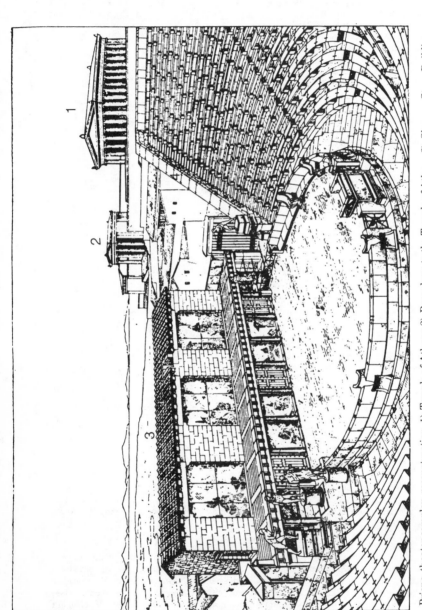

Priene, theater complex, reconstruction. 1) Temple of Athena 2) Propylaea to the Temple of Athena 3) *Skene* or Stage Building 4) *Cavea*. The architectural elements of the city became the physical symbol for the abstraction of life. The city was defined as a social relationship of citizens which possessed the complex institutional statements of life. In this respect the physical world of the city was secondary to the abstract relationships created by the society of citizens. This point has a concrete expression in the tourist Pausanius who, in his *Description of Greece* states "From Chaeronia it is twenty stadia to Panopeus, a city of the Phocians, an give the name of city to those who possess no government offices, no gymnasium, no theater, no market-place, no water descending to a fountain, but live in bare shelters just like mountain cabins, right on a ravine. Nevertheless, they have boundaries with their neighbors, and even send delegates to the Phocian assembly . . ." (IV. iv. 1-4). Without the physical elements the quality of life expressed in the city ceased to exist.

Aphrodisias. 1) Stadium 2) Temple of Aphrodite 3) Theater Complex. The spatial quality of life was of extreme importance to the city-dweller and was not neglected. Urban sprawl existed in many cities of the ancient world. The spatial aspects of the city, however, revolved around well-designated social areas—areas which enhanced the quality of life in the private sector.

Aphrodisias, stadium. Almost every city of note had an elaborate stadium complex. With a seating capacity of 30,000 the stadium became the center for religious and secular games. Sponsored by the community, festivals of this nature became major attractions.

Aphrodisias, Odeion, second century A.D. One of the many public structures which dominated the city, the odeion served a dualistic function: as a cultural and social focal point for dramatic and comic performances and festivals; and as a chamber for the city senate or municipal council. A building of note, the once roofed structure, was a source of civic pride. Though the initial expenditure of municipal revenues was great for the construction, embellishment, and general upkeep of the structure, its lifespan was one of centuries. The ancient city became an accumulative expression of design, style, and wealth as public structures were constantly added to the city landscape.

Aphrodisias, theater complex, Hellenistic in date. 1) *Skene* or Stage Building 2) Lower *Cavea* 3) Roadway and Paved Plaza with Fountain. A major focus in any city, the theater enhanced the social, cultural, and political aspects of life. Life in the ancient city was expressed in the out-of-doors. Thus, a unique combination of environmental and social factors created as harmonious expression of quality living in the city. The natural world became a backdrop for the physical realm of man.

Aphrodisias, Temple of Aphrodite, Hellenistic in date. The ancient city was summed up in its major religious cult. A source of constant elaboration, the temple went through numerous phases of reconstruction and embellishment. It was the unifying factor between the urbanite and the rustic. As the ancient world changed, so changed its most important part, the city. In the ebb and flow of religious movements, Christianity eventually captured the spirit of the ancient world—a spirit which was centered in the city. Temple complexes, formally dedicated to the patron god or goddess of the community, eventually were turned into Christian shrines and monuments. Their function, however, remained essentially the same; that is the focus and point of unification

V

Images of Physicians in Classical Times

Fans of television, comicstrips and best sellers will recognize that doctors and their patients are almost as ubiquitous in popular literature as are cops and robbers. Dr. Kildare, for example, set the standard for one convention in a series of novels that continued as a daytime radio serial and later as a television drama. In this essay, Darrel W. Amundsen introduces us to images of doctors in classical times, drawing on such popular sources as folktales, joke books and romantic novels. The similarities with modern conventions are startling, until we realize that physicians have always occupied a singularly democratic role in all societies. In addition, their privileged access to the sickrooms of the wealthy, to the bedrooms of women and to the means of ending human lives has always made physicians the objects of sensational speculation in the popular consciousness. Amundsen's article takes all these characteristics into consideration, and in his discussion of lovesickness, touches on some of the same territory as does Gerald Erickson in the following article. Deathbed stories in Amundsen's article also relate to some of the essays following on medieval and gothic death themes.

Darrel W. Amundsen is a member of the Foreign Languages Department at Western Washington University. He has written extensively on medicine and medical ethics in the ancient and medieval worlds, two of his more recent articles in the Journal of the History of Medicine *being on "Medical Deontology and Pestilential Disease in the Late Middle Ages" and "The Liability of the Physician in Classical Greek Legal Theory and Practice."*

Images of Physicians in Classical Times

Darrel W. Amundsen

Will Durant writes that "in all civilized lands and times physicians have rivaled women for the distinction of being the most desirable and satirized of mankind."[1] Even a cursory look at the entries under "physician" (and related terms) in Stith Thompson's *Motif-Index of Folk-Literature*[2] will impress upon one the pervasiveness of the sundry motifs that impinge upon the healer in disparate cultures. The attitudes range from contempt to adoration for the physician with a vast, neutral, area in between, where the foibles to which the physician is most susceptible are exploited, sometimes with a grace bordering on tenderness but more frequently with scathing sarcasm.

In Greco-Roman literature the attitudes toward physicians are ambivalent. Indeed, even where the physician is held in esteem and awe, there is often an underlying tension generated by the patient's feeling of helplessness, of being at the physician's mercy. Generally people who excessively venerate the medical art, attaching an unrealistic aura to its practitioners, naively crediting to them the ability to cure nearly all of man's physical or mental ills, may, when the physician fails, suspect him of evil intent and/or negligence, for surely, if the physician had really wanted and tried, he could have cured the patient. Or, if the physician was unsuccessful in treatment, he might be considered as grossly incompetent in comparison with an unrealistic ideal imagined by the patient. Even in classical culture, where the healing art had many obvious deficiencies, at least from the perspectives of twentieth-century medicine, frequent attestations of faith in medical practitioners are found. On the other hand, there are those who hold the medical profession in contempt. Such people often believe that all or most physicians are unprincipled men, greedy for wealth and position, cozening the naive, victimizing the innocent and defrauding the unwary: evil if competent but usually incompetent as well.

It was commonly recognized that the competent physician had a tremendous potential for good and evil by virtue of his medical knowledge. In *The Republic,* Socrates asks "Who then is the most

94

able to benefit friends when they are ill and harm enemies in respect to disease and health?" The answer given immediately is "the physician."[3] Aristotle was also aware of this reality: "...when people even suspect physicians of being in the confidence of their enemies and of trying to do away with them for gain, they prefer to treat themselves 'by the book'."[4] There is, indeed, in the historical literature rather frequent mention of physicians employed or considered as political assassins.[5] On the more mundane level the sentiments of Plato and Aristotle just quoted were manifest in the fear that one's heirs might use one's physician to expedite their coming into their inheritance. Pliny the Elder, probably the most outspoken and vituperative critic of the medical profession, maintains that there is no more fertile source of conspiracies against wills than the medical art.[6] Perhaps the worst mistake a man could make would be to include his physician in his will. As Publilius Syrus writes, "The patient who makes an heir of his physician treats himself badly."[7] The anecdotal value of this theme is recognized by Hierocles and Philagrius, late classical compilers of a joke book. In one of their stories a physician was to receive a bequest of 1000 drachmas from a patient of his who had died. Since much of the bequest was being used up for the funeral, the physician followed the funeral procession and kept loudly lamenting how little of the bequest was left for him. Later the son of the deceased became ill and sent for the same physician. When he arrived the physician said, "If you leave me a bequest of 5000 drachmas, I shall treat you just as I treated your father."[8]

It was particularly as poisoners that physicians were most feared. Lucian was aware of their susceptibility to such accusations: "Slanderers...generally make their charges credible by distorting the real attributes of the man they are slandering. Thus they insinuate that a physician is a poisoner...."[9] The motif of the physician as poisoner was exploited by rhetoricians[10] and provided the authors of prose fiction with a theme quite suitable for the ancient romances.[11] In Apuleius' *Golden Ass* (also known as the *Metamorphoses*) a notoriously corrupt physician was approached by a woman who wished to have her ill husband poisoned. The woman ensured that some of her husband's relatives would be present when the physician arrived. After the physician had gone through the motions of examining the man, he was at the point of administering the drug, saying that it was never known to fail in alleviating intestinal trouble and carrying off the bile. The woman, however, insisted that the physician take a drink of the drug first so that her husband's relatives would know that it was not poison. He was thrown into confusion and drank some of the medicine, hoping that he could get home quickly enough to take an antidote. After the rest of the drug had been administered to her husband, the woman detained the physician until the poison began to take effect. The physician managed to get home before dying and instructed his wife to collect the fee.[12] This, no doubt, was intended to emphasize the physician's greed, a topic that was popular in the classical world.[13] The role of the physician in this tale is undoubtedly one of pure poetic justice, where the murderous and conniving physician received his just deserts.

Other physicians in the ancient romances who were approached for poison react differently from the one we have just seen. In the *Ephesian Tale* of Xenophon of Ephesus, a girl was being compelled to marry against her will. After exacting from a physician an oath that he would assist her, she begged him to provide her with poison so that she might commit suicide. After she gave him some money and her jewelry, he anguished over the problem for some time, but finally agreed and left to get the poison. He returned shortly with a drug, however not a poisonous one, but a soporific, so that no real harm would come to the girl. She waited to take the drug until just before the marriage was to be consummated and was taken for dead and put in a tomb where she was later discovered alive by grave robbers.[14]

The substitution of a soporific for a poisonous drug is a commonplace in folk-literature and provides many obvious possibilities for writers of fiction. Apuleius weaves a tale of a woman who, lusting after her stepson, was spurned and then determined to kill him. She sent her slave to obtain poison from a physician, mixed it with wine and awaited the appropriate moment to administer it. Quite by accident the woman's own son drank the concoction and was then entombed. She then charged her stepson with murder. It happened that the physician from whom the drug had been obtained was one of the judges. At the moment when the disclosure would have the greatest impact, this physician described how the woman's slave had come to him saying that he wanted the drug for a friend who was suffering from an incurable disease. Suspicious of the slave's intentions, the physician had substituted a soporific, in this case mandragora. Needless to say, the episode ends happily with the stepson acquitted, the stepmother banished, and the slave crucified.[15]

These last two physicians come off as characters by no means to be despised. Both, by substituting a soporific for a poison, perform a laudable role, Xenophon's by preventing the suicide of an innocent maiden and Apuleius' by averting homicide. A physician who provided poison used for murder was liable for prosecution for homicide, under Greek[16] and Roman[17] law. If Apuleius' physician had supplied poison, the burden would have been on his shoulders to prove that he had no knowledge that the drug was to be used for murder. It was in part this that prompted him to substitute a soporific, for it is clear from his speech that, if he had believed that the drug was actually intended for use in a suicide, he would have had no qualms about supplying it. Suicide for any reason except by soldiers or slaves, was not generally prohibited by law and only rarely do the sources suggest that a terminally ill person deserved reprobation for putting an end to his suffering. Nor was a physician generally criticized for assisting even a healthy person in committing suicide. For most physicians, helping a person commit suicide would not have been construed as violating the ethics of the profession.[18]

A fable attributed to Aesop tells of a cat who heard that there were some sick hens on a farm, disguised himself as a physician and presented himself at the farmhouse. When he had called to the hens asking how they were, they replied, "Fine, if you will just go away."[19] The golden opportunities for dishonest and dishonorable activity that the physician-patient relationship provides the medical practitioner were recognized. Another of Aesop's fables relates the story of an old woman whose sight was bad offering a physician a fee to cure her. While treating her he kept stealing her possessions. After she was cured and found all her possessions gone, she refused to pay him. When summoned to court, she claimed that the physician's treatment was ineffective: "Before he began, I could see all the things in the house, but now I can't see anything."[20] Somewhat similar is a joke in the collection by Hierocles and Philagrius: A thievish physician who was treating a witty man for a disease of the eyes stole a lamp that he himself had previously lent him. One day the physician asked him, "How are your eyes?" and the wit replied, "I do not see the lamp you lent me."[21]

In the sphere of love and lust the sexual opportunities that laymen thought were available to the physician occasionally appear in the literature. Pliny the Elder simply remarks that through the medical arts adulteries also occur.[22] Martial writes an epigram that involves a woman who tells her aged husband that intercourse was prescribed as necessary for her health but that she is not willing to undergo such treatment. He orders her to submit to what he himself is not able to provide. "Immediately the men physicians come in, the lady physicians depart, and her feet are hoisted up. Oh, what stringent treatment!"[23] In the deontological medical literature there is some mention of the importance of avoiding sexual relations with patients or with members of the patients' households[24] but in lay literature there is little mention of actual sexual exploitation by physicians. Hierocles and Philagrius, however, preserve the following anecdote: A witty man, seeing a young physician rubbing down a woman in the very bloom of youth, said, "While you're treating the outside, don't violate the inside."[25] And in a completely different vein, Martial writes that a man who entrusts his care to a physician who is a rival in love will then become a eunuch.[26]

An anonymous epigram in the *Greek Anthology* describes the mutually beneficial dishonesty of an undertaker and a physician who make an arrangement whereby the former sends the latter the wrappings he steals from the grave-clothes. In return the physician sends him all his patients to bury.[27] In many of the quips at the physician it is difficult to determine whether the root of the matter lies in his dishonesty, negligence, incompetence or bad luck. Dio Chrysostom writes that "the lack of physicians or else their incompetence accounts for the increase in the number of undertakers"[28] and Seneca observes that "numerous executions are not less discreditable to a prince than are numerous funerals to a physician."[29] It is true indeed that physicians have, perhaps often unfairly, been judged to a large degree by the recovery or death of their patients, although the apparent results of treatment may be due to many causes other than the ability or incompetence of the physicians. But the death of a physician's patients has provided the epigrammatists with a plethora of gibes. Hedylus writes that one physician killed his patients merely by coming into their presence,[30] Lucilius remarks on a man dying by dreaming about a particular physician,[31] and Callicter says that simply the mention of a certain physician's name was enough to kill a patient.[32] Nicarchus goes so far as to maintain that a physician named Marcus killed a stone statue of Zeus merely by laying his hand on it.[33] In his art the physician is deemed more efficient than the astrologer. Both Niarchus[34] and Ausonius[35] tell of an astrologer predicting that a certain physician would die within nine months. Thereupon the physician merely touched him with his hand and immediately the astrologer died. Callicter writes of a physician who was so proficient that he treated three groups of five patients with different procedures and succeeded in killing all fifteen of them.[36] Lucian describes a physician, who was quite aware of his particular skills, sending his son for elementary grammar lessons. The son returns from the lesson reciting this verse from Homer: "Many strong souls he sped to Hades." The father then withdrew his son with the remark "That boy can learn that at home, for I speed many souls down to Hades."[37] Palladas expresses the sentiments that it is better to fall into the hands of an executioner than into those of a particular surgeon. For the former executes criminals justly, but the latter extorts a fee for sending his patients to Hades.[38]

Martial has two epigrams on physicians who have changed their professions. One has become an undertaker and now puts his patients to bed in his old effective way.[39] The other physician, who had been an eye-specialist, has become a gladiator. He did as a physician what he now does in his new profession.[40] The reverse process is sometimes seen, as in a fable attributed to Aesop[41] and retold by Phaedrus.[42] In this story a bungling cobbler, who was so incompetent in his profession that he could not make a living, resorting to peddling an "antidote" in areas where he was not known. By so doing he acquired quite a splendid reputation as a physician. Finally he was summoned by the king of a particular city who tricked him into confessing that his reputation was based on the gullibility of the crowd and not on any knowledge of the medical art. The king then called an assembly of his people and said: "Don't you see what idiots you are? You don't hesitate to put your lives into the hands of a man to whom no one in need of shoes ever entrusted his feet."

There were in the ancient world no medical licensure requirements.[43] Anyone could call himself a physician and set up a practice or become an itinerant healer. While there were some legal concepts of "professional" liability that could be brought against any dolose, negligent or incompetent physician,[44] there were few means of protecting the public from the quack who possessed no legitimate claim to be called a physician. In the deontological medical literature it is evident that many of the ethical principles of the art were motivated by the physician's concern for his reputation. For the physician's only credential was his reputation[45] and the protection of his reputation was of paramount concern to him. While physicians in a society where rigid licensure requirements both exist and are enforced, may be only mildly annoyed or even somewhat amused at times by being the butt of humorous attacks, physicians in the classical world, particularly those who were competent and protective of their reputations, may have been but little pleased by wholesale attacks against members of their profession.

Some classical authors were quite capable of lampooning the incompetent or stupid medical practitioner. Callicter writes an epigram on a physician who attempted to straighten a hunchback's spine. Although he killed him, he made him straighter than a ruler.[46] Nicarchus tells of the ophthalmologist Dion who was so successful that he even put out the eyes of his patient's portraits.[47]

Hierocles and Philagrius pass on a *bon mot* concerning a physician operating on a patient who was screaming in excruciating pain, so he switched to a duller knife.[48] Babrius[49] and Ausonius[50] both describe an unskilful physician who would tell his patients that they would not live beyond the next day and then would visit them no longer. One patient thus deserted recovered and when he encountered the physician was asked how things were in Hades. The man replied that Persephone and Pluto were extremely angry at physicians for not allowing the sick to die and were set on punishing them, but "I asserted under oath that you were in reality no physician but had been falsely defamed."

Physicians recognized that it was important that they look healthy and be of suitable weight. In a treatise in the Hippocratic corpus appears the statement that "the common crowd considers those who are not of excellent bodily condition to be unable to take care of others."[51] In classical culture health was held to be both a virtue itself and an indicator of virtue. Prophylaxis played an extremely important role in Greco-Roman medicine and a physician who did not appear capable of preserving his own physical excellence would probably have been considered as unable to assist others in the preservation or restoration of health. Cicero writes, "Do not imitate bad physicians who, in treating the diseases of others, claim to have mastered the whole art of healing but cannot cure themselves."[52] "Physician, heal yourself," is a proverb that knows no cultural boundaries.[53] Babrius[54] and Avianus[55] both preserve a fable involving a distended frog who tried to comfort afflicted beasts with the assurance of the efficacy of her medicines for relieving their diseases and prolonging their lives. The cattle were credulous but a perspicacious vixen said, "How is this frog, whose pale countenance is marked by a sickly hue, going to prescribe medicines for others?"

The ostentatious or pompous physician was frowned on by both his peers[56] and by many lay authors. A fable attributed to Aesop relates the following story: At the funeral of one of his friends a physician commented: "If this man had abstained from wine and taken cathartics, he wouldn't have died." One of those present replied, "You shouldn't be saying this now, when it's too late. You should have given him this advice at a time when he could have used it."[57] There are other types of ostentation criticized. Plutarch, for example, castigates physicians who perform operations in the theaters with an eye to attracting patients.[58] Dio Chrysostom distinguishes between the "so-called" physician who enchants the throng with his lectures and the "genuine" physician who actually treats patients conscientiously and without fanfare.[59] Simply being competent, however, was, in the opinion of some sources, an insufficient criterion for establishing the excellence of a physician. Aristotle, for example, maintains that "accomplished" physicians will deal with theory.[60] If they have subtle and inquiring minds, they will have something to say about natural science and claim to derive their principles from it.[61] He contrasts those who depend strictly on theory with those who work only from experience and admits that those who practice on the basis of experience succeed more frequently than those who have theory without experience. Nevertheless he maintains that men of theory are wiser than men of experience since the former recognize "the cause" where the latter do not.[62] Aristotle distinguishes between three types of physicians: "But 'physician' means both the ordinary practitioner and the master of the craft and, thirdly, the man who, as part of his general education, has studied medicine; for in almost all the arts there are some students of this type, and we assign the right of judgment as much to those generally educated in the field as to the experts."[63] Many cultivated laymen disdained the unlettered physician. Aulus Gellius, for example, relates an incident where the philosopher Calvisius Taurus mildly admonishes a physician for confusing veins and arteries. Gellius then comments, "I said that it was shameful, not only for a physician, but for all cultivated and liberally educated men, not to know even such facts pertaining to the knowledge of our bodies as are not deep and recondite, but which nature, for the purpose of maintaining our health, has allowed to be evident and obvious."[64] There are quite precise and detailed criteria for determining standards of competence for physicians delineated both in medical and in some cultivated lay literature from the classical period. In the ancient novels, where the characters whom we encounter are highly romanticized, the physician is made to respond to two types of challenges. One involves the moral dilemma that arises from the physician's frequent opportunity for unethical conduct, which has been discussed above. The second category illustrates the extent of his proficiency in circumstances different from those normally encountered in the mundane atmosphere of routine treatment of patients. This second category includes both the reanimation of a comatose person and the diagnosis of lovesickness.

Apollonius, Prince of Tyre, an anonymous Latin romance, tells about a physician who, while strolling along the seashore with some of his students, came upon a coffin. The coffin contained the body of a beautiful girl, a bag of money and a note requesting that the girl be given a proper burial. The physician instructed one of his students, who was described as a youth in appearance but in ability an old man, to prepare the body for burial. The young man took some ointment and, with an inquisitive hand, spread it over her body. To his astonishment, he thought that he had detected signs of life. He felt for her pulse, checked her nose and mouth for signs of breathing, instructed his companions to apply heat over her entire body, and then exercised her limbs. When he had completely revived her, he rushed to his mentor and said, "Come and see your student's achievement!" When the physician came and saw that the girl he had believed dead was alive, he said to his pupil, "I approve of your skill, I praise your practical knowledge, I admire your diligence. But listen, student: I don't want you to be deprived of the benefit of your skill. Here, take your fee. For this girl has brought her money with her." He then gave him half the money that had been found in the girl's coffin and ordered poultices and nourishing food for her.[65]

The fear of being buried alive appears to be deeply rooted in the psyche and is a common motif in folk-literature. Also, tales, often apocryphal, frequently are attached to various famous physicians and healers, illustrating their ability to detect life in the body of one assumed to be dead. The most famous story of this nature from the classical world involves the famous Asclepiades of Prusa, who practiced in Rome during the first century B.C. One scholar has remarked: "The multitude acclaimed Asclepiades as a god—to the annoyance, no doubt, of rival practitioners."[66] The sensation that such an event would have created among the general public is obvious. The motif is one suitable for exploitation in romance.

The diagnosis of the enervation and depression of a person suffering from lovesickness was a subject to which medical authors, both Greco-Roman and medieval,[67] devoted a great deal of attention. The view was popularly held that love (Eros) was a divinity that could afflict men as a disease, and physicians of the highest caliber (e.g. Galen, Aretaeus, Caelius Aurelianus and Oribasius) addressed themselves to the effects that love could have on an individual. Some physicians, most notably Galen, divorced lovesickness from the preternatural, recognizing its psychosomatic basis. The ability to diagnose lovesickness was popularly held to be a mark of the most skillful physicians. Highly romanticized stories were created that describe physicians such as Hippocrates and Erasistratus diagnosing lovesickness.[68] Galen himself tells of somewhat similar experiences he had encountered in his practice.[69]

In the ancient romances lovesickness is common. In the *Ephesian Tale* by Xenophon of Ephesus the hero and heroine were both love-sick but their parents, rather than consulting a physician, inquired of the oracle of Apollo in Colophon concerning the cause of the ailment. In describing the lovesickness of one of his characters in *The Golden Ass,* Apuleius laments "the shallow intellect of physicians. What does the beating of the pulse indicate, what does the immoderate heat mean, why the weary panting and the incessant tossing and turning back and forth, from side to side? Good gods! How easy is the diagnosis although not to the ingenious physician, nevertheless to anyone who has experienced Venus' passion, when you see anyone burning without any bodily fire."[70] In *Apollonius, Prince of Tyre,* the physicians who were called upon to treat a love-sick girl examined her thoroughly but were unable to discover the cause of her illness.[71] In Heliodorus' *Ethiopian Romance* a physician called in for a similar problem possessed the perspicacious acumen to recognize the nature of the complaint.[72] So also does the physician in a short love story written by Aristainetos:

Charicles, the son of the most worthy Polycles, was ill in bed on account of a desire for his father's concubine. Although he feigned a hidden physical ailment, in reality the problem was lovesickness. At any rate, the father, being a good parent and loving his son very much, immediately summoned Panakeos, a suitably-named physician, who, putting his fingers on the youth's pulse, observed skillfully his unsteady mood and noted with his eyes a diagnosable problem of the mind, but noticed no sickness at all well-known to physicians. For a long time, indeed, although he was a great physician, he was helpless. Then, by chance, the one whom the young man loved passed by. At once his pulse leapt erratically and his appearance seemed troubled and his countenance was no better than his pulse. From both sources Panakeos discovered what the youth's illness was and he did not arrive at that simply by skill but it came by chance and his gift of providence he kept to himself until the right time.

This was the first step he took in conducting his investigation. As he once again stood nearby, he ordered every girl and woman of the house to pass before the sick youth, not all together but individually, separated from each other by a short interval. And while this was happening, he took the youth's pulse, the unfailing guide for physicians, the unlying displayer of the condition residing within us. Now the youth, bedridden by desire, was unmoved by the rest of the women, but when the concubine whom he loved appeared, immediately both his appearance and his pulse again changed.

But the wise and excessively lucky physician still was going to make the proof of the ailment more certain in his own judgment, "saving the third for the saviour," as they say. Using as an excuse that the illness required the preparation of medicines for the youth, he departed for a time. As he left, promising that he would supply the medicines on the next day, he encouraged both the patient and the grieved father to be of good cheer.

When, at the appointed time, he returned, the father and all the rest of the household addressed him as saviour and, coming forward, greeted him cheerfully. The physician, being bitterly troubled, responded harshly, shouting that he was withdrawing himself from the case. While Polycles was persistently begging and inquiring about the cause of the rejection, Panakeos, shouting quite immoderately, continued to be angry and acted as though he intended to depart immediately. But the father begged still more earnestly, kissing the physician's breast and embracing his knees. Then, pretending that he was yielding to force, Panakeos heatedly expressed his reason as follows: "Your son loves my wife desperately and wastes away with an unlawful lust; I resent him now and cannot endure the sight of this would-be adulterer." Then Polycles, when he had heard, was ashamed of his son's illness, and blushed before Panakeos. But, when he had gained control of himself, he did not hesitate to beg the physician to give up his wife, calling the matter a necessary, not an adulterous, means of deliverance. While Polycles was begging in this fashion, Panakeos cried out loudly such responses as one might expect from a man to whom it had been suggested that he should change from a physician into a pimp to promote adultery, especially that of his own wife, regardless of what words were used to describe the action. When Polycles again pressed him with entreaties and kept calling the affair a necessary solution, not an adulterous one, the calculating physician, as if he were seriously debating the matter, said to Polycles: "Now really, by Zeus, if your son were in love with your concubine, you wouldn't marry her off to him because he desired her." After Polycles replied, "Yes indeed, I would, by Zeus," the wise Panakeos said, "Then direct your entreaties to yourself, Polycles, and urge the right things. For this lad loves your concubine. Now, if it is right for me to hand over my spouse to anyone whatever for the sake of his deliverance, as you say, it is indeed much more right fo you to give your concubine to your endangered son." He spoke logically, he concluded powerfully, and he persuaded the father to be obedient to his own advice.[73]

The motif of the clever, witty or harsh physician appears in several jokes included by Hierocles and Philagrius in their *Facetiae*. One involves a physician bringing a man suffering from tertian fever into a semi-tertian state. The physician then demanded half his fee.[74] A certain man approached an erudite physician and said, "Doctor, whenever I wake up, I'm dizzy for a half-hour; then I immediately return to normal." The physician replied, "Wake up a half-hour later."[75] Another story involves a man with bad breath who encountered a physician and said, "Sir, my uvula is drooping." The physician, reeling back from the man's open mouth, said," Your uvula is not drooping, but your bowels are rising."[76] Two jokes deal with harsh physicians: A harsh, one-eyed physician asked a sick man how he was. The patient replied, "Just as you see." "If you are as I see," remarked the physician, you are half dead."[77] A man went to a harsh physician and said, "Sir, I am not able to lie down, stand up, or even to sit." And the physician said, "There is nothing left for you but to be hanged up."[78] In real life harsh physicians were encountered occasionally. Galen criticizes those who were not only tactless but downright cruel in informing a patient of impending death. He mentions a physician who, in response to his patient's question whether he would die, answered, "If you are not the child of Leto, who is blessed with fair children, you will die." To another patient who asked the same question the reply was, "Patroclus [a legendary Greek hero] too, died, and he was a better man than you.[79]

Those who have been patients in training hospitals may emphathize with Martial: "I was ailing, but you attended me at once, Symmachus, with a train of a hundred apprentices. A hundred hands frosted by the north wind have pawed me. I had no fever before, Symmachus; now I have."[80] Some today perhaps share the opinions expressed by a semi-literate ex-slave at Trimalchio's table. Speaking of a friend's death, he said, "The doctors killed him. Maybe not doctors; call it fate. Anyway, a doctor's only good for your peace of mind."[81] Others were quite outspoken in their contempt for physicians. The emperor Tiberius is said always to have had a sneer for physicians.[82] Plutarch, in his "Spartan Apothegms," includes seven sayings attributed to Pausanias, King of Sparta 445-426 and 408-394 B.C. Four of these are deprecatory of physicians: When a physician paid him a visit and said, "There's nothing wrong with you," Pausanias remarked, "No there isn't; for I don't have you as my physician." Once, when one of his friends chastized him for castigating a certain physician who had never had him as a patient or harmed him in any way, Pausanias replied, "If I had ever had anything to do with him I wouldn't be alive now." On another occasion, when a physician remarked, "You've lived to be an old man," he said, "That's because I've never had you as a doctor." Pausanias summed up his attitude toward physicians in his maxim that "The best physician is the man who does not allow his patients to rot, but buries them quickly."[83]

Perhaps the most censoriously abusive excoriator of physicians in classical times was Pliny the Elder. He took as his model Cato the Censor whose loathing for the medical profession knew no bounds. But Pliny hastens to emphasize that "it was not medicine that our forefathers condemned, but the medical profession, chiefly because they refused to pay fees to profiteers in order to save their lives."[84] Indeed it is over the large income of many physicians that Pliny waxes most indignant, and he maintains that "the brightest side of the picture is the vast number of frauds. For it is not shame but the competition of rivals that keeps the fees down."[85] He accuses physicians of using patients as guinea pigs in their incessant search for novelties that will increase their fame.[86] "Physicians acquire their knowledge from our dangers, making experiments at the cost of our lives."[87] Underlying all of Pliny's berating of the medical profession is his ardent belief in the superiority of traditional folk medicine as the means of preserving and restoring health, a means available to anyone who should wish to avail himself of Pliny's *Natural History* and doctor himself naturally. Pliny does sound much the same as many of the more fanatical health food enthusiasts of the present day. Not only do physicians exploit the credulous and trusting public but also they are themselves wilfully, obstinately, stubbornly ignorant of the remarkably efficacious and inexpensive panaceas easily plucked from the fields or readily available at the local health food store.

The gamut of attitudes toward physicians in the classical world is as broad and diverse as in nearly any culture. The parallels with those of contemporary civilization appear striking until one realizes that the majority of motifs associated with the medical practitioner transcend time, place and ethnocultural barriers.

Notes

Note: The *Oxford Classical Dictionary* may be consulted for references to texts and translations of classical authors cited.

[1] *The Story of Civilization.* Part V: *The Renaissance,* New York, 1953, p. 531.

[2] 6 vols., Bloomington, 1955-1958.

[3] Plato, *The Republic* 360 E.

[4] Aristotle, *Politics* 1287 a.

[5] E.g., Cicero *De Haruspicum responsis* 16, 35; Livy *History* 40, 56, 11; 42, 47, 6; Tacitus *Annals* 12, 67, 2; *Agricola* 43, 2; Plutarch *Moralia* 195 B; Capitolinus *Gordiani Tres* 38, 5 f., in *Scriptores Historiae Augustae.*

[6] Pliny the Elder *Historia Naturalis* 29, 8, 20.

[7] Publilius Syrus *Sententiae* 373.

[8] Hierocles and Philagrius *Facetiae* 139.

[9] Lucian *Slander* 13.

[10] E.g., Quintilian *Institutio oratoria* 7, 2, 17 f.; 2, 16, 5; Calpurnius Flaccus *Declamationes* 13; pseudo-Quinrilian *Declamationes minores* 321; Libanius *Progymnasmata* 7, 3.

[11] For a discussion of the role of the physician in the ancient romances, see Darrel W. Amundsen, "Romanticizing the Ancient Medical Profession: The Characterization of the Physician in the Graeco-Roman Novel," *Bulletin of the History of Medicine,* 48, 1974, pp. 320-337.

[12] Apuleius *The Golden Ass,* 10, 23.

[13] Usually a subordinate theme, however, in individual narratives.

[14] Xenophon of Ephesus *Ephesian Tale,* 3, 5ff.

[15] Apuleius *The Golden Ass,* 10, 11.

[16] See Darrel W. Amundsen, "The Liability of the Physician in Classical Greek Legal Theory and Practice, *Journal of the History of Medicine and Allied Sciences,* 32, 1977, pp. 172-203.

[17] See Darrel W. Amundsen, "The Liability of the Physician in Roman Law," in *International Symposium on Society, Medicine and Law,* ed. H. Karplus, *Amsterdam and New York, 1973, pp. 17-30.*

[18] See Darrel W. Amundsen, "History of Medical Ethics. IV. Europe and the Americas. A. Greece and Rome," to be published in the *Encyclopedia of Bioethics.*

[19] S.A. Handford (trans.), *Fables of Aesop,* Maryland, 1954, number 95. Similar to Babrius *Fables,* 121.

[20] Handford (n. 19), number 161.

[21] Hierocles and Philagrius *Facetiae,* 142.

[2] Pliny the Elder *Historia naturalis,* 29, 8, 20f.

[23] Martial *Epigrams,* 11, 71.

[24] See Amundsen (n. 18).

[25] Hierocles and Philagrius *Facetiae,* 260.

[26] Martial *Epigrams,* 11, 74.

[27] *Greek Anthology* 125.

[28] Dio Chrysostom *Discourses,* 32, 19.

[29] Seneca *On mercy,* 1, 24, 1.

[30] Hedylus in *Greek Anthology,* 123.

[31] Lucilius in *Greek Anthology,* 257.

[32] Callicter in *Greek Anthology,* 118.

[33] Nicarchus in *Greek Anthology,* 113. Nearly identical to Ausonius *Epigrams,* 81.

[34]Nicharchus in *Greek Anthology*, 112.

[35]Ausonius *Epigrams*, 80.

[36]Calicter in *Greek Anthology*, 122.

[37]Lucian in *Greek Anthology*, 401.

[38]Palladas in *Greek Anthology*, 280.

[39]Martial *Epigrams*, 1, 30; cp. 1, 47.

[40]Ibid., 7, 74.

[41]Handford (n. 19), number 169.

[42]Phaedrus *Fables*, 1, 14.

[43]The closest parallel to licensure was in the appointment of "public physicians"; *demosieuontes iatroi* of Greece, *demosioi iatroi of* Roman Egypt, and *archiatri populares* of Rome. There is much confusion concerning their functions. It can be said with certainty, however, that these "public physicians" were not in any modern sense of the word "licensed" to practice medicine and that many if not a majority of physicians were not "public physicians."

[44]See the articles by Amundsen cited above (nn. 16, 17).

[45]See Amundsen (n. 18).

[46]Callicter in *Greek Anthology*, 120.

[47]Nicarchus in *Greek Anthology*, 112; cp. anonymous epigram in *Greek Anthology*, 126.

[48]Hierocles and Philagrius *Facetiae*, 177.

[49]Babrius *Fables*, 75.

[50]Ansonius *Epigrams*, 4.

[51]*The Physician*, 1.

[52]Cicero *Epistulae ad familiares*, 4, 5, 5.

[53]Cf. Luke 4:23; Euripides Fragment 1086.

[54]Babrius *Fables*, 120.

[55]Avianus *Fables*, 6.

[56]See Amundsen (n. 18).

[57]L.W. Daly, *Aesop without Morals*, New York and London, 1961, number 114.

[58]Plutarch *Moralia*, 71 A.

[59]Dio Chrysostom *Discourses*, 33, 6f.

[60]Aristotle *Nicomachean Ethics*, 1180 b.

[61]Aristotle *On Respiration*, 480 b.

[62]Aristotle *Metaphysics*, 981 a.

[63]Aristotle *Poetics*, 1282 a.

[64]Aulus Gellius *Noctes Atticae*, 18, 10.

[65]*Apollonius, Prince of Tyre*, 25 ff.

[66]T.C. Allbutt, *Greek Medicine in Rome*, New York, 1921, p. 184.

[67]See J.L. Lowes, "The Loveres Maladye of Hereos," *Modern Philology*, 11, 1914, pp. 491 ff.

[68]On these see Amundsen (n. 11), pp. 333 ff.

[69]Ibid., pp. 335 f.

[70]Apuleius *The Golden Ass*, 10, 2.

[71]*Apollonius, Prince of Tyre*, 18.

[72]Heliodorus *Ethiopian Romance*, 4, 7.

[73]Aristainetos *Epistulae*, 1, 13; translation quoted from Amundsen (n. 11), pp. 329 ff.

[74]Heirocles and Philagrius *Facetiae*, 175 a.

[75]Ibid., 3.

[76]Ibid., 235.

[77]Ibid., 185.

[78]Ibid., 183.

[79]Quoted from Ludwig Edelstein, "Hippocratic Prognosis," in *Ancient Medicine: Selected Papers of Ludwig Edelstein*, ed. Owsei Temkin and C. Lilian Temkin, Baltimore, 1967, p. 76, n. 13.

[80]Martian *Epigrams*, 5, 9.

[81]Petronius *Satyricon*, 42.

[82]Tacitus *Annals*, 6, 46; Suetonius *Life of Tiberius*, 68, 4; Plutarch *Moralia*, 794.

[83]Plutarch *Moralia*, 231 A.

[84]Pliny the Elder *Historia naturalis*, 29, 8, 16.

[85]Ibid., 29, 8, 21.

[86]Ibid., 29, 5, 11.

[87]Ibid., 29, 8, 18.

VI

Possession, Sex and Hysteria: The Growth of Demonism in Later Antiquity

Gerald Erickson's essay is really three articles in one, each of which illuminates some important aspects of popular culture in today's world. From the comedian Flip Wilson's "the devil made me do it," which is regarded as silly duplicity; to the more than frivolous popularity of The Exorcist *that points to real concerns about the nature of evil in a world marked by terrorism, atrocity and a dangerous manipulation of power; to the serious incidence of mental illnesses in the face of scientific advances in medicine, popular concepts of irrationality and possession dominate tabloid newspapers, television, science fiction and pseudo-religous cults today. In the first part of his essay, Erickson takes us to the Fifth Century B.C., when possession was sanctioned as a beneficial gift by the intellectual and priestly establishment. In the second part, Erickson recounts the shift from an elite, positive tradition to a popular movement that provided demonic explanation for the deteriorating values and rapidly changing social and economic system that characterized Rome in the First Century A.D. In the third part, we see popular pagan traditions of possession combine with ancient medical theories about hysteria and with the doomsday psychology of the early nazarene cult to bring us to the threshold of the Christian era.*

Gerald Erickson is a member of the Classics Department of the University of Minnesota. In addition to teaching courses in Latin and Greek languages and literature, he has developed and teaches such courses as Madness and Deviant Behavior in Ancient Rome and Greece, Eroticism and Family Life in the Greco-Roman World, *and* Witchcraft and the Occult in Greece and Rome.

Possession, Sex and Hysteria: The Growth of Demonism In Later Antiquity

Gerald Erickson

Traditional history texts customarily give short shrift to what was one of the most significant changes which occurred in a period of less than five hundred years in Classical antiquity—the change from possession viewed as a blessing conferred by the gods on a select few to possession as a common affliction inflicted by demons. Why this topic, so pregnant with suggestions about the interaction between popular culture and the philosophical speculations of the ruling classes, should be neglected by conventional historians is in itself a fascinating question and certainly worthy of extensive treatment, but what I propose to do in this paper is much more modest, to give a brief description of the change and to suggest a somewhat esoteric hypothesis which may at least in part account for the ready acceptance of demonism by the Christian church.

The emergence of demonism in later antiquity, i.e. from the first century A.D., is a complex issue, which involves an analysis of socio-economic factors and their effects on the ideological superstructure. In keeping with the more limited scope of this paper, I shall attempt merely to present some of the evidence for this change and to suggest one factor which predisposed Christians to accept and propagate demonic possession as something which was both imminent and to be feared.

Only by an analysis of the origins of the circumstances predisposing early Christian communities to the belief in demonism can we begin to make any assessment of the reasons for the inordinate, by artistic criteria, success of Peter Blatty's *The Exorcist* and the inevitable progeny of D grade movies which followed in its wake. The first step of our inquiry will be to demonstrate the early (5th century B.C.) attitude toward possession, the palpable change which was occurring in the first century A.D., and one of the considerations which made the phenomenon of demonic possession so compatible to Christianity.

Divine Possession in the Fifth Century B.C.

In a remarkable passage in the *Phaedrus,* Plato sets forth the view accepted in the fifth century B.C. toward the madness which comes from being possessed by a god.

If it were simply that madness is an evil, the saying would be true. The greatest things, however, come to us from madness, sent as divine gift. For the prophetess at Delphi and the priestesses at Dodona gave, when they were mad, many splendid benefits to Greece both in the realm of public and private matters, but when they were sane gave little or nothing. If we should speak of the Sibyl and the others who have used prophetic inspiration foretold many things to many and afterwards made them fortunate in what followed, then we would have to speak for a long time.[1]

Plato, through the persona of Socrates, goes so far in his encomium of divine madness that he connects the derivation of *mania* (madness) with *mantike* (the prophetic art). In so doing he indicates that this possession by a god confers even more than foreknowledge from the gods:

The ancients attest that madness which comes from a god is in name and fact as much superior to augury as to sanity which comes from humans. Moreover, when diseases and the greatest troubles have come upon certain families from ancient guilt, madness has come and by prophecy has found a way of release for those in need of it. By taking refuge in prayer and service to the gods, he who has this madness is made safe for the present and following time by purifications and sacred rites, for whoever has this madness finds a release from present evils.[2]

It would be interesting to note here that Plato's view of a madness as a possible balm in times of intense grief and as an escape from an untenable situation has considerable similarity to R.D. Laing's definition of madness as an effort to reconstruct a more viable personality:

In over 100 cases where we studied the actual circumstance around a social event when one person becomes to be regarded as schizophrenic, it seems to us that *without exception* the experience and behavior that gets labeled schizophrenic is a *special strategy that a person invents in order to live in an unlivable situation.* In his life situation the person has come to feel he is in an untenable position. He cannot make a move, or make no more, without being beset by contradictory and paradoxical pressures and demands, pushes and pulls, both internally from himself and externally from those around him. He is, as it were, in a position of checkmate. (emphasis by Laing).[3]

If one follows Plato's and Laing's views of madness as a potential blessing, then psychiatric intervention can only disturb or frustrate this salutary process. This sequence, the destruction and reconstruction of self in madness, "is very seldom allowed to occur because we are so busy treating the patient, whether by chemotherapy, shock therapy, milieu therapy, group therapy, psychotherapy, family therapy—sometimes now, in the very best, most advanced places, by the lot."[4]

Without pressing the similarities between Plato's and Laing's views of beneficial madness, it may not be amiss to suggest that the "new" principles rediscovered by the anti-psychiatry movement have been around for a long time.

Prophetic madness is not the only variety of divine madness which Plato regards as beneficial to mankind:

Socrates: And we made four divisions of the divine madness, ascribing them to the four gods, saying that prophecy was inspired by Apollo, the mystical (*telestike*) madness by Dionysus, the poetic by the Muses, and the madness of love, inspired by Eros we said was best.[5]

It should be emphasized that the divine madness referred to by Plato is in Greek *enthusiasmos,* meaning literally "having the god within." All four kinds were envisioned as a kind of possession by the appropriate god to be conferred as a special dispensation on favored or deserving mortals. Manic or prophetic possession was almost invariably associated with Apollo and institutionalized in temples dedicated to that deity. Although not the only such institutionalized source of prophecy in antiquity, the oracle of Apollo at Delphi was certainly the most famous. There the Pythoness, priestess of Apollo, sat on a tripod in the inner chamber and after achieving a state of possession would issue prophecies which were normally interpreted by the attendant priests of Apollo. Needless to say, offerings were accepted; in fact, the wealth accumulated at Delphi became legendary.

The most detailed and dramatic description of mantic possession is found in Lucan's *Pharsalia,* in which Appius, a Roman general during the Civil War between Caesar and Pompey, went to the oracle at Delphi to learn the outcome of the conflict. Since the oracle had fallen into desuetude centuries earlier, the priestess of Apollo, Phemonoe, was reluctant to become possessed. When Appius persisted and threatened her, she attempted to simulate possession, but was unconvincing. Finally, under duress she allowed the god. Lucan's description, although probably based on traditional accounts and not on personal observation, is so vivid that it will be quoted here at some length:

Fearing to take her stand on that dread threshold, Apollo's priestess sought by vain deceit to discourage Appius from his eagerness to learn the future. "Why," she asked, "does presumptuous hope of learning the truth draw you hither, O Roman? The chasm of Parnassus, fallen dumb and silent, has buried its god. Either the breath of inspiration has failed yonder outlet and has shifted its path to a distant region of the world; or, when Pytho was burned by the brands of barbarians, the ashes sank into the vast caverns and blocked the passage of Phoebus; or Delphi is dumb by the will of Heaven, and it is thought enough that the verses of the ancient Sibyl, entrusted to your nation, should tell forth the hidden future; or else Apollo, accustomed to exclude the guilty from his shrine, finds none in our age for whose sake to unseal his lips."

The maiden's craft was plain, and even her fears proved the reality of the deity she denied. Then the circling band confined the tresses above her brow; and the hair that streamed down her back was bound by the white fillet and the laurel of Phocis. When still she paused and hesitated, the priest thrust her by force into the temple. Dreading the oracular recess of the inner shrine, she halted by the entrance, counterfeiting inspiration and uttering feigned words from a bosom unstirred; and no inarticulate cry of indistinct utterance proved that her mind was inspired with the divine frenzy. To appius, who heard her false prophecy, she could do less harm than to the oracle and Apollo's repute for truth. Her words, that rushed not forth with tremulous cry; her voice, which had not power to fill the space of the vast cavern; her laurel wreath, which was not raised off her head by the bristling hair; the unmoved floor of the temple and the motionless trees—all these betrayed her dread of trusting herself to Apollo. Appius perceived that the oracle was dumb, and cried out in fury: "Profane wretch, I myself and the gods whom you counterfeit will punish you even as you deserve, unless you go down into the cave and cease, when consulted concerning the mighty turmoil of a terrified world, to speak your own words." Scared at last the maiden took refuge by the tripods; she drew near to the vast chasm and there stayed; and her bosom for the first time drew in the divine power, which the inspiration of the rock, still active after so many centuries, forced upon her. At last Apollo mastered the breast of the Delphian priestess; as fully as ever in the past, he forced his way into her body, driving out her former thoughts, and bidding her human nature to come forth and leave her heart at his disposal. Frantic she careers about the cave, with her neck under possession; the fillets and garlands of Apollo, dislodged by her bristling hair, she whirls with tossing head through the void spaces of the temple; she scatters the tripods that impede her random course; she boils over with fierce fire, while enduring the wrath of Phoebus. Nor does he ply the ship and goad alone, and dart flame into her vitals: she has to bear the curb as well, and is not permitted to reveal as much as she is suffered to know. All time is gathered up together: all the centuries crowd her breast and torture it; the endless chain of events is revealed; all the future struggles to the light; destiny contends with destiny, seeking to be uttered. The creation of the world and its destruction, the compass of the Ocean and the sum of the sands—all these are before her. Even as the Sibyl of Cumae in her Euboean cave resenting that her inspiration should be at the service of many nations, chose among them with haughty hand and picked out from the great heap of destiny the fate of Rome, so Phemonoe, possessed by Phoebus, as troubled and sought long ere she found the name of Appius concealed among the names of mightier men—Appius, who came to question the god hidden in the land of Castalia. When she found it, first the wild frenzy overflowed through her foaming lips; she groaned and uttered loud inarticulate cries with panting breath; next, a dismal wailing filled the vast cave; and at last, when she was mastered, came the sound of articulate speech: "Roman, thou shalt have no part in the mighty ordeal and shalt escape the awful threats of war, and thou alone shalt stay at peace in a broad hollow of the Euboean coast." Then Apollo closed up her throat and cut short her tale.[6]

Lucan then described her as still possessed after giving the oracle. After some time she slipped into unconsciousness whereupon Apollo filled her mind with forgetfulness so that she would not be burdened with knowledge of the future.

Apollo's prophecy was accurate, but as often happened, misunderstood. Appius died before the battle and was buried on the Euboean shore.

The best known literary example of mantic possession is found in Priam's daughter, Cassandra, whose states of possession by Apollo were considerably less frenetic than Phemonoe's. The gift, as is well known, became a curse by revealing impending doom.[7]

Telestic or ritual possession was associated almost exclusively with the god Dionysus. In this type of possession the altered state of consciousness was induced in a group through participation in a ritual resulting in possession of each participant by the god. Although the benefits resulting from telestic possession are less explicit than for mantic possession, in which knowledge of the future is promised, ritual possession can be seen as a transcendence of normality, a communion joining participants with elemental nature, each other, and the god. It is not without significance that Dionysus was most popular among the lower classes and women, who were in most Greek communities, especially Athens, a most oppressed and repressed group. Telestic possession either in voluntary or spontaneous form seems to have been throughout subsequent history associated with social groups experiencing oppression and to be particularly likely to increase during times of social tension, conflict and uncertainty.

As might be expected, some classicists have found the process of telestic possession with its emphasis on the irrational to be alien to the classical ideal and have had few compunctions of conscience about attempting to reconstruct our perception of ancient reality to fit their idealized image of classical antiquity. As an example of this kind of attempt, we cite Sandys, an eminent Victorian classicist:

In art as well as poetry, the representation of these wild states of enthusiasm was apparently due to imagination alone, for in prose literature we have very little evidence, in historic times, of women actually holding revels in the open air. Such a practice would have been alien to the spirit of seclusion which pervaded the life of womankind in Greece.[8]

The available evidence, however, quite clearly contradicts this assertion. Numerous ancient historical sources affirm the existence of outdoor rituals frequented primarily by women. Diodorus Siculus, for example, asserts:

In many Greek states congregations (*Bakheiai*) of women assemble every second year, and the unmarried are allowed to carry the Thyrsus and share the transports (*synenthousiazein*) of their elders.[9]

Other historical attestations are found in Pausanias for Arcadia, in Aelian for Mytilene, in Firmicus Maternus for Crete, and Herodotus for Thrace.[10] In addition, Plutarch described an incident which occurred apparently during his lifetime when a rescue party had to be sent out to help a group of women who had been cut off by a snowstorm in the mountains.[11] Inscriptional evidence, discovered after Sandys had penned his skeptical view of the actual occurrence of outdoor Bacchic rites, also clearly points to such rituals in Thebes, Opus, Melos, Pergamum, Priene and Rhodes. In any event it seems to be quite certain that the existence of these rituals is more than a figment of the literary imagination.[12]

The most famous and dramatic description of the Dionysiac rites is found in Euripides' *Bacchae,* in which King Pentheus of Thebes attempts to prevent the entrance of the new god and his rituals into Thebes. We may be more confident today than scholars of the past have been that the ritual described by Euripides is essentially accurate. Because Dodds has made the most thorough and unprejudiced study of the Dionysiac ritual, his conclusion has special significance:

To sum up: I have tried to show that Euripides' description of maenadism is not to be accounted for in terms of "the imagination alone"; that inscriptional evidence (incomplete as it is) reveals a closer relationship with actual cult than Victorian scholars realised; and that the maenad, however mythical certain of her acts, is not in essence a mythological character but an observed and still observable human type. Dionysus has still his votaries or victims, though we call them by other names; and Pentheus was confronted by a problem which other civil authorities have had to face in real life.[13]

Poetic madness, the inspiration which the Muses breathe into the poet during the act of creating or performing, finds formulaic expression in the traditional invocation of the Muse at the beginning of an epic poem. In the *Ion* Plato gives a description of this poetic madness:

For a poet is a light and winged and sacred thing, and is unable ever to indite until he has been inspired and put out of his senses, and his mind is no longer in him: every man, while he retains possession of that is powerless to indite a verse or chant an oracle. Seeing then that it is not by art that they compose and utter so many things about the deeds of men—as you do about Homer—but by a divine dispensation, each is able only to compose that to which the Muse has stirred him, this man dithyrambs, another laudatory odes, another dance-songs, another epic or else iambic verse, but each is at fault in any other kind. For not by art do they utter these things, but by divine influence.[14]

The madness of love, possession by Eros or Aphrodite, is a central theme of the *Phaedrus,* in which it is extolled as the highest form of madness:

All my discourses so far have been about the fourth kind of madness, which causes him to be regarded as mad, who, when he sees the beauty on earth, remembering the true beauty, feels his wings growing and longs to stretch them for an upward flight, but cannot do so, and, like a bird, gazes upward and neglects the things below. My discourse has shown that this, of all inspirations *(ton enthousiaseon),* is the best and of the highest origin to him who has it or shares in it, and that he who loves the beautiful, partaking in this madness, is called a lover.[15]

These examples of beneficial madness from possession bring out with sufficient clarity the favorable attitude of the 5th century Athenians toward madness arising from possession by a deity. The idea persisted, especially among those conversant with Greek philosophy; Cicero, for example, is not far from Plato when he says: "therefore no great man ever existed who did not enjoy some portion of divine inspiration."[16]

The Death of These Blessings

These beneficent aspects of possession either disappeared from the popular consciousness or were greatly attenuated during the period between the fifth century B.C. and the first century A.D. By the third century B.C., the major oracles of antiquity were not functioning. Lucan, for example, in the description which we gave earlier, mentions that the Delphic oracle had been silent for two centuries. The immediate reasons for their demise may be found in the growing skepticism toward the old Olympic pantheon and their replacement by the various mystery religions.

Ritual possession had always been considered suspect by the ruling classes for several reasons: the direct experience of and contact with the god eliminated the need for intermediaries, priests who could use the religious belief for state purpose and channel activities away from those which were potentially inimical to the ruling classes. In the rites themselves the boundaries of normal everyday life were transcended; the ruling classes feared that people accustomed to cross these boundaries may also be increasingly disposed to cross other boundaries such as the class stratification of the political order. Dionysus had always been primarily a god associated with the lower social classes. The Romans particularly feared any mass gathering of the commoners which was not under the control and supervision of the state, in other words the ruling classes.

That early Christianity also incorporated telestic possession into religious practice is evidenced by Acts 2:11:

And, when the days of Pentecost were fulfilled, all were together in the same place and suddenly from the sky there was a sound like a violent wind coming, and it filled the whole building where they were sitting. Separate tongues as of fire appeared to them, and it sat above each of them. All were filled with the holy Spirit and all began to speak in various tongues as the holy Spirit gave them to speak.[17]

The attitudes of the developing church hierarchy toward telestic possession is a large topic, which would require a massive tome for complete documentation. It should suffice here to observe that the hierarchy did oppose the encouragement of this phenomenon for reasons quite similar to those of the Roman ruling classes: they felt the need to establish their functionaries as necessary intermediaries and to create dependence of the laity upon them for all the sacraments. Direct experience with the deity would diminish the intermediary role of the priest, would provide a fertile source of heretical movements, and possibly a base for movements that would acquire a political and revolutionary significance. The church was, of course, not uniformly successful in suppressing these spontaneous outbreaks of possession, and groups arising from telestic ritual did in fact prove to be troublesome sources of heresy and revolution during the Middle Ages.[18]

Poetic inspiration became in later antiquity little more than a cliché, a generic formula. Increasingly, poetry became a craft as in Horace's *Ars Poetica*. The imitative nature of much of the literature of later classical antiquity would serve to reinforce this observation; if divine inspiration of the act of literary creation was ever operative, it ceased to function, and increasingly the effort was made merely to emulate the old models.

The change in attitude toward love from the fifth century B.C. is extremely significant and, in a global way, quite demonstrable. Evidence for a change in attitude toward love is quite apparent from the first century B.C. on. Among the lyric poets the wasting away of the unrequited lover is a *locus tritus,* but it is Lucretius who in the first century B.C. paints the grimmest view of the madness of love.

This, then, is what we term Venus. This is the origin of the thing called love—that drop of Venus' honey that first drips into our heart, to be followed by numbing heart-ache; though the object of your love may be absent, images of it still haunt you and the beloved name chimes sweetly in your ears. If you find yourself thus passionately enamoured of an individual, you should keep well away from such images, thrust

from you anything that might feed your passion, and turn your mind elsewhere. Vent
the seed of love upon other objects. By clinging to it you assure yourself the certainty
of heart-sickness and pain. With nourishment the festering sore quickens and
strengthens. Day by day the frenzy heightens and the grief deepens. Your only
remedy is to lance the first wound with new incisions; to salve it, while it is still fresh,
with promiscuous attachments; to guide the motions of your mind into some other
channel.[19]

This of course reflects the Epicurean view and does come from
the first century B.C., which fact may not be without significance.
We should bear in mind that the Epicureans were not opposed to sex
in moderation, but to romantic love.

A similar change of attitude toward sexual love is clearly
indicated in a physician of the first century A.D., Soranus, whose
work, except for one treatise on gynecology, has been preserved only
in a Latin translation by Caelius Aurelianus, probably from the
fifth century A.D.:

Some physicians hold that love is a proper remedy for insanity, on the ground that it
frees the patient's mind from the agitation caused by madness and thus purifies it.
They are not aware of the obvious truth that in many cases love is the very cause of
madness. Thus one man through love for Proserpina sought to enter the lower world,
thinking he could rightly take to wife a goddess wedded to another. Another threw
himself into the sea because of his longing for the sea nymph Amphitrite. In the rich
mythology of the Greeks there is a story that a woman of divine descent, harried by
human fates and beset by the grim pangs of vengeance, killed her offspring with her
own hand. Nor should we disdain the view of those who have actually called love a
form of insanity because of the similarity of the symptoms which the victims show.
And surely it is absurd and wrong to recommend, of all remedies for the disease, the
very thing that you are trying to treat.[20]

Again Soranus reflects a conspicuously negative attitude
toward sexual love:

And coitus or venery, which these physicians recommend in cases of epilepsy, has
itself been called minor epilepsy; various parts are subject to spasms, and at the same
time there occur panting, sweating, rolling of eyes, flushing of the face. And the
completion of coitus brings with it a feeling of malaise along with pallor, weakness, or
dejection. Moreover, the harmful effect of it on the nerves and sinews of an epileptic is
seen in the fact that often when an attack is imminent the patient first suffers an
ejaculation of semen during sleep.[21]

In later antiquity, however, asceticism—a revulsion against the
sensual and particularly the sexual—swept across the ancient
world. It should be emphasized that this was not just a Christian
phenomenon, but rather that the Christians partook of what was a
growing trend. Musonius Rufus, a non-Christian philosopher
banished from Rome in 66 A.D., held that sexual acts (even for men)

outside of marriage were not permissible. Apollonius of Tyana, an ascetic philosopher and mystic regarded as a competitor to Jesus by the early Christians, maintained that even married love was impure. Precursors of Neo-Platonism adapted Plato's doctrine of ideas so that flesh and the world were considered to be impure, and spirituality and ideality timeless and good.[22]

Although the adducing of these few passages does not prove the transition of attitude from the earlier view of love as a blessing to one of fear and disgust, I would suggest that they do reflect the general trend toward asceticism in later antiquity, which will be discussed later in this paper.

By the first century A.D. the idea of divine possession as a blessing conferred on select individuals or groups had become little more than a literary concept. A few exceptions remained: the early Christian practices as described in *Acts* and, perhaps, the rites of Cybele as described in Lucian's *On the Syrian Goddess* and by Apuleius in *The Golden Ass*. This did not, however, result in the disappearance of belief in possession, but over the period from the fifth century B.C. to the first century A.D. a curious metamorphosis in attitude toward possession can be observed—from a blessing in the form of divine possession to a curse in the form of demonic possession. As Harnack observed:

The distinguishing trait of belief in demons in the second century consists first of all in the fact that it spreads from the obscure and lower strata of society to the upper ones, and even finds its way into literature, becoming far more important than before; secondly in that it no longer has beside it a strong, simple, and open religion to keep it under; furthermore in that the power of the demon, hitherto considered as morally indifferent, is now conceived as evil; finally in the individual application of the new religion which at at that time numbered the mental affections also among its consequences. If all these causes are taken into consideration, the extraordinary spread of belief in demons and the numerous outbursts of demoniacal affections must be attributed to the combined effects of the well-known fact that in imperial times faith in the ancient religions was disappearing.[23]

The perceptions of demonic possession in later antiquity are best known from New Testament accounts. The most frequent and recurring type of miracles performed by Jesus is the administering of healing exorcisms of demons. In the Gospel of Mark the very first miracle which Jesus performed after emerging from the wilderness is an exorcism. In fact, just for illustration, we'll cite the exorcisms performed by Jesus from only one Gospel, Mark's.

And there was in their synagogue a man with an unclean spirit. He shouted out and said, "what do you have to do with us, Jesus Nazarene? Have you come to destroy us? I know who you are, the Holy one of God!" And Jesus threatened him, saying, "Be silent, and come out of that man." The unclean spirit convulsed, shouted loudly, and came out of him. (Mark 1:23-26)

Clearly casting out demons was a major activity of his ministry:

And he cured many who were suffering from various afflictions, and he cast out many demons. He did not allow them to speak, because they knew him. (Mark 1:34)

And he was preaching in their synagogues, and in all Galilee, and casting out demons. (Mark 1:39)

And the unclean spirits, when they saw him, fell before him and shouted saying, "You are the Son of God." He threatened them vehemently that they should not reveal him. (Mark 3:11-12)

Jesus also conferred the power of exorcism on his disciples:

And he gave them the power of curing illnesses and of casting out demons. (Mark 3:15)

Most vivid of all the exorcisms is the description of the demoniac of the Gerasenes:

And they went to the other side of the lake into the region of the Gerasenes. Immediately a man with an unclean spirit ran up from the tombs to him as he was disembarking. The man had his home in the tombs and no one was able to bind him with chains, because, although often bound with chains and stocks, he smashed the chains and broke the stocks and no one was able to tame him. Day and night he was among the tombs and in the mountains, shouting and beating himself with stones. When he saw Jesus from a distance, the demoniac ran up and worshipped him. Shouting loudly, he said, "Jesus, Son of the Highest God, what business do you have with me? I adjure you in the name of God not to torture me," and Jesus said to him, "Come out from the man, unclean spirit." Jesus asked him, "What is your name?" He answered, "My name is Legion, for we are many." He begged Jesus insistently that he not be driven out of the region. There was around the mountain a flock of pigs grazing. The spirits entreated him, "Send us into the pigs so that we can enter them." Immediately Jesus agreed. The unclean spirits left the man and entered into the pigs; in one great rush the flock, around two thousand of them, went headlong into the sea and were drowned. (Mark 5:1-13)

Apparently the apostles sent out by Jesus were also successful in performing exorcisms:

And they (the apostles) went out and preached that people should repent, they cast out many demons, anointed with oil many sick persons, and healed them. (Mark 6:12-13)

The last exorcism performed in the Gospel of Mark is perhaps the most interesting because of its graphic description of the effects

of possession:

Coming to his disciples, he saw a large crowd around them as well as scribes arguing with them. As soon as all the people saw him, they were dumbfounded and afraid. They ran up and greeted him. Jesus asked them, "What are you arguing about among yourselves?" An individual in the crowd answered, "Teacher, I brought to you my son who has a dumb spirit. Every time this spirit seizes him, he dashes him to the ground and he froths at the mouth, gnashes his teeth, and goes rigid. I asked your disciples to cast him out, but they were not able to do it." Jesus answered them, "You unbelieving generation, how long will I be among you? How long must I put up with you? Bring him to me." They brought him and when he saw Jesus, the spirit threw the boy into convulsions. After falling onto the ground he rolled frothing at the mouth. Jesus asked the boy's father, "How long has it been since this first happened?" He answered, "From infancy. The spirit often cast him into fire and water to destroy him, but, if you can do anything, take pity and help us." Jesus answered him, "If you can believe, all things are possible to a believer." Immediately, the boy's father exclaimed and with tears responded, "I believe, master. Help my unbelief." When Jesus saw the crowd gathering, he threatened the unclean spirit and said to it, "Deaf and speechless spirit, I order you, come out of him and do not enter him any more." Shouting and convulsing the boy, the unclean spirit came out of him, who so resembled a corpse that many said he was dead. Jesus, however, held his hand and raised him up and the boy rose. (Mark 9:13-26)

The citations from the Gospel of Mark should indicate that at the time of the composition of this Gospel—probably the last quarter of the 1st century A.D.—demonic possession was such a central concern that any great mystical teacher had to demonstrate power over demons to establish credibility among the multitudes.

It should be pointed out that the almost obsessional concern of this period with demonic possession was not limited to Christians. It seemed to pervade all strata of society and provided a challenge to any prophet or mystical teacher of that period. One such was Apollonius of Tyana, who lived and taught in the first century A.D. Since his career is contemporaneous with the authorship of the Gospel of Mark, exorcisms performed by him should be of special interest. Flavius Philostratus, whose lengthy biography of Apollonius, written probably at the end of the second century from several written sources, recounts his teachings, travels and miracles. One particularly interesting parallel is described in considerable detail:

Now while he was discussing the question of libations, there chanced to be present in his audience a young dandy who bore so evil a reputation for licentiousness, that his conduct had once been the subject of coarse street-corner songs. His home was Corcyra, and he traced his pedigree to Alcinous, the Phaeacian who entertained Odysseus. Apollonius then was talking about libations, and was urging them not to drink out of a particular cup, but to reserve it for the gods, without ever touching it or drinking out of it. But when he also urged them to have handles on the cup, and to pour the libation over the handle, because that is the part of the cup at which men are least likely to drink, the youth burst out into loud and coarse laughter, and quite drowned his voice. Then Apollonius looked up at him and said: "It is not yourself that perpetrates this insult, but the demon, who drives you on without your knowing it." And in fact the youth was, without knowing it, possessed by a devil; for he would laugh at things that no one else laughed at, and then he would fall to weeping for no reason at all, and he would talk and sing to himself. Now most people thought that it was the boisterous humour of youth which led him into such excesses; but he was really the mouth-piece of a devil, though it only seemed a drunken frolic in which on that occasion he was indulging. Now when Apollonius gazed on him, the demon in him began to utter cries of fear and rage, such as one hears from people who are being branded or racked; and the demon swore that he would leave the young man alone and never take possession of any man again. But Apollonius addressed him with anger, as a master might a shifty, rascally, and shameless slave and so on, and he ordered him to quit the young man and show by a visible sign that he had done so. "I will throw down yonder statue," said the devil, and pointed to one of the images which was in the king's portico, for there it was that the scene took place. But when the statue began by moving gently, and then fell down, it would defy anyone to describe the hubbub which arose thereat and the way they clapped their hands with wonder. But the young man rubbed his eyes as if he had just woke up, and he looked towards the rays of the sun, and won the consideration of all, who now had turned their attention to him; for he no longer showed himself licentious, nor did he stare madly about, but he had returned to his own self, as thoroughly as if he had been treated with drugs; and he gave up his dainty dress and summery garments and the rest of his sybaritic way of life, and he fell in love with the austerity of philosophers, and donned their cloak, and stripping off his old self modelled his life in the future upon that of Apollonius.[24]

The parallels between the careers and teaching of Jesus and Apollonius were for early Christianity a source of considerable concern and embarrassment. Eusebius in an attempt at refutation of Apollonius' teachings and denigration of his miracles reveals much about the Christian attitude toward demons:

These then are the achievements which preceded his accusation, and it behoves us to notice throughout the treatise that, even if we admit the author to tell the truth in his stories of miracles, he yet clearly shows that they were severally performed by Apollonius with the cooperation of a demon. For his presentiment of the plague, though it might not seem to be magical and uncanny, if he owed it, as he himself said, to the lightness and purity of his diet, yet might quite as well have been a premonition imparted to him in intercourse with a demon. For though the other stories of his having grasped and foretold the future by virtue of his prescience can be refuted by a thousand arguments which Philostratus' own text supplies, nevertheless, it we allow this particular story to be true, I should certainly say that his apprehension of futurity was anyhow in some cases, though it was not so in all, due to some uncanny contrivance of a demon that was his familiar. This is clearly proved by the fact that he did not retain his gift of foreknowledge uniformly and in all cases; but was at fault in most cases, and had through ignorance to make enquiries, as he would not have needed to do, if he had been endowed with divine power and virtue. And the very cessation of the plague, according to the particular turn which was given to the drama, has already been shown to have been a delusion and nothing more.

Moreover, the soul of Achilles should not have been lingering about his own monument, quitting the Islands of the Blest and the places of repose, as people would probably say. In this case too it was surely a demon that appeared to Apollonius and in whose presence he found himself? Then again the licentious youth was clearly the victim of an indwelling demon; and both it and the Empusa and the Lamia, which is said to have played off its mad pranks on Menippus, were probably driven out by him with the help of a more important demon; the same is true also of the youth who had been driven out of his mind by the mad dogs; and the frenzied dog itself was restored to its senses by the same method. You must then, as I said, regard the whole series of miracles wrought by him, as having been accomplished through a ministry of demons; for the resuscitation of the girl must be divested of any miraculous character, if she was really alive all the time and still bore in herself a vital spark, as the author says, and if a vapour rose over her face. For it is impossible, as I said before, that such a miracle should have been passed over in silence in Rome itself, if it happened when the sovereign was close by.[24]

It is interesting that Eusebius, reflecting the Christian viewpoint, does not deny the reality of the exorcisms or even of the miracles, but attributes his success to the complicity of demons. Interestingly, this was the very charge laid against Jesus by the scribes:

The scribes, who had come down from Jerusalem, said, "Beelzebub (Beelzeboul—lord of the flies) possesses him, because he is casting out demons under the leadership of demons. (Mark 3:22)

Nevertheless it does appear that the early Christians accepted the concept of demonic possession with great alacrity and fostered this belief as an integral part of their doctrine. Osterreich, who along with the early nineteeenth century Tambonino,[25] has made perhaps the most exhaustive study of the phenomenon of possession, makes a comparison of demonic possession among pagans and Christians:

The contrast between the pre-Christian and Christian eras is striking enough, according to documents adduced by Tamborino. Judging by the number of pages, the difference is not great; the whole bulk of documents relating to the non-Christian epoch occupies twenty-four pages, while those of the Christian period occupies twenty-eight. But on closer inspection it appears that for the first part all quotations relating in a general way to states of enthusiasm have been collected, even the briefest references in detached phrases, while the second admits only real states of possession and veritable descriptions. In addition the Christian testimonies are not even complete, as may be convincingly shown by a simple comparison with the index of *Bibliothek der Kirchenvater,* and in order to make the second correspond to the first its scope would have to be extended, and all evidence relating to states considered as inspired by the Holy Ghost included. The space occupied by the testimonies of the Christian era would then be infinitely greater. This contrast between the two groups of evidence can scarcely be explained, except by admitting that possession has played a much more important part during the Christian era than in earlier times.[26]

The Christians, although certainly not the only segment of the population in the imperial period which believed in demonic possession, did indeed find it most compatible with their basic doctrines, and in the ensuing centuries exerted themselves to foster and promote belief in demonic possession. Why the early Christians accepted and promoted demonic possession with such (*sit venia verbo*) enthusiasm is a question to which neither Christian apologetics nor the Classicists' wish-fulfilling idealizations have been able to offer even a plausible explanation. In the following paragraphs I would like to suggest some hypotheses which may, at least in part, account for the Christians' ready acceptance and incorporation of demonic possession.

Christianity, Hysteria, and Demonic Possession

That elusive affliction called hysteria may at first glance appear to be quite remote from the rise of demonism, yet by observing the relationship between the ancient medical and popular view of the etiology of hysteria and the marked tendency toward asceticism, we may be able not only to perceive one of the factors predisposing early Christianity toward a ready acceptance of demonism, but we may also see a clear illustration of how economic, social and psychological factors may interact to produce a given emphasis in theology. The following hypothesis, although admittedly speculative, does seem to offer a rational explanation.

Hysteria, one of the oldest identified diseases in western civilization, is described in the Egyptian Kahun Papyrus dated from probably the twentieth century B.C. In it the following symptoms are described:

> A woman who loves bed; she does not use it and does not shake it.
> Ill in seeing and has pain in the neck.
> Woman pained in her teeth and jaws and does not know how to open her mouth.
> A woman aching in all her limbs with pain in the sockets of her eyes.[27]

The cause of these afflictions is ascribed in this same papyrus to a wandering uterus, with fumigation of the uterus as the recommended cure. The sixteenth century B.C. Ebers Papyrus, the greatest of the Egyptian medical documents, has an entire chapter on diseases of women, in which hysteria is described in a very similar fashion, but treatments are more elaborately described:

> Dry excrement of men is placed on frankincense and the woman is fumigated

therewith; let the fumes enter the vulva.[28]

The early Egyptian medical documents, as distinguished from later ones, are remarkably free of the magical and superstitious. The Ebers papyrus does have one prescription for hysteria which has both magical and rational elements: an ibis of wax is placed on charcoal; the charcoal is ignited and the resultant fumes are placed to enter the vulva. Fumigation is, assuming the theory of the wandering womb, a rational treatment; the womb which has moved upwards must be attracted downwards by the fumes of pleasant smelling substances and the womb which has moved downward is driven upward by fumigation with evil smelling substances. The ibis is the magical element: it is the symbol of the god Thoth, who is the personification of the moon and is therefore related to female functions.

Ancient Greek medicine and popular tradition retained the same etiology and similar treatments for hysteria. Plato reflects the continuity of this tradition:

And the marrow, inasmuch as it is animate and has been granted an outlet, has endowed the part where its outlet lies with a love for generating by implanting therein a lively desire for emission. Wherefore in men the nature of the genital organs is disobedient and self-willed, like a creature that is deaf to reason, and it attempts to dominate all because of its frenzied lusts. And in women again, owing to the same causes, whenever the matrix or womb, as it is called—which is an indwelling creature desirous of childbearing—remains without fruit long beyond due season, it is vexed and takes it ill; and by straying all ways through the body and blocking up the passages of breath and preventing respiration it casts the body into the uttermost distress and causes, moreover, all kinds of maladies; until the desire and love of the two sexes unite them.[29]

The etiology of hysteria expressed by Plato is almost identical with the Hippocratic, which dominated medical thought throughout antiquity with the notable exception of the Methodists and Galen. Most of the later Graeco-Roman physicians including Celsus, Aretaeus and Soranus retained essentially the same description of hysteria. For example, Arataeus:

In the middle of the flanks of women lies the womb, a female viscus, closely resembling an animal; for it is moved of itself here and there in the flanks, also upwards in a direct line to below the cartilage of the thorax, and also obliquely to the right or to the left, either to the liver or spleen; and it likewise is subject to prolapses downwards, and in a word, it is altogether erratic.[30]

Soranus, who practiced medicine in Rome from 98-138 A.D., wrote the first work exclusively dedicated to the diseases of women.

In this treatise he gives the following description of hysteria:

Suffocation of the womb, which is called *hysterike* by the Greeks, receives its name from the fact that it suffocates women. This is, however, a retention of the breath in all silence, for the womb itself suffocates the woman as it ascends to the chest, so that she lies as if dead. This disease is brought about by frequent miscarriages, by premature childbirth, also by prolonged widowhood, by retention of the menses, and by swelling of the uterus.

He also mentions fumigation as a treatment:

Indeed the ancient physicians would place before the nostrils all kinds of putrid and stinking substances, such as burned hairs and lamp fumes; they would smear the nose with castor and resin and generally used all sorts of stinking substances upwards, and below in the region of the womb they would put pleasant smelling substances of nard and storax so that the womb would flee from the stinking substances and descend to the pleasant smelling.[31].

Some ancient physicians, although a definite minority, did not accept the wandering womb theory. They were the Methodists, who attempted to explain illness as the result of abnormal states of constriction (*status strictus*) or excessive relaxation (*status laxus*) of the pores. Hysteria was regarded as a condition of constriction to be cured by the application of relaxants.

The most famous of the later ancient physicians, Galen of Pergamon (129-199 A.D.), also rejected the wandering womb theory. He did, however, posit a close interactional relationship between mind and body. Although he rejected the wandering uterus as the etiology of hysteria, he was convinced of its somatic nature and ascribed it to the retention of secretion as a result of sexual abstention.[32] A fascinating document from later antiquity (second century A.D.), is Apuleius' *Apologia,* in which the author defended himself against the charge of using magic to induce a wealthy older woman to marry him. In his defense Apuleius gives the reason why this woman, Pudentilla, desired to marry after over a dozen years of widowhood:

She was now freed from all embarrassment, and being sought in marriage by so many distinguished persons, resolved to remain a widow no longer. The dreariness of her solitary life she might have borne, but her bodily infirmities had become intolerable. This chaste and saintly lady, after so many years of blameless widowhood without even a breath of scandal, owing to her long absence from a husband's embraces, began to suffer internal pains so severe that they brought her to the brink of the grave. Doctors and wise women agreed that the disease had its origin in her long widowhood, that the evil was increasing daily and her illness was steadily assuming a more serious character; the remedy was that she would marry before her youth finally departed from her.[33]

We have here clear testimony again of an hysterical condition, which was almost universally ascribed by the ancient physicians to sexual deprivation and of the most common prescription for it—sex.

From all available evidence we can conclude with considerable certitude that the overwhelming majority of Graeco-Roman physicians continued to believe well into the imperial period that hysteria was the result of a wandering womb and that, although other palliative measures such as fumigation could be employed, the really effective therapy and preventive for hysteria was heterosexual coitus. Both the antiquity of the belief and non-medical references to this theory (as in Plato) suggest that it was also widely accepted in popular culture that sexual activity was a necessary and beneficial function for the relief and prevention of an affliction which, from the amount of medical and non-medical references to hysteria in antiquity, was a common malady at that time.

In order to appreciate fully the relationship between the medical/popular view of hysteria and the early Christians' acceptance of demonism, we should look more closely at their view of sexuality. We have already noted a tendency toward asceticism in later antiquity. The Christians not only seized upon this trend, but carried it to extremes which today could only be described as pathological. In part this was because they were constricted by a double set of influences. In the Old Testament heterosexual coitus for purposes of procreation was considered natural, although there was evidence of gynephobic tendencies such as ritual purifications required for child birth and also segregation and avoidance of menstruating women. The Christians, however, emphasized woman's role as temptress and agent in man's fall. This change toward gynephobia was decidely a Greek contribution to the new religion. This new emphasis, coupled with the severe Hebrew injunctions against pederasty, a dominant form of "romantic" love in Greek culture, left the Christian without either outlet.

It is difficult today to appreciate fully the irrational lengths to which the early Christian went to deny sexual pleasures of the flesh. The early Christian communities held to an ideal of total chastity, celibacy. Not even sex for reproduction was necessary, because the world as constituted was soon to end. The basis for this belief is found in Mark 9:1, in which Jesus is reported to have said:

Amen, I say unto you that there are some of you standing here who will not taste death until they see the kingdom of God coming in its power.

When it became apparent that not all new converts could be won over to celibacy and that the end was not coming within the predicted time, it became necessary to make concession for institutional survival. Marriage for purposes of procreation was permitted, but celibacy remained as the purer and more desirable state. As Paul said, reflecting this fundamental idea:

It is good for a man not to touch a woman. Nevertheless, to avoid fornication, let every man have his own wife, and let every woman have her own husband.... I would that all men were even as myself.... I say therefore to the unmarried and widows, it is good for them if they abide even as I. But if they cannot contain, let them marry, for it is better to marry than to burn. (I Corinthians 7:1-2, 8-9)

Clement of Alexandria (3rd century A.D.) dictated in his *Paidagogus* at times of the month that married couples could lie together. He also exhorted the *man* to be constrained and not enjoy himself too much in the sex act. Two centuries later St. Jerome wrote:

It is disgraceful to love another man's wife, or one's own too much. A wise man ought to love his wife with judgment, not with passion. Let a man govern his voluptuous impulses, and not rush headlong into intercourse.... He who too ardently loves his own wife is an adulterer.[34]

Many others of the faithful attempted to follow the injunction implied in Matthew 19:12:

For there are eunuchs who were born from their mother's womb, and there are eunuchs who were made so by men, and there are eunuchs who have castrated themselves for the kingdom of heaven.

Thousands did castrate themselves. Origen, the leading intellectual of the Christian Fathers is perhaps the most famous instance. Others, however, attempted to fight the battle against lust by running away from the temptations of civilization. In the fourth century the Egyptian desert was swarming with refugees from lust. (Estimates run as high as 22,000.) The feats ascribed to these men defy belief. Out of fear of a nocturnal emission the monk Besarian did not lie down for forty years. St. Simeon Stylites spent thirty years on top of a sixty foot pillar. His clothes were clotted with filth and a rope was bound so tightly around his waist that it produced a maggot infested putrefaction. Worms filled his bed, and when they fell from him, he would put them back saying, "Eat what God has given you."

The *Verba Seniorum* (sayings of the Elders), a work of edifying purport, tells an amusing, but illustrative, little narrative. Whether the story is actual or apocryphal is of little concern for our purposes, because it was used as an exemplar of the ascetic ideal. According to the Verba practical jokers from a nearby village sent a prostitute out to a monk inhabiting a cave in the lower Egyptian desert. The prostitute was instructed to explain that she was lost and afraid of the wild beasts. Naturally the monk felt compelled to let the woman in. As she used her charms to tempt the hapless ascetic, he was so overcome with desire that he lit a lamp and put his finger in it as a distraction. By morning the fingers were burned away, but his purity had remained intact.[35]

A pronounced strain of gynephobia runs through the writings of many of the Church Fathers. Perhaps this is best exemplified by a letter written by John Chrysostom (Golden Mouth) in an attempt to dissuade a young friend from the marriage that he was planning:

The groundwork of this corporeal beauty is nothing else but phlegm and blood and humor and bile, and the fluid of masticated food.... If you consider what is stored up in those beautiful eyes, and that straight nose, and the mouth and cheeks, you will affirm the well-shaped body to be nothing else but a whited sepulchre... Moreover, when you see a rag with any of these things on it, such as phlegm, or spittle, you cannot bear to touch it even with the tips of your fingers, nay you can't endure looking at it; are you then in a flutter of excitement about the storehouses and repositories of these things?[36]

Clement of Alexandria voiced a similar view of women:

You are the gate of Hell, the unsealer of the forbidden tree, the first deserter of the divine law.[37]

Although all the early Christian churches shared the ascetic ideal, they did not all respond to the temptations of the flesh in the same way. To some, to resort to refuge and isolation was to run from the field of battle; true virtue was demonstrated by confronting temptation head on, and even more so by deliberately making the sources of enticement constantly available. From this type of reasoning the curious institution of the *agapetae* became widespread in some of the Christian communities. The *agapetae* were virgins who lived in close, but presumably asexual, cohabitation with the Christian ascetics. It was reported that in some instances they even slept together. Some of the more stodgy of the Church Fathers evinced considerable scepticism about the reality of these heroic measures of self-denial. Saint Cyprian, Bishop of Carthage, finally wrote a letter in 249 A.D. attempting to "blow the whistle" on the cohabitation of the *agapetae* with men of the cloth:

Don't let anyone think that she can be defended by the excuse that she can be examined and proved whether she is a virgin or not, since the hand and eye of the midwives are often deceived, so that, even if a woman be found to be uncorrupted in that part by which she is a woman, she nevertheless can have sinned in another part of her body which can be corrupted and still cannot be inspected. Certainly the very lying together, the very embracing, the very small talk and kissing and the shameful and foul sleeping of two lying together—how much of shame and accusation does all this confess? If a husband arrives and finds his spouse lying with another, doesn't he get angry and rage and even take sword in hand through the pain of his jealousy? What then when Christ the Lord, our judge, sees that his virgin who is pledged to him and his sanctity is lying with another man? How angry he becomes, and how enraged, and what penalties does he threaten for such unchaste copulations of this sort! For it is his spiritual word and coming day of judgment that we must labor and plan with every measure to enable each one of the brothers to avoid. And, although it is necessary that all hold to the discipline, how much more necessary is it that officials and deacons, who should offer an example and model for character and intercourse, do so. How can they be in charge of integrity and continence, if the very teaching of corruption and vice come from them?[38]

The practice of keeping *agapetae* quickly fell into official disfavor, but the practice never completely disappeared until relatively modern times.

One Christian Father, Tertullian, unwilling to leave any aspect of the evils of sex unexplicated, even ventured to answer the age old question, "Is there sex after death?"

To Christians, after their departure from the world, no restoration of marriage is promised in the day of resurrection, translated as they will be into the condition and sanctity of angels.... There will at that day be no resumption of voluptuous disgrace between us. No such frivolities, no such impurities, does God promise to His servants.[39]

In sum, from earliest Christian times, when sex was considered unnecessary, even for reproduction, through the Medieval period, when sex was tolerated solely for purposes of generation, it was impossible for the shapers of Christian doctrine to acknowledge that sexual coitus could confer preventive and therapeutic benefits. Thus the organic basis of hysteria had to be denied; to do otherwise would be to acknowledge that sex was natural—a continuing human need. It was likewise necessary to deny that it was a functional disorder (as implied by Galen) because the use of sex to restore the balance between *soma* and *psyche* would require a sinful activity to accomplish this therapeutic purpose.

Demonic possession as an explanation for hysteria required no concession to sexual etiology, although demons were usually described as lascivious and characterized by prurient interests. In addition, emphasis upon demons as a source of disease and psychic malfunction also conformed conveniently with other trends taking place in later antiquity.

One pronounced trend was a growing lack of confidence in the scientific approach which characterized the Hippocratic school and its successors. In later antiquity there were many severe epidemics with which the practice of medicine seemed to be unable to cope. (We should note in passing that the Black Death of the late middle ages was also a precursor of increased interest in demonic possession and the presence of evil occult forces.) In addition, this period saw many natural disasters and famines. The rapidly diminishing productivity of the land and the growing dysfunctionality of the slave system led people increasingly to perceive themselves as pawns manipulated by unseen forces, and out of a lack of confidence in the possibility of progress toward human felicity in this world to cast their gaze at a compensatory *post mortem* existence.

Belief in demons also aided the new Christian religion in reconciling the old pagan beliefs with the new, and provided a rationale comprehensible to the popular culture for the existence of evil. Rather than denying the existence of the old pagan deities, the Christians tended to assert that they were in reality mortals who had become demons. Clement of Alexandria in his *Exhortation to the Greeks* articulates this view clearly:

Those whom you worship were once men, who afterwards died. Legend and the lapse of time have given them their honours. For somehow the present is wont to be despised through our familiarity with it, whereas the past, being cut off from immediate exposure by the obscurity which time brings, is invested with a fictitious honour; and while events of the present are distrusted, those of the past are regarded with reverent wonder. As an example, the dead men of old, being exalted by the long period of error, are believed to be gods by those who come after. You have proof of all this in your mysteries themselves, in the solemn festivals, in fetters, wounds and weeping gods:

Woe, yea, woe to me! that Sarpedon, dearest of mortals, doomed is to fall by the spear of Patroclus son of Menoetius. (Homer, *Iliad,* XVI. 433-434)

The will of Zeus has been overcome, and your supreme god, defeated, is lamenting for Sarpedon's sake.

You are right then in having yourselves called the gods "shadows" and "daemons." For Homer spoke of Athena herself and her fellow-deities as "daemons," paying them a malicious compliment.

But she was gone to Olympus, Home of shield-bearing Zeus, to join the rest of the daemons. (*Iliad,* i. 221-222)
How then can the shadows and daemons any longer be gods, when they are in reality

unclean and loathsome spirits admitted by all to be earthy and foul, weighted down
to the ground, and "prowling round graves and tombs," where also they dimly appear
as "ghostly apparitions"? These are your gods, these shadows and ghosts; and along
with them go those "lame and wrinkled cross-eyed deities," the Prayers, daughters of
Zeus, though they are more like daughters of Thersites.[40]

Conclusion

In a period encompassing slightly more than a millenium the
possession model of madness underwent a strange evolution. From
a gift conferred by a deity upon a favored individual it became a
curse which we may judge from the recorded demand for exorcists,
and from the large number who came to them, to be an affliction
which affected increasing numbers of people as the general trends of
later antiquity became more pronounced.

Although this is not the appropriate place to develop the point, I
would like to suggest that the changes which occurred in the ancient
world in socio-economic relations, medicine, philosophy and
religion are closely concatenated and reflect the growing
contradictions of the slave society and its evolution to a higher level
of economic organization— feudalism. The recrudescence of interest
and credence in demonic possession in our contemporary society
may very well also be the reflection of a social system which is
collapsing because of its intensifying contradictions.

Notes

[1]*Plato.* Vol. I (*Phaedrus* 244 A & B). Translated by Harold North Fowler. Cambridge, Mass.:
Harvard Univ. Press, 1971, pp. 465-7. (Loeb Classical Library 36).
[2]Ibid., pp. 467-9.
[3]Laing, R.D. *The Politics of Experience.* New York: Ballantine Books, 1968, pp. 114-5.
[4]Ibid., p. 123.
[5]*Plato (Phaedrus* 265 B) Vol. I. p. 533. (Loeb Classical Library 36).
[6]Lucan, *The Civil War (Pharsalia* V, 128-97). Translated by J.D. Duff. Cambridge, Mass.:
Harvard Univ. Press, 1962, pp. 249-53. (Loeb Classical Library 220).
[7]See, for example, the *Oresteia* of Aeschylus.
[8]Dodds, E.R., *The Greeks and the Irrational.* Berkeley: Univ. of California Press, 1971, p. 270.
[9]*Diodorus of Sicily* (IV.3). Translated by C.H. Oldfather. Cambridge, Mass.: Harvard Univ.
Press, 1967, p. 347. (Loeb Classical Library 303).
[10]*The Greeks and the Irrational,* p. 270.
[11]*Plutarch's Moralia* XII (*De Primo Frigido* 18.953D). Translated by Harold Cherniss and
William C. Helmbold. Cambridge, Mass.: Harvard Univ. Press, 1968, p. 273. (Loeb Classical
Library 406).
[12]Dodds has compiled much of the available evidence for the historical reality of the Bacchic
rites in his appendix on Maenadism in *The Greeks and the Irrational,* pp., 270-82.
[13]Ibid., p. 278.
[14]*Plato (Ion* 534 B). Translated by W.R.M. Lamb. Cambridge, Mass.: Harvard Univ. Press, p.
424. (Loeb Classical Library 164).
[15]*Plato* Vol. I (*Phaedrus* 249 D & E), p. 483. (Loeb Classical Library 36).
[16]*Cicero: De Natura Deorum, Academica. (De Natura Deorum* II, 167). Translated by H.
Rackham. Cambridge, Mass.: Harvard Univ. Press, 1967, p. 283. (Loeb Classical Library 268).

[17]This and all subsequent quotations from the New Testament are the author's translation made from the Latin Vulgate version and compared to the Greek.

[18]An excellent description of peasant religious movements which acquired a political significance can be found in Harris, Marvin, *Cows, Pigs, Wars and Witches*. New York: Vintage Books, 1975, pp. 155-203.

[19]*Lucretius. De Rerum Natura* (IV, 1058-1072). Translated by W.H.D. Rouse. Cambridge, Mass.: Harvard Univ. Press, 1967, p. 323. (Loeb Classical Library 181).

[20]Caelius Aurelianus, *On Acute Diseases and Chronic Diseases*. Translated by I.E. Drabkin. Chicago: Univ. of Chicago Press, 1950, pp. 557-9.

[21]Ibid., p. 523.

[22]This is clearly and astutely developed in Dodds, E.R. *Pagan and Christian in an Age of Anxiety*. New York: W.W. Norton, 1965.

[23]Quoted from Harnack in Oesterreich, Traugot K., *Possession and Exorcism*. Translated by D. Ibberson. New York: Causeway Books, 1974, p. 158.

[24]*Flavius Philostratus—The Life of Apollonius of Tyana*. (IV, xx). Translated by F.C. Conybeare. Cambridge, Mass.: Harvard Univ. Press, 1912, pp. 389-393. (Loeb Classical Library 16).

[25]Tamborino, Julius. *De Antiquorum Daemonismo*. Giessen: Religionsgeschictliche Versuche und Vorarbeiten vol. vii. 3.

[26]*Possession and Exorcism*, p. 155.

[27]Veith, Ilza. *Hysteria: The History of a Disease*. Chicago: Univ. of Chicago Press, 1965, p. 3.

[28]Ibid., p. 5.

[29]*Plato* Vol. VII (*Timaeus* 91 B & C). Translated by R.G. Bury. Cambridge, Mass.: Harvard Univ. Press, 1952. (Loeb Classical Library 234).

[30]*The Extant Works of Aretaeus, The Cappadocian*. Translated and edited by Francis Adams. London: Sydenham Society, 1857, pp. 285-87.

[31]*Soranus' Gynaecology* (III, iv). Translated and with an Introduction by Oswei Temkin. Baltimore: Johns Hopkins Univ. Press, 1956, pp. 149, 152.

[32]*Hysteria: The History of a Disease*, pp. 31-39.

[33]*The Apology and Florida of Apuleius of Madaura* (69). Translated by H.E. Butler, Oxford: Clarendon Press, 1909, p. 114.

[34]Hunt, Morton. *The Natural History of Love*. New York: Funk & Wagnall's, 1959, p. 115.

[35]Merton, Thomas (trans.). *The Wisdom of the Desert*. New York: New Directions, 1960, pp. 55-56.

[36]*The Natural History of Love*, p. 110.

[37]Ibid., 109.

[38]*Corpus Scriptorum Ecclesiasticorum*. Vindobanae: Academia Litterarum Caesarea, 1868, pp. 474-75.

[39]*The Natural History of Love*, p. 116.

[40]*Clement of Alexandria* (Exhortation to the Greeks). Translated by G.W. Butterworth. Cambridge, Mass.: Harvard Univ. Press, 1968, p. 127. (Loeb Classical Library 92).

Bibliographical Essay

The bibliography for a topic such as this is extensive and forbidding. In this short essay I shall indicate only those sources which I think are of special value and which would provide a convenient entrée for someone interested in pursuing the subject of the paper further. To conserve space, a work cited here will be identified by the number with which it is first entered in the footnotes. Complete references can be found there.

Absolutely essential for any study of the phenomenon of possession is Traugot Oesterreich's *Possession and Exorcism* (23). Although somewhat old, it still contains an impartial analysis of most of the source material and represents a distinguished scholar's life-long work. A more recent analysis of possession in ancient Greece, E.R. Dodds' *The Greeks and the Irrational* (8), places the phenomenon in literary and cultural perspective. It is both a scholarly and an innovative work.

The economic changes which precipitated the metamorphosis of world-view in antiquity are summarized succinctly in Karl Kautsky's *The Foundations of Christianity,* New York: Russel, 1953). The distinctive *zeitgeist* of later antiquity is described very well in E.R. Dodds' *Pagan and Christian in an Age of Anxiety* (22).

The views of the ancient Greek and Roman physicians and their interaction with the general trends of philosophy in antiquity are treated in Gregory Zilboorg's *A History of Medical Psychology.* New York: Norton, 1967. Hysteria as an affliction is treated historically in a work which is really so well written that it stands out as a model of historical medical writing, Ilza Veith's *Hysteria: The History of a Disease* (27). All research into the ancient medical views must start with Hippocrates; fortunately the *Hippocratic Corpus* is available in an adequate translation in the Loeb Library series. Three later medical writers are of special value for treatments of, diagnosis of and therapy for "mental illness"; they are Aulus Cornelius Celsus, available in the Loeb series, Aretaeus (30), and Caelius Aurelianus (20). The last is a somewhat later translation (probably fifth century A.D.) into Latin of an earlier work written in Greek by Soranus in the first century A.D.

The attitudes of the early Christians is described in a witty and scholarly fashion by the popular writer, Morton Hunt, in his *The Natural History of Love* (34). Revolutionary movements rising out of religious movements and messianic expectations are discussed from an anthropological point of view by Marvin Harris in *Cows, Pigs, Wars, and Witches* (18)—highly recommended.

The Loeb Classical Library is an excellent source for the ancient authors whom you may wish to consult. The translations are generally accurate, although their literary qualities are quite uneven, and some of the volumes released early in the series are marred by a Victorian squeamishness. Another advantage of the Loeb series is that a reader who has learned some Latin or Greek can compare the original text, which is printed opposite, with the translation.

For any who may wish more extensive bibliographies, the following are available upon request and payment of postage to Gerald Erickson, Classics Department, 310 Folwell Hall, University of Minnesota, Minneapolis, MN 55455.

1. Madness in Antiquity
    A. Ancient sources
    B. Secondary treatments

2. Eroticism and Family Life in Greece and Rome

3. Dreams in antiquity
    A. Primary sources
    B. Secondary treatments

4. Magic and Witchcraft in Classical Antiquity
    A. Primary sources
    B. Secondary treatments

VII

Greek and Roman Witches:
Literary Conventions or Agrarian
Fertility Priestesses?

Witchcraft as an academic reconstruction is still practiced as a cult religion in the modern English-speaking world, while practices associated with witchcraft (curses, sympathetic cures and charms, etc.) remain active in the western world, especially in traditional rural societies. But the witch as type of person has been almost completely reduced to a literary convention in popular children's entertainment. However, the conventional appearance of witches that we know so well from commercial Halloween decorations and from the film The Wizard of Oz *is directly descended from classical models, as Steve Oberhelman demonstrates in some hair-raising descriptions in the first part of this essay. "The witch image," he concludes, "has not changed over the past 2400 years, whether one examines Greek and Latin poetry, medieval literature, King James'* Daemonology *in 1597, or modern film-making."*

In the second part of the article Oberhelman inquires into the possible reality underlying the convention. What he discovers touches upon several aspects of popular life and beliefs of the Greek and Roman world, but even more relates to universal fertility practices. Finally, Oberhelman proposes an original and interesting explanation for the almost exclusive ascription of the witch conventions to women in western society. On all of these matters, Oberhelman's footnotes are recommended as being of particular interest. Steve Oberhelman held a dissertation fellowship at the American School of Classical Studies in Athens in 1978-79. He was a contributor to the collection of articles in the Journal of Popular Culture *that preceded this volume with an equally engrossing study of "Popular Dream—Interpretation in Ancient Greece and Freudian Psychoanalysis" JPC XI: 3, 682-695).*

Greek and Roman Witches:
Literary Conventions or Agrarian Fertility Priestesses?

Steve Oberhelman

If someone asked you to write a description of a witch you would probably write about an old woman who is ugly, long-nosed, wart-covered, dressed in black, who casts evil spells upon her enemies, has a black caldron boiling with brews, transforms herself and others into different animal and human shapes, flies about on a magic stick or broom and carries on her secret rites at midnight during a full moon. This is the witch that we as children saw in *The Wizard of Oz*, Walt Disney's movies and Grimm's fairy tales.

If you had asked an ancient Greek to write a description of a witch, the conception would have been essentially the same. In fact, our present-day notion of witchcraft is derived directly from the descriptions of the witches of Greek and Latin literature. The purpose of this paper is first to establish the close connection between ancient witchcraft and modern popular stereotyping of witches by discussing the rites and actions of the most famous witches in Greek and Latin literature. We will then attempt to ascertain the extent to which the witch descriptions in ancient literature, which present a consistent picture, were due to literary convention and how much they were due to the existence of contemporary witches. At the end we will make an hypothesis as to the probable origin of magic and witchcraft.

* * *

The earliest witch in Greek and Latin literature is Circe, who appears in the Homeric *Odyssey* written about 700-675 B.C. It is noteworthy that witchcraft does not appear in the *Iliad,* which dates from about 740-725 B.C. The reason for its appearance in the later work is clear. The seventh century B.C. in Greece was a period of immense troubles—economic, political, social and religious. On the religious side alone, this century saw the advent of new gods, Dionysian cults, mystery religions, new centers of worship such as the oracle at Delphi, a belief in the immortality of the soul (which was absent in Greek thought before), asceticism and the tenet of the

138

transmigration of the soul. Magic makes its first literary appearance during this time in the *Opera et Dies (Work and Days)* of Hesiod and in the *Odyssey:* obviously magic was widespread enough to capture the attention of the intellectuals of the time.

All these new religions and magical practices reflect an attempt by the Greeks to solve their emotional and spiritual problems. These problems arose with the inability of the existing social and religious institutions to keep pace with the growing complexity of Greek life,[1] and so caused the individual Greek to cope with new anxieties and pressures. Magic and new forms of religious experience were sought out by the Greek in his quest for emotional comfort which could not be acquired elsewhere.[2]

Circe's main claim to fame is her ability to transform people into various shapes. In the *Odyssey* she transforms the crew of Odysseus into swine by mixing "baleful drugs" into their food and by then striking them with her magic wand. Odysseus, however, escapes the same fate, since he had eaten the moly plant through the god Hermes' orders; this plant has the power to counteract any magical potion's effects. Odysseus enters Circe's palace and with sword drawn demands that she change his crew back into human form. Circe complies and changes them from their pig form by touching them again with her wand.

This predilection of Circe for *metamorphosis,* or transformation, is evidenced by two stories found in Ovid's *Metamorphoses,* which was written in the first century A.D. The first story, found in book XIII, tells how a certain fisherman named Glaucus comes to Circe to seek her help in winning over the love of Scylla, a beautiful sea-nymph. Circe, however, immediately falls in love with Glaucus, and begs him to forsake Scylla and love her instead. Glaucus refuses, and so Circe plots revenge on her rival:

She bruised together uncanny herbs with juices of dreadful power, singing while she mixed them with Hecate's own charms. Then putting on a blue cloak she went to Rhegium. Here, there was a peaceful place where Scylla loved to come; this pool she befouls with her baleful poisons, she sprinkles liquors brewed from noxious roots and a charm, dark with its maze of uncanny words; thrice nine times she murmurs over it with lips well skilled in magic.

Scylla later came to the pool and went in for a swim. But, to her horror, her legs and feet turned into gaping dogs, and thereby she became the infamous half-woman, half-dog monster of the *Odyssey* (where she fittingly wreaks her revenge by eating the crew of Circe's lover Odysseus).

Another story, found in book XIV, describes the fate of Picus the son of Saturn, the king of Latium. One day Picus was hunting with his servants in the deep woods. Circe spotted him and fell in love on the spot; she tried to approach Picus, but was ordered away by the prince. Circe went away in a rage to plot her revenge. She fashioned a phantom of a wild boar and ordered it to rush in front of the king and then to "take cover in thickets where no horse could enter." Picus followed the boar, while Circe prevented his attendants from following the king by raising up from the ground a thick mist through incantations and prayers to unknown gods. Circe then found Picus; she touched him with her wand three times, repeated her charms three times, and watched while wings grew on Picus' back, his purple cloak turned into purple plumage and his crest of gold into gold feathers. Picus had turned into a woodpecker![3] His attendants chased Circe, but she sprinkled them with drugs and poisons and called upon Night, Chaos and Hecate (the patron deity of witchcraft). Immediately the woods sprang up from their place, the earth groaned, ghosts of dead people flew among the trees, the grass turned red from blood, and the ground became black with countless crawling things. The servants took fright and ran away.

Circe's other great claim to fame besides metamorphosis, is that she was the aunt of the queen of ancient witches—Medea. Most of us know her adventures with Jason and the Argonauts, as related in the *Argonautica* of Apollonius Rhodius and in three Italian movie versions, and therefore we need not mention her magic practices in that context. She did appear in many other ancient texts, and in each instance she was a witch.[4] Her most famous act of magic, according to our sources, is her restoration of youth to Aeson, the father of Jason. The scene is midnight during a full moon. Medea enters barefoot, with hair streaming, her robes flowing.[5] Three times she turns about, three times sprinkles water upon her head, three times utters wailing cries. She prays to Night, Hecate and Earth; in her prayer she boasts of how she can draw the moon down from the sky, raise the ghosts of the dead from graveyards, break the jaws of snakes, move asunder streams, trees, rocks and mountains. She then climbs into her golden chariot and travels nine days and nine nights, gathering herbs from every place. Having returned, she builds two altars, one to Hecate, the other to Youth. Upon these altars she slaughters black sheep and pours out milk and wine from goblets. She then casts Aeson into a deep sleep, and places on top of him magic herbs. She circles around the altar, plunges sticks into the black pools of blood and then lights them. She purifies the old man three times with fire, three times with water and three times with sulphur. All the while, a magic brew is boiling in her caldron: roots and flowers gathered on her chariot trip, pebbles, sand, hoarfrost, the wings and flesh of a vampire screechowl, the entrails of a werewolf, the skin of a watersnake, the liver of a long-lived stag, the head of a crow and a thousand nameless things. The grass turns green around the caldron whenever the mixture boils over. Medea cuts the throat of Aeson and fills the veins with the broth. Aeson immediately jumps up, a man of only forty years.

Medea also appears in *Heroides, Epistola* VI of Ovid.[6]. The description of Medea by Hypsile, Jason's forsaken mistress, can serve as the *communis opinio* of the ancients of what a witch should be; each phrase in the letter reveals a characteristic which is found in all our other ancient sources. She writes:

Tis not by good looks, nor by her goodness, that she wins thee, but she knows incantations, and cuts poisonous herbs with a charmed knife. She essays to bring down the struggling moon from her course, and to plunge the sun's steeds in darkness. She bridles the waters and stays the flowing streams. She moves forests and living rocks from their places. She wanders through tombs with steaming hair, and collects bones from the pyres still warm. She dooms men to death in their absence, fashions figures in wax, and drives the fine needle into the tortured heart and does more things which I am not desirous of knowing.

This is the same type of witch whom we meet in the late first century A.D. epic *Pharsalia,* by Lucan. The witch is Erichtho, who lives in Thessaly, the home of all witches. She is a foul creature: a lean, filthy old woman of horrible visage and of deathly pale color— even her breath befouls the air. She offers no prayers to the gods above, but haunts tombs and funeral pyres. She snatches bodies from their graves and collects fragments of bodies from fiery biers. If she needs living blood, she will cut the throats of innocent men; if she needs parts of a corpse, she will tear its cheeks with her own teeth, or cut off its locks of hair, or club off the head and bite off the tongue.

One day she is asked to perform the rites of necromancy, or the raising of the dead to foretell the future. She locates a body which has had its throat recently slit, and drags it home by means of a hook. She then puts on a multi-colored cloak and places vipers in her hair. Then she opens the corpse's breast and fills it with blood. She bathes the marrow with gore, and adds venom from the moon, the marrow of a stag fed on snakes, the foam of a mad dog, the entrails of a lynx, the spine of a hyena, the eyes of a dragon, a sucking fish, a winged serpent, the ashes of a phoenix, vipers, herbs which she had spit upon as they shot up, leaves steeped in dreadful spells, and her own secret poison. Then she chants in a voice resembling the barking of a dog, the howl of a wolf, the screech of an owl and the hiss of a snake. The corpse's owner comes out from the ground and stands next to Erichtho; but it refuses to re-enter his body, and so Erichtho beats the body with snakes until the ghost enters his body again and thereupon foretells the future.

Not all witches were so professional: some were amateurs such as Simaetha in Theocritus' *Idyll* II, written in the third century B.C. Simaetha is seeking to put a spell on her faithless lover Delphis, who has deserted her for twelve days past. The scene of the poem is midnight during a full moon. Simaetha is at the crossroads, which is the special place of Hecate the goddess of witchcraft. She is aided by her slave-girl who wreathes a magic bowl with bay-leaves, love charms and crimson wool. Simaetha invokes Hecate, and whirls a love-wheel in the air to the refrain "Wheel, bring my lover back to me." Then she calls for barley-meal, and as her slave throws it into the fire, Simaetha says "May these be Delphis' bones that she throws." When the crackling of the leaves has died down, she thrusts into the flames a waxen image of her lover, and says "As this puppet melts for me before Hecate, so may Delphis as speedily melt with love; and as this bronze wheel turns by the grace of Aphrodite, so may Delphis turn again before my threshold." As she flings bran into the flames, she hears the howling of the dogs in town—the waves and the winds are hushed: Hecate is approaching! Three times Simaetha pours libations, adding the herb *hippomanes*.[7] Next she produces a fragment of Delphis' cloak and flings it into the fire, while she mutters a threat that on the following day she will pound a lizard into a love potion.[8] Then Simaetha gathers up the remains and takes them to Delphis' house, where she smears the threshold with the liquid. At the end of the poem, however, she despairs of the potion's efficaciousness, and goes home dejected.[9]

The Roman elegiac poets of the first century A.D. gave us four descriptions of witches, and these can be discussed in a summary fashion.[10] Our first witch is Delia, who appears in the *Elegiae,* 1.2.4ff, of Tibullus. Delia possesses strong powers: she draws the stars from the sky; she turns the courses of rivers; she cleaves the ground with her spells; she lures spirits from the tombs and the bony frame from the funeral pyre. She commands the clouds in the sky and can make snow in the summer. She knows all the secrets of Medea's deadly herbs and can call forth Hecate's hounds. She even used a charm on Tibullus himself, which she had chanted three times and spat on three times. Later she released him from it by using the torch rite (the method of which is not known to us).

Dipsias, the witch in Ovid's *Amores,* 1.8, is also very knowledgeable in magic rites and charms. She can turn rivers back to their source, and she is thoroughly well-versed in the workings of herbs, whirling-wheels and love charms. Whenever she so desires, she can draw clouds across the sky or sweep them from the heavens; she can make the stars drip with blood, darken the moon's face or cleave the ground with her incantations. She can even fly like a bird into the night, and call forth ancestors from their tombs.

Propertius, writing in his *Elegiae,* 4.5, describes a brothel madam who is also a powerful sorceress. She can put spells upon the moon; she can disguise herself as a wolf; she tears out the eyes of crows for her spells; she gathers charms which drip from pregnant mares, and she consults owls for advice on how to get rid of Propertius! This old woman, named Acanthis, has had an evil influence upon Propertius' mistress. Acanthis has told her every trick in the trade on how to get more money from him; for example, she should feign that she has a husband—this of course will heighten Propertius' interest and consequently raise the price; or she can plead a headache, for this will cause Propertius to return with added fire after having missed a night of love. But now Propertius is celebrating in the poem the old woman's death: "I saw the cough clot in her wrinkled throat, and the bloodstained spittle trickling down through her hollow teeth." He is certainly gloating in his hour of joy!

Horace devotes three poems to his witch Canidia—*Epode* 5, *Epode* XVII and *Sermones* 1.8. For the sake of brevity we shall examine only the latter poem. The scene is Campus Esquilinus (which used to be a burial place for the lowest classes, but had been turned into a garden by a Roman aristocrat during Horace's lifetime). The speaker of the poem is a wooden statue of Priapus, the fertility god of Roman religion. He complains not of the abuse of birds, jackals or thieves but of the practice of witches. Suddenly Canidia, an ugly old woman, enters the scene: her black mantle is girt high, her feet are bare and her hair is loose and flowing. While howling in a terrible voice she digs into the ground; she tears apart a black ewe-lamb with her teeth, and collects the blood in the trench in order to draw up the spirits of the dead. Then she places two effigies upon the ground: one is made of wool and represents Canidia, while the other is made of wax and represents an unfaithful lover whom she wants to torture with her love charms; the waxen image is kneeling in a suppliant's position, as if expecting a sentence of death. Canidia calls upon Hecate: suddenly serpents and hell-hounds move about, and the moon disappears lest it should see such sights. Canidia buries in the ground a wolf's beard and the tooth of a spotted snake, and then burns the waxen image. At this point Priapus' buttocks split apart from a loud fart, and off runs Canidia, frightened, into town—her herbs and charmed loveknots falling everywhere from her arms.

Many other witches appear in Greek and Latin literature, e.g. Pamphile in the *Metamorphoses* of Apuleius, the sorceress in Virgil's *Eclogue* VIII, the witch in Petronius' *Satyricon*, Tacita in Ovid's *Fasti*, yet the information which we receive does not substantially differ from that already given. In fact, all our ancient sources give a consistent picture of what the Greek and Roman witch was: an ugly old woman, who knew various evil incantations and brews, flew about during the night, transformed herself and others into different shapes, cast spells upon her enemies, carried out her rites at midnight during a full moon, raised the dead from the grave, and, what will become important later in this paper, controlled natural phenomena such as clouds, rivers, weather and crop growth. If we compare this composite picture with the one we gave at the beginning of this paper, it can be seen that the two correspond very closely. Indeed, the witch image has not changed over the past 2400 years, whether one examines Greek and Latin poetry, medieval literature, King James' *Daemonology* published in 1597 or modern film-making.

*   *   *

Since ancient literature presents such a persistent portrayal of the witch, the question arises as to what extent witchcraft was a literary convention and how much of it actually existed. First of all, one may remark that conventions are not possible unless there is a substantial body of popular or personal belief behind them; as in satire and comedy, conventions are most effective when they deal with topical subjects. Moreover, the fact that witchcraft appears in the *Odyssey*, which does not use conventions (except for epic devices such as heroic subjects and oral formulae), points to the prominent role of witchcraft in everyday life; indeed, magic and witchcraft form an integral part in the *Odyssey*, and there is nothing in the poem to contradict the view that magic like that in the Circe scene was quite in line with contemporary popular opinion. And since the *Iliad* is totally free of all forms of magic and superstition, while on the other hand the *Odyssey* abounds with both, we can point to the date of c. 700 B.C. as the time when magic began to occupy the thoughts of the Greeks. The reasons for this have been stated earlier, but here we can note the role of the gods in each poem. In the *Iliad* everyone and everything comes under the providence of the gods; in the *Odyssey*, however, the gods are more removed from the action, and man is left to choose and act more according to his own will. Perhaps magic filled the widening gap in the man/god relationship, and thus provided psychological security for those who feared freedom of action and its consequences.[11]

Witchcraft appears in other written sources besides literature. It is the chief concern of the *defixionum tabellae*[12] and of the demotic papyri, which can teach you how to inflict impotency upon your enemy and how to make your lover sleepless for nights on end. These magical hand-books imply the marketability of, if not the practice and existence of, witchcraft. Moreover, legislative measures were frequently initiated against witchcraft. Plato mentions specific penalties to be assessed against practicers of magic in his dialogue *Hoi Nomoi (The Laws),* while at Rome witchcraft legislation covered the entire span of the Roman state. For example, there were laws passed against magic in 450 B.C., 212 B.C., 186 B.C., 139 B.C., 97 B.C., 82 B.C., 32 B.C., 12 B.C., 16 A.D., 58 A.D., and 69 A.D. Obviously witchcraft was very real to the government of Rome for over 500 years.

If magic and witchcraft were indeed practiced in antiquity, as it has been up to the present day, can we detect their origins? Many scholars have previously brought forward theories to answer this question; some of their theories are patently false, others more meritorious. For example, it has been hypothesized that witchcraft is due to psychological factors: either a kind of mass hysteria (we may compare the dancing manias and flagellant movements of the Middle Ages) or individual psychoses. Witchcraft phenomena, however, are on the whole universal and consistent: the practices and rites are essentially the same for all cultures both past and present. We cannot suppose that hallucinations occur in the same pattern for every person; mind and environment are in endlessly varying and interreacting relationships, and thus hallucinations will always be as a rule idiosyncratic. Others have adduced the origin of witchcraft to ergot substances or other such drugs, but the previous argument applies here as well.[13] It has also been asserted that witchcraft was a hoax created by the Christian Church in order to eliminate heretics and dissenters. This is very true when the European witchcraft trials of the eleventh through seventeenth centuries are considered,[14] but it does not at all explain other forms of witchcraft such as those found in African or Native American cultures. Margaret Murray established her school of disciples in the 1920s with the publication of her "Horned God" theory; however, at close scrutiny her theory becomes so flawed that its former popularity is a source of wonderment.[15] Finally, the views of the early twentieth century anthropologists such as Frazer and Malinowski, who advocated an evolution in primitive consciousness from magic to religion, are unacceptable; no clear distinction between magic and religion can be made, and at best

Frazer and Malinowski have achieved in their theories a cultural and spiritual racism.

Magic and witchcraft, in my opinion, should rather be thought of as remnants of ancient agrarian fertility rites, which were formerly under the direction of women. This theory supposes the first communities to have been primarily agricultural and matrilinear.[16] For while men were still roving about in search of game during the paleolithic and early mesolithic periods (when mankind was still at the hunting and food-gathering stage), women stayed behind and supervised the village affairs; (village must, of course, be taken in a very broad sense, i.e., the habitation of a small band or group of families or clan). This division of duties for men and women is based, according to Briffault, upon spontaneous instincts and dispositions.[17] The male is a confirmed, restless hunter, a rover and wanderer in search of food and adventure. The female, however, is the home-maker in the true sense of the word: it was the woman who fashioned the first homes, huts and tents—in some tribes even today men sleep in the open while the women live in shelters. Because the woman stayed at home, while the male was absent for long periods of time, she was in control of the family and communal concerns.

The position of women was enhanced further by other factors. Firstly the act of conception and childbirth elicited awe from the males, who in the ignorance of natural processes attributed mysterious powers to the woman. The same applies to menstruation which is considered unclean only in male-oriented societies. Moreover, the human baby is the most maternally dependent creature in the animal kingdom. It takes longer to mature and break away from the mother than with any other species. With the father absent for much of the child's early life, the mother supervised the care and training of the child, and so it was the mother who received the filial respect and love, the father being a mere source of food. More importantly, women most likely learned first the domestication of the seed. This is verified by myth: almost every mythology which discusses the origin of agriculture has imputed its discovery to women.[18] This is very probable, for since the woman was the one who gathered the collectable food growing wild such as grain and fruit, she would have been the first to notice how seeds when placed in the ground grow and produce food. Even granted that it was a male who first learned the secret of cultivation, the woman at any rate cultivated the fields, seeing that the male still was hunting animals or herding them (herding is practiced from the middle mesolithic age onwards). Therefore, at this early stage, the woman enjoyed by natural right a much higher status than she does now in our patrilinear societies, and was closely connected with agriculture.

Agriculture at first must have been a risky affair. There was much excellent soil available such as the alluvial land basins, but until agriculture became more certain in methods and techniques, failure was probably a frequent occurrence. Thus early mankind would have turned to certain rites, whether prayers or magico-religious ceremonies, to promote fertility and ensure good crops. The women were chosen to carry out these rites, for as we have seen they were very closely associated with agriculture, they were fertile like the land and thus could communicate their fertility to the soil by close contact, and they already enjoyed a status of awe and respect. These rites, which would be concerned with fertility, cultivation and weather control, can be divided into six specific categories for easy discussion:

Agricultural magic. As was pointed out already, in the primitive division of labor the gathering and cultivation of vegetable food was the special domain of the women, while the hunting was that of the men. The magical/religious rites which were intended to secure the fertility of the fields were naturally within the actions of women. For example, in one tribe in India the chief function of women is to prepare "medicine" or magical charms which are sprinkled over the rice fields to ensure fertility. Most cultures have similar beliefs; one of the readiest causes for divorce is the sterility of the wife, since it is believed that her unfruitfulness will be transferred to the man's crops; conversely nothing could be more desirable than a fruitful wife. We can note here a remedy for protecting crops against caterpillars which is found in the *de Re Rustica* of Cato, a second century B.C. Roman writer: find a woman in the midst of her menstrual period and have her walk around the field three times; this will protect the crops for the coming year. We have another example from Rome—this time from the law books. The law code of 451/450 B.C., which contains the first written evidence of magic in ancient Rome, assesses the death penalty on anyone who causes his neighbor's crops to wither and transfers the fertility into his own land through magic spells.

Vestal fires. The practice of lighting fires or of carrying lighted torches around newly sown fields to ensure fruitfulness is another function of women in most cultures. In one culture a fire is lit in the middle of each cornfield; in these fires special magic herbs which have been made by the women are burnt. This is considered an infallible means of causing crop growth. In ancient Rome it was customary to light fires around a field, and then send young girls with torches about it to make the land fertile. Also, sacred fires are set up in holy places and are dedicated to moon goddesses and other female deities. These fires serve the same function as those lit in the fields. They were perpetually kept lit, lest the fields lose their richness, and they were tended by sacred women called vestal priestesses. At Rome alone there were vestal fires dedicated to Demeter, Kore and Luna, all of whom were fertility goddesses.

Rain-making. No rites connected with the success of agricultural operations are as important as those designed to control rainfall. These rites are commonly regarded as belonging to the woman's special sphere. For not only is rain the primary condition for successful cultivation of the soil, but rain is always associated with the moon which is the patron of women. Thus, most cultures have sacred women, priestesses or sorceresses perform rites to procure rain. For example, in Southern India, whenever rain is needed, the women make a small clay figure of a man, place it on a cart and carry it from house to house; they then place it in the dry field. The ceremony is regarded as a powerful rain-charm and fertilizer. In ancient Rome, on May 15, the vestal priestesses used to throw 24 to 27 straw puppets into the Tiber river, thereby ensuring good rainfall for the growing season.[19]

Childbirth/menstruation beliefs. We can easily predict an ambivalent attitude toward feminine functions in a particular society, depending on whether it is patrilineal or matrilineal. In the latter type of societies childbirth and menstruation are treated with awe; during these times women are holy and cannot be approached lest they be polluted. Also, while in menstruation women would most communicate their fertility to the earth, and therefore pregnant and menstruating women often go into orchards and fields for this very purpose (see Cato's remedy above). We may add that one of the most effective charms in ancient witchcraft was the discharge of a menstrual cycle. In patrilineal societies, on the other hand, the attitude is the opposite. Women during these times are considered unclean and unholy, and are not approached, lest they pollute those whom they meet. For example, an ancient Greek inscription states that women are not allowed in temples for ten days after menstruation or childbirth. Also, exclusion from the Greek Eleusian mysteries, as another inscription tells us, was mandatory for anyone who had committed manslaughter, touched a corpse or approached a woman in her childbed. The seventh century B.C. poet Hesiod writes that a man should never wash in the same water as that used by a woman, for otherwise he will be polluted. In societies which recently became patrilinear from an original matrilineality, as ancient Greek and Roman societies were, we should expect a mixture of both attitudes. This is indeed the case: the older beliefs survived in magic and popular superstition, while the patrilinear views were fixed in state religion; this is a pattern which is consistent in Greek and Roman religion.

Moon worship. It is a commonplace among different peoples that the reproductive functions of women are regulated by the moon, since the menstrual period coincides so closely with the lunar cycle. In many societies the moon is considered the cause of menstruation: e.g. the moon is a young man who ravishes the women and thereby causes discharges of blood. The moon is the cause of impregnation according to many cultures, who believe that it is the real husband of all women. The idea of the moon as a source of fertility was supported by the interpretation of actual lunar phenomena: the moon waxes and wanes, grows and decays, just as life does. In ancient Greece the moon was popularly regarded as the source of fertilizing moisture such as dew, which in poetry is called the daughter of the moon; Cicero, the first century B.C. writer/statesman, said that the moon releases a flow of moisture which fosters the growth of living creatures.

Herbal magic. In the earliest societies women were the doctors; for originally medical skill depended upon the use of herbs and plants, of which the women would have had excellent knowledge, seeing that they took care of the vegetation and crops. Later it was always one of the talents of the witch to know what herbs to pick for a brew or spell and where they could be found. It seems very probable that the infamous witches' brew developed out of what were originally medicinal cures, which had been formulated by women in early agrarian communities.

* * *

Each of the above categories finds expression in Greek and Roman witchcraft, and therefore we may conclude that a number of the rites and spells of the classical witch were descended directly from a fertility religion which was designed to maintain sustenance and livelihood. The early fertility priestesses could cause crops to grow, the seasons to be mild, rain to fall, children to be born. The Greek and Roman witches were no longer such priestesses: men had long before usurped the majority of their powers and functions in the transition from matrilineality to patrilineality. Yet rites still lingered on among the lower classes who preserved to some extent their more ancient religion; some of these rites retained only some small semblance to their original significance, while the purpose of other rites remained unchanged. This is why the remedy for caterpillar-infested fields was still used in the lifetime of Cato; why love magic is the most important part of classical witchcraft; why enemies of a witch were afraid that they would be inflicted with impotency or sterility, while her friends expected success and fruitfulness; why herbal potions were concocted by all witches; why the Roman vestal priestesses enjoyed such high status in society; why the first mention of magic in Rome is a law forbidding the bereavement of fertility from a neighbor's crops; why the first god was the Mother Earth goddess who looked after vegetation and crops; why in fact all witches were, and are, always women. We can indeed say that the Greek and Roman witch was much more than a literary device: she looks as much ahead to the witches of the twentieth century A.D., as she glances back to her remote ancestors who were priestesses that conducted agricultural fertility ceremonies as part of their duties for the community.

Notes

[1]For a similar situation in the third century A.D., see E.R. Dodds, *Pagan and Christian in an Age of Anxiety: Some Aspects of Religious experience From Marcus Aurelius to Constantine* (Cambridge Univ. Press, 1965).

[2]One can always discern a close nexus between witchcraft and social phenomena. For example, the Salem witchcraft trials can only be properly understood in the light of the contemporary social, political, economic and religious factors. For it was not only religious fanaticism which caused the witch craze, but other factors such as famine, changes in the village charter, breakdown in social structure, wars, new religious heresy from England. The same relationship of sociological phenomena and witchcraft trials can be discerned in the McCarthyism of the 1950s; see A.R. Cardozo, "A Modern American Witch-Craze," in M. Marwick, *Witchcraft and Sorcery* (Middlesex, England, 1970), pp. 369-77. Marwick's book contains many excellent essays which should not be overlooked by anyone who studies witchcraft, whether it be African, Greek, medieval or New World.

[3]*Picus* is a Latin word which means "Woodpecker."

[4]Medea of course is the subject of the famous tragedy by Euripides who wrote it in 431 B.C. Medea's magic is non-existent in this play except for the poisonous robe and chariot. It is purposely down-played by Euripides who wished to depict the psychological conflicts within the mind of Medea, namely the conflicts of passion and reason and of motherly love and revenge. To have portrayed Medea as a witch would have deprived her of her crucial character traits and would have made the audience unsympathetic. Medea was the subject of another tragedy, which was written by Seneca in the first century A.D. Here Medea the witch appears from the very beginning and the magic is sustained throughout the play. Thus Euripides deviated from the tradition which was at least 100 years older than he was (cf. the four Pythian Odes of Pindar).

[5]According to our ancient sources, there could be no constriction anywhere, even a ring, on the witch's body while she was conducting her rites.

[6]Since Ovid is one of our latest sources for classical witchcraft, he represents in many respects the culmination of witchcraft stories; consequently he is our most important source for Greek and Roman witches. Pliny the Younger is our best source for magic and superstition.

[7]The *hippomanes* was considered by the ancients to be a most powerful love charm. It is the

tubercle on the forehead of a newly-born foal; the mare eats it immediately, or, as believed, the foal goes insane. It was the witch's job to snatch it off the foal before the mare got it.

⁸This threat of pounding a lizard into a potion is indicative of her amateurism. Any knowledgeable witch would always use a toad in this situation!

⁹One can see here the great principles of sympathetic magic in action. Homeopathic magic, i.e. like affects like, or the result is the same as the cause, is reflected here by the waxen image. It is a universal practice (cf. voodoo) to form a doll of your enemy and then subject it to various tortures; whatever the image suffers the person will suffer as well. The cloak symbolizes contagious magic, or "whatever has once been in contact with something or someone is always in contact, no matter the distance involved." Thus, you can be harmed if someone places sharp glass in your footprints. The burning of Delphis' cloak signifies that Delphis will burn too (probably with fever).

¹⁰The question of whether or not the following four poets believed in magic is not a relevant question, as S. Lilja, *The Roman Elegists' Attitude to Women* (Helsinki, 1965), pp. 104, 118-9, believes. The important point is that these poets were writing for their audience which did believe in magic and witchcraft. For witchcraft and these four poets, see I. Bruns, "Der Liebeszauber bei den augusteischen dichtern," *Preussische Jahrbucher,* CIII (1901), pp. 193-220.

¹¹The situation also applies for the second century A.D.: see the chapter "Freedom and Fear" in E.R. Dodds, *The Greeks and the Irrational* (Berkeley, 1951).

¹²*Defixionum tabellae* are curse tablets. If someone wished to place a curse upon his enemy, he would write a magical saying on a lead tablet, bind it with a thread or drive a nail through it, and then place it where it could not be found, e.g. in the ocean or in a coffin. The definitive book on the subject is *Defixionum Tabellae* (written in Latin) by A. Audollent (published by Albertus Fontemoing, Paris, 1904).

¹³It is interesting that a recent study which analyzed three ointments used by Middle Age witches, showed that all the potions contained substances which could give the illusion of flying. The first compound contained hemlock and aconite, which together cause mental confusion. The second ointment contained belladona which produces excitement that might pass into delirium. The third compound contained both aconite and belladona which together produce excitement and irregular action of the heart. These ointments were taken either internally or externally (if the latter, it still entered the bloodstream through the vaginal area or broken skin). They produced hallucinations and elevation of spirit; impression of flying was brought about through the cardiac arrhythmia.

¹⁴In the eleventh century the Catholic Church did a complete turnabout on its stance on witchcraft. Early in the century it had published the *Canon Episcopi,* in which it was stated that witchcraft was a mere delusion and that anyone who practiced it was performing vain rites. The penalties were light, as they had been for the past 800 years, involving certain periods of fasting and prayers. Later in the century, however, a papal bull was published which called witchcraft the work of the devil and witches satanists. All witches were to be rounded up and executed. The reason for this change in part lies in the Church's reaction to internal schism and heresy. Political factors can not be excluded. Kings and popes often collaborated on witch-hunts to enrich their treasures; an example of this involves King Philip II of France who received papal permission to exterminate the Templar Knights for their money. Witch-hunts also provided an excellent means of suppressing revolts or of diverting the masses from the horrible economic conditions of the time. A fairly good discussion of this can be found in the third chapter "The European Witch-Craze of the Sixteenth and Seventeenth Centuries" of *Religion, Reformation and Social Change* (London, 1967) by H.R. Trevor-Roper.

¹⁵Murray published her thesis in *The Witch-Cult in Western Europe* and in *The God of the Witches.* The gist of her theory is that witchcraft was an actual phenomenon, in fact it was a pagan religion which existed all over the Mediterranean and Europe; the followers worshipped a god with horns which promoted fertility. To prove this theory Murray extracted isolated phenomena from various European cultures and fitted them to her thesis. This method of extraction and quoting out of context led her to intolerable mistakes. See G.L. Burr, "A Review of M.A. Murray's *Witch-Cult in Western Europe,"* *American Historical Review,* XXVII, 4 (1922), pp. 780-83. In her section on ancient Greece and the Horned God I have noticed errors in each of her arguments. First, she says that Pan was the horned god of the Greeks and that he was so as his name proves (*pan* in Greek means "all," thus showing that he was the only god). Murray failed to realize that Pan is a very late god, since his earliest representation is in fifth century B.C. and he

was not listed with the other major deities in the Linear Tables written in 1250 B.C. (though Murray could not have known this last fact, since the tablets were not deciphered until 1952); moreover, Pan comes from the word *pa-sco which means "to feed"—the association with the adjective *pan* ("all") being based upon a false analogy, as Kern has shown (*Die Religion der Griechen*, iii, 127). She also said that Dionysos was a late importation, probably around 700 B.C.; yet we know that he was worshipped as early as 1250 B.C. according to the Linear B tablets (see Ventris-Chadwick, *Documents in Mycenaean Greek*, p. 127 and note). Further, she states that the legend of Phrixus and Hellene dates to the Early Bronze Age (3000-2200 B.C.), yet how she knows this is perplexing, since mention of the legend does not occur until 2000 years later. Even more indicative of her method is the fact that she does not mention the heavy preponderance of religious significance of the bull on Crete during the Bronze Age; this would be very supportive of her theory, yet she never seems to have consulted archaeological evidence.

[16]It must be kept in mind that matrilineal does not mean matriarchal. The latter signifies "rule by women," while matrilineal simple means "a society wherein the woman enjoys a higher position than the male." In a matrilineal society there is exogamy, descent traced through the female, transmission of property through the mother and an emphasis on female functions and fertility. For further reading see the article "matrilineal" in *Encyclopedia of Religion and Ethics.* That Greece and Rome were formerly matrilineal societies can be shown by many facts. See J. Bachofen's *Mutterecht* and Briffault's book listed below, and especially G. Thompson's *Studies in Prehistoric Greek Society.*

[17]See R. Briffault, *The Mothers: A Study of the Origins of Sentiments and Institutions* (New York, 1927), vols. I-III. I have incorporated many of his ideas in the next few paragraphs.

[18]See the first chapter of volume II of Briffault's work.

[19]For a complete discussion of Greek and Latin rain magic see M. Morgan, "Greek and Roman Rain-Gods and Rain Charms," *Transactions of the American Philological Association,* XXXII (1901), pp. 83-109.

Selected Bibliography

The trouble when dealing with Greek and Roman witchcraft is that no one has ever devoted a book to the subject. There are, for example, some books which discuss witches, others amulets, others lycanthropy, others specific rites and ceremonies; however, to date no book has appeared which treats the subject in full. The place to begin, if you wish to read up on this topic, is the article "magic" in *Oxford Classical Dictionary* by S. Eitrem; then the article "mageia" in Pauly-Wissowa, *Real-Encyclopadie der Klassischen Altertumswissenschaft,* vierzehnter band, 301-393; H. Hubert has a superb article entitled "magic" in *Dictionaire des antiquites grecques et romaines;* equally excellent is the article "Magic—Greek and Roman" in *Encyclopedia of Religion and Ethics* by K. Smith. These four articles give background information which should satisfy both the expert and the layperson.

The most important books are E. Tavenner, *Studies in Magic from Latin Literature* (New York, 1916); B. Bekker, *De Betoverde Weereld* (Amsterdam, 1961); K. DeJong, *De Magie Bij De Grieken en Romeinen* (Haarlem, 1948); J. Lowe, *Magic in Greek and Latin Literature* (Oxford, 1929); L. Maury, *La Magie et l'astrologie* (Paris, 1923); and L. Thorndike, *A History of Magic and Experimental Science* (London, 1923). Specialized studies on amulets and charms include M. Blumler, *A History of Amulets* (Edinburgh, 1887); D.

Albert, *Secrets marvelleux de la magic naturelle et cabalistique* (Lyon, 1782); E. Budge, *Amulets and Talismans* (New York, 1970). The evil eye has been studied by F. Elworthy, *The Evil Eye* (London, 1895) and by E. Gifford, *The Evil Eye* (New York, 1958). Magical papyri are dealt with by K. Preisendanz, *Papyri Graecae Magicae* (Leipzig, 1928-31); the texts are not translated but there are good discussions and notes. Lycanthropy is treated by K. Smith, *The Werewolf in Latin Literature* (Baltimore, 1892) and by M. Summers, *The Vampire* (London, 1928); there is a complete annotated bibliography on werewolfism in G. Black, *A List of Works Relating to Lycanthropy* (New York, 1920). For magic and Roman religion, see E. Burriss, *Taboo, Magic and Spirits* (New York, 1931); F. Cumont, *After-Life in Roman Paganism* (New York, 1922); and W. Adams, *Dwellers on the Threshold* (London, 1865).

VIII

Roman Domestic Religion: The Archaeology of Roman Popular Art

One of the most characteristic aspects of popular Roman Catholic Christianity today is the household shrine. These range from niches containing plaster renditions of the Madonna with votive candles and palm leaves to grottoes formed from discarded bathtubs, to mass-produced images that glow in the dark, to simple wall decorations such as crucifixes and Sacred Heart chromos. In this article David Gerald Orr suggests a continuing tradition deriving from classical Roman domestic religion. Using the evidence of some five hundred examples preserved at Pompeii, Orr describes the four primary types of household shrines, including those for Vesta, the living flame of the hearth; the Lares, personal protective spirits; the Penates, home deities; and the Genius, the spiritual alter-ego of the individual Roman.

These Pompeiian shrines are truly popular culture. As Orr says, there was "no priestly college to make the cult concrete... no written dogma" to guide ancient Romans or modern scholars. Highly individual and artistically unsophisticated in style, these shrines, like so much popular culture of the past have been ignored by archaeologists and art historians whose interests and prejudices have usually focussed attention on high-style expressions.

David Gerald Orr currently serves as Regional Archaeologist for the National Park Service's Mid-Atlantic Region in Philadelphia. Formerly he was an Assistant Professor of American Civilization at the University of Pennsylvania where he was also Curator of American Historical Archaeology at the University Museum. His interests include vernacular architecture, folk ethnographies, industrial archaeology, Roman religion and American popular culture.

Roman Domestic Religion:
The Archaeology of Roman Popular Art

David Gerald Orr

"sed patrii servate Lares: aluistis et idem,
cursarem vestros cum tener ante pedes."

Tibullus 1. 10. 15-16.

The Roman poet Tibullus summed up the essence of all Roman domestic forces when he mentioned in his poem *Against War* that his Lares (tutelary domestic deities) watched over him and reared him when he was a boy. Beyond every other element contained in the cult of the Roman domestic deities stretched the idea that these religious forces of the hearth and home guarded their wards and averted evil from the home. A Roman's protective gods followed him throughout life and their favor was sought through the continual practice of an ancient ritual and the maintenance of traditional concepts of piety. It was this venerable household cult that persisted late into the waning years of the Roman Empire. It was this cult which meshed with Christianity in the home and it is this cult which still survives in domestic Italian religious practices. The idea that one popularly conceived domestic institution syncretically blended some of its material culture and much of its mental template with a later cultural change is not a new one. Yet, the simple domestic ceremony and practices of the Roman household does unite physical objects (the shrines of Campania) with what little we know from other sources left to us from ancient Rome. The result forms what George Kubler[1] denotes as the "collective identity," a point of reference to the future. With such a "community of objects"[2] linkages can be clearly structured which depict the visual flow from the world we have lost to the world we live in. In such a perspective the remarkable persistence of aspects of the Roman household ritual may not seem so remarkable. This essay hopes only to elucidate the cult as it existed under the Roman Empire. Those elements suggesting its survival in various areas of the Mediterranean will only be generally described. It is a clear invitation to more extensive modern ethnographic research.

For the ancient Roman the cult of the domestic deities primarily concerns itself with a quest for their special individual protection.[3]

156

As the cult evolved, separate and distinct groups of divine powers (or *numina*) were venerated in a clearly defined household ritual.[4] Although we are not clear on the exact nature of this ritual, it nevertheless played an important role in the household, first by the ancient male head of the family (the *paterfamilias*) and his own servants and family, and then later by non-Romans, freedmen and eventually Christians. This worship survived and its material forms creates the background for much of the iconography found in modern Italian domiciles. The domestic cult signified much to the Roman: reliance of the family for its survival on the household deities, ritual piety and simplicity, and encouragement to the family for well-being to name just a few functions. The formal religions of the Roman Empire, both indigenous and oriental, offered status, gregarious social activity, but little intimacy. Within the private seclusion of the Roman household the Lares and Penates were propitiated in quiet and deep devotion. The nexus of all activities relating to the domestic cult was the household shrine (lararium).[5] Here also was demonstrated the flexibility of the cult since it enabled the worshipper to introduce into the home many strange deities and sects. Perhaps Christianity penetrated into the Roman home as such a newcomer in the simple lararium niche, altar, miniature temple, or painting. Three peculiar sets of powers were incorporated within the framework offered by the domestic shrine and its ritual. Each of these was represented by separate deities and by special ceremonies.[6] The central protective force caring for the health and continuance of the family was propitiated at the hearth and was in fact symbolized by the living fire of Vesta, goddess of the hearth. Originally agricultural deities, another group moved from the field into the home at some early point in time. Here they were honored as an additional set of tutelary *numina* within the home. The final group of deities guarded the storerooms and cupboards and never were iconographically depicted. Simply reduced, these above three sets of powers were known as Vesta, the Lares, and the Penates, respectively. Each of these elements needs to be examined.

One characteristic of Roman domestic worship which must constantly be kept in mind is that there was no priestly college to make the cult concrete and there was no written dogma to express its ancient history. No area in the Roman house better expresses this aspect of household worship than the hearth. From earliest times it was the center for religious activity in the home.[7] Here was found the "living flame" of Vesta.[8] Vesta's public cult in which her fire was tended as a symbol of Roman permanence and power is fairly well understood but her more primitive and intimate nature is only to be comprehended in relationship to the domestic hearth. Here, in simple paintings located in kitchens, near the hearth fire, Vesta was depicted anthropomorphically.[9] Since Pompeii became a Roman town rather late in its historic existence, the presence of Vesta in the lararium painting indicates the Romanization of the town. She was the patron deity of millers and bakers and in Pompeii is found on shrines located near ovens and mills. The round shape of Vesta's temple in the forum in Rome may have antecedents going back to the prehistoric period of the city.[10] Her presence in the houseshrines thus connoted both ancient tradition and political power. Yet her early amorphous religious power was reflected in her Roman temple where she was not represented by images but by fire.[11] Similarly, Vesta preserved her abstract nature in the household where her fire was tended by the daughters or wife of the *paterfamilias*. She maintained her close linkages to the purity symbolized by flame at the domestic hearth.[12]

The origins and early history of the Lares are sharply disputed.[13] Simply put it was the nature of these *numina* to resist precise areas of influence and defy clearly delineated functions.[14] The evidence suggests that the vague character of the Lares and their position in Roman domestic worship led to the practice in imperial times of using the word "Lar" as a substitute for home, household, hearth and even areas far removed from a domestic ambience.[15] The cult of the Lares had developed by the first century A.D. into a highly diversified one which could offer different services to the family. In the home, however, the tutelary character of the Lares never lost its force. The Lar (or Lares) of the family protected a Roman sent out on military service,[16] watched closely the daily lives of the home's residents,[17] and exercised constantly the role of the familial protector.[18] The survival of ancient agricultural festivals, like the *Compitalia,* demonstrates the manner in which the Lares prospered in the Roman household.[19] By the early imperial epoch, the Lares were guarding particular places, not necessarily homes. Thus there existed Lares of roads and travelers, soldiers and military camps, games, the imperial residences and even the state of Rome itself.[20]

In the household the Lares were offered sacrifices of grapes, table scraps, garlands, grain, honeycakes and wine.[21] They were worshipped on special feast days and probably were venerated in daily acts of homage. When a Roman boy and girl came of age, they dedicated to their Lares the small emblem of their childhood, the *bulla,* which was worn around their necks before adulthood.[22] A *bulla* was found in a house in Pompeii tied carefully around the figure of a domestic deity. In the house the Lares promoted the health and welfare of the family.

The image of the Lar as it is known to us from the days of the late Roman Republic and from the pictorialization of it in ancient Pompeii somehow does not convey the *gravitatas* and sobriety generally associated with the *paterfamilias* of a Roman home (fig. 1). They are shown as happy sprites, holding a wine cup overflowing with the fruits of Campanian harvests, and pose in a light, tip-toes dancing position. Their total impression is one which relates to Hellenic Dionysiac depictions; indeed their source probably was located in Magna Graecia to the south of Pompeii.[23] Non-Roman elements in the Lar's costume and makeup include the rhyton (Greek drinking vessel), the posture of the Lar itself, and the treatment of the footwear.[24] Hair length differs greatly from Lar to Lar; some are shown with closely cropped locks while others are given long flowing curls. The "Liberty Cap" (*pileus*) is also occasionally shown on Lares (fig. 2) and probably reflects the political status of their masters.[25] The high-girded skirt, however, is definitely meant to represent the Roman *tunica*.[26] Iconographically, the idea of placing paired Lares in lararium painting became popular and was the commonest canon in which the domestic deities were couched (fig. 3).

Fig. 1 Lar depicted holding rhyton (wine vessel) which is shown spouting wine into a small sacrificial pail. This is from a lararium painting found in Pompeii. The numbers refer to the Region, insula (block), and house number respectively. First Century A.D. I. xii. 3.

Fig. 2 Lararium niche with flanking Lares, each wearing the Liberty Cap *(pileus)*. A crescent moon (perhaps the moon god *Men)* crowns a finely modeledgorgon head within the niche. An incredibly thin serpent is shown beneath the lararium. Pompeii, First Century A.D. I. xii. 15.

Fig. 3 The standard lararia painting canon. Two Lares flanking a togate and sacrificing Genius figure (with female equivalent (?) Juno (?)). Two small sacrificial attendants complete the painting. First Century A.D., Pompeii, House of Polybius, IX. xiii. 3.

The position of the Penates in the Roman home is not disputed. Their function clearly related to the *penus,* a place usually located at the back of the atrium (open roofed central court) of the home.[27] Although they were also present at the hearth in company with the Lares, their main activity centered on the storeroom. Their abstract nature resulted from their earlier utilization as wards of the cereal storehouse.[28] Yet, at ancient Pompeii the Penates have significantly changed. Here, the meaning of the Penates encompasses all the domestic numina of the home.[29] Thus the Penates mean Vesta, the Lares, and any diety who is worshipped in the home. Making the muddied picture of the Penates even more difficult to see is the fact that the state cult of the Imperial Penates must have filtered down into the Roman home of the first century A.D., especially in the domiciles of those freedmen who felt strong allegiance to the imperial house. The worship of the Penates, at any rate, was an integral part of the household cult.[30] Unfortunately, our understanding of its relationship to the ancient Roman deities of the storehouse is, at the best, imperfect.

Other religious forces were present in the house shrines of ancient Roman homes. The most significant by far is the Genius. The genius was the alter-ego or spiritual "double" of an ancient Roman.[31] He was responsible for the procreative force present in the *Paterfamilias* and encouraged the continuation of the Roman family.[32] Versatile and flexible, it too could be used to protect places and things like the Lar and other fixtures of the domestic cult.[33] Both kinds of Geniuses were found in the domestic shrine. The household Genius was honored on the *dies natalis* (birthday) of the Paterfamilias.[34] Sacrifices included not only the customary honeycakes and wine but blood offerings such as pigs and lambs.[35] Oaths were sworn by the Genius and members of the Roman home regarded the concept as one of blood relationship.[36] Yet its most important power was that of continuing the roman *gens* and insuring its maintenance from one generation to another.

In ancient Pompeii, the Genius appears as both a public and a private religious being. Street shrines dedicated at the *compita* held imperial dedications and gestures (mostly by Freedmen) while in the lararia of the residential quarter the Genius was venerated as a domestic numen.[37] The Lares also seem to share in this duality; perhaps it was the simple idea that the household shrine and deities of the emperor protected the entire empire. At any rate the Genius is depicted in the shrines as a togate male figure, usually carrying a cornucopia and sacrificing with a small *patera* (fig. 4).

Closely associated with the Genius and also an ubiquitous element of the Roman household shrine is the house snake. This is

Fig. 4 Togate Genius figure sacrificing over lighted altar; Genius serpent before. First Century A.D., Pompeii, I. xvi. 2.

not the place to examine the multitudinous ways in which serpents penetrated Roman religion and the diverse character of that symbolic force.[38] In the home the serpent plays two roles. First, he is the guardian of a particular spot; the Genius of the place.[39] Here he and the earlier cult of the Genius have obviously been combined. One aspect of the Genius serpent's role in the home has apparently survived in Calabria (Italy) today. Harmless snakes are still welcomed in the home as protectors and even pets.[40] This use of the "house snake" is still common in Balkan areas of the Mediterranean and even as far north as Sweden.[41] In rural South Italy serpents are seen as examples of "bon fortuna" whenever they are encountered in the fields. All these aforementioned examples attest to the second and most important role played by the serpent in Roman domestic religion—that of familiar protector and Genius attribute.

Both the Genius (depicted anthropomorphically) and the serpent are common in the house shrines of Campania. Most of the reptiles are shown as viperine, large necked, rough-scaled animals (fig. 5). It must be stressed that the depictions of both Hellenic and Roman house serpents iconographically related to long established Mediterranean forms and are not indicative of those snakes introduced into Italy as part of the cult of Oriental or Egyptian sects.[42] They not only serve apotropaically in the home but are used frequently on mural frescoes both inside and outside the Roman house or building.[43] Here they mean simply that the place is sacred and should not be treated impiously. Curiously enough, when the Roman house cult serpent confronted Christianity (and with it the connotation of the snake as evil) it yielded its formal precedence but preserved its deep-rooted agrarian nature. Thus the house snake endured as animate arm of the procreative Genius force, together with its tutelary function of guarding special spots and places. Able to accommodate a great many religious ideas, the Genius (and its serpent) became a significant element in Roman domestic worship.

Fig. 5 Crested and bearded Genius serpent approaching altar upon which is an egg and pine cone. Pompeii, I. xii. 3. First Century A.D. Lararium painting.

All the aforementioned elements are bound together by the ceremonies and rituals which once centered on the house shrines themselves. Pompeii has by far the most dazzling assemblage of objects and shrines to be found anywhere in the Roman world. By the fortuitous and timely application of basic volcanism some 1900 years ago, Pompeii has preserved for us a collection of about five hundred lararia. The entire remaining portion of known Roman house shrines from sites other than ancient Campania actually amounts to about twenty examples. Nevertheless, certain caveats should be underscored at the onset of our final discussion. First, the surviving shrines are typical of the immediate region surrounding Vesuvius, "happy Campania," and may in fact be atypical of those found in Rome and other more densely populated areas and provinces. Specific details of the iconography encountered in Pompeian lararia, for example, probably were not indicative of those common, let us say, to Iberia or Africa. Yet the literary evidence does confirm the presence of the main elements of the Roman house shrine; elements we have summarized above. Thus their general character is not singularly distinctive and may respond closely to a general canon found elsewhere; perhaps couched in different styles and symbols.[44] They must, moreover, be considered typological reference points for what we know of Roman culture elsewhere.[45]

All the shrines excavated in Pompeii have two basic key attributes. They must provide for the veneration of deities symbolized by the paintings and sculpture found on the shrine, and they must accommodate the simple needs presented by the worshipper. Since portions of the sacrifice ritual involves burnt offerings, the lararia area must have access to the open sky. Altars can be provided as tile shelves attached to the shrine or can be temporary in nature and used wherever the need arises. Scale does not seem to be a factor; lararia range from tiny foot square niches to the freestanding platformed "temples" occasionally present in the central halls of Roman houses. Of course, it must be admitted that sacrifice can be accomplished along with acts of domestic piety without lararia or altars. Yet, in the formal domestic ritual, the lararium becomes indispensable. Three major areas of the Roman house appear to be the most frequently encountered sites for house shrines. The grandest and most monumental shrines are usually found in the atria (central open roofed hall) of Roman domiciles. Kitchens, the room containing the hearth fire, and gardens account for most of the lararia present in Pompeii. Many houses (and shops) have multiple shrines and some rooms within Roman homes may have more than one shrine.

Four types of shrine are present in Pompeii. The most common form is simply an arcuated niche or recess in the masonry wall; either painted or unpainted. These niches are usually furnished with a roof tile or masonry ledge for sacrifice and object display[46] (fig. 6). More elaborate variations on this type is repeated by adding

Fig. 6 Niche-type lararium. The painting shows a togate Genius figure sacrificing before a small altar; an attendant can be seen behind him. Pompeii, First Century A.D., I. xvii. 4.

two-dimensional temple facade surrounds.[47] Some shrines are created by wall paintings fronted with small portable altars[48] (fig. 3). Most impressive of all forms is the miniature freestanding temple type, or aedicula (fig. 7). This lararium is generally built of rubble masonry stuccoed and painted, and roofed by rubble masonry columns; one unique example even sheathed with marble slabs covered with bas-relief depictions of the earthquake which demolished Pompeii in 62 A.D.[49] Rare indeed is the sacellum; a separate building devoted exclusively to the propitiation of the household deities.[50] Only a small group of these structures are

Fig. 7 Aedicula-type lararium. The roof has been destroyed but the stuccoed brick columns are still present. Two painted and stuccoed serpents can be seen on the shrine's inner panels. Painted winged griffons are also visible on either side of the aedicula. Pompeii, Probably first century A.D., I. xvi. 2.

known.

The paintings and sculptures found in the Pompeian house shrines document an incredible spectrum of religious concepts and practices. Fortuna, Vesta and Bacchus are among the most popular

Roman deities and they respectively referred to basic aspects of Pompeii's economic and social makeup. Fortuna, more precisely the good luck of Pompeian commerce and trade, reflected the mercantile character of Pompeii. Vesta mirrored the newly acquired "Romanity" and with it its central Italic religious traditions. She was also the patroness of bakers: an important industry in Pompeii.[51] Like Vesta, the wine god Bacchus embodied the economic activity of Campania. The rich viticultural farming land surrounding Pompeii is encapsulated in the iconography of Bacchus shown sometimes as a figure completely enveloped in grapes! He is additionally the most popular patron deity for the numerous hostels and taverns located in the town. Pompeii's Roman protectoress was Venus, the family goddesses of Sulla who captured the town in the first century A.D. and who later became an important deity in the imperial pantheon. Finally let us not ignore the presence of Mercury in the household shrines; the god of tavern owners, commerce, finance and thieves.

But it was the dramatic infusion of oriental religions into the Pompeian home which gives the shrines their most exciting character. Egyptian gods and goddesses, most notably those of the Isis and Serapis cults, are found in many of the lararia. The active commercial links with Alexandria probably accounted for their great popularity. Stranger still were the Hellenistic Greek-Egyptian syncretisms such as Isis-Artemis and Isis-Fortuna. Even the river Sarnus which flowed by Pompeii was honored by an elaborately painted household shrine which depicts scenes of trade and pleasure on the river.[52] Lastly, Christianity may be present in Herculaneum during the same period as Pompeii, i.e. the late first century A.D. A possible imprint in the wall near a wooden lararium found in a Herculaneum house appears to be cruciform in shape.[53]

The paintings found in Pompeian lararia differ markedly from the regular mural decoration encountered as one visits the houses and public structures of the city. Even more remarkable is the fact that each individual depiction, although many follow the canon previously described, displays its own personal hallmark. No two house shrines have been found to display similar qualities of line, color and design. More often than not the work is spontaneously rendered and intimately postured. Thus the Pompeian house shrines confront us with a "primitive" quality not found in the more elitist "high-style" standard mural compositions scattered throughout the city. These paintings have long been ignored since they do not take part in the "loftier" and more Olympian world of the great four Pompeian styles. But the study of art is an historical and sociological phenomenon which must not bog itself down in the swamps of truth and teleology. More to the point, the Pompeian shrines reflect a different intellectual and phenomenological sense of time and place. As such they partake in traditional passages of time and share attributes which usually are more permanently immeshed in the cults of house and hearth. At the same time the paintings show interesting innovations. For example, the full face frontality more generally associated with early Christian and later Byzantine art can be found in many kitchen paintings found in Pompeii. The sense of humor deeply ingrained in many of the shrines, e.g. a painted smiling snake emerging from a real hole in the plaster, underscore an additional quality present in such paintings. The eighteenth-century aestheticians chose to ignore high style Roman painting as well as popular depictions since they were not consistent with a Polyclitan ideal they so much admired in Hellenic sculpture. Here at Pompeii, on the lararia surfaces, these paintings serve as strong testators for the continuing debate as to the nature of art and the nature of the designed material world. Another essay may offer some clarity on these troubling waters.

It may be that the individually executed house shrine paintings, with their attendant variety, expressed ideas which were later to mature into a new European artistic force. In the House of Polybius, a fine lararium painting was recently discovered; one which was apparently left unfinished at the time of the eruption in 79 A.D. (fig. 3). A detail of one of the Lares shows the thin drawing which preceded the shading and coloring that completed the painting (fig. 8). Here we can appreciate the personal nature of these paintings with the greatest attention given to facial physiognomy and expression. Exceptional as this painting is (few are as monumental in scale and detail), the Polybius shrine manages to convey to us the force and power of the Roman house shrine. One imagines the Roman youths, male and female, who first donned their adult clothes before it in their "coming of age" rituals. It truly gives us a participatory experience in the traditional power of religious images.

Roman household worship, as exemplified by these shrines, became the vehicle used by Christianity to penetrate into the Mediterranean home. Christians quickly took advantage of the simple provisions for domestic piety already framed by the household shrine. As Christianity spread throughout Europe, the house cult, now duly converted, went with it. It easily combined with sacred house corner traditions already present in Germanic lore and prospered in every European region. In the Mediterranean it survived practically unscathed. The graceful polychromed terracotta garden shrines now seen in the Naples area recall the Roman

Fig. 8 Detail of the head of the left Lar present on the shrine illustrated *in toto* as Figure Three. The unfinished character of the work demonstrates the painting techniques utilized. Pompeii, 79 A.D. ca., IX. xiii. 3.

house cult vividly. Madonnas, proudly ensconced in Neapolitan homes, evoke still the tutelary nature of the Lares. The mountain shrine in Greece still serves the weary traveller in much the same manner as the Roman roadside lararium. Above all, the continual flow of domestic numen still protects and keeps the home. The importance of Roman domestic religion as a significant catalyst in this process is undisputed. The needs so wondrously identified by Roman household rituals never have been displaced by the violent patterns of western history.

Notes

[1]George Kubler, *The Shape of Time,* New Haven: 1962, especially p. 9.

[2]Bernard Herman and David Orr, "Pear Valley, *et al:* An Excursion into the Analysis of Southern Vernacular Architecture," *Southern Folklore Quarterly* V. 39, no. 4, Dec., 1975, pp. 307-325.

[3]See Warde Fowler, *Roman Ideas of Deity in the Last Century B.C.*, London: 1914, pp. 15, 25. See also R.M. Ogilvie, *The Romans and Their Gods in the Age of Augustus*, London: 1969, pp. 102-105.

[4]For the early development of the cult see Jesse Benedict Carter, *The Religion of Numa*, London: 1906.

[5]For *lararia* see George K. Boyce, *Corpus of the Lararia of Pompeii, Memoirs of the American Academy in Rome*, 14, Rome: 1937, and David Gerald Orr, *Roman Domestic Religion: A Study of the Roman Household Deities and their Shrines* (Ph.D. dissertation, University of Maryland, College Park, Md, 1972).

[6]David Gerald Orr, "Roman Domestic Religion: The Evidence of the Household Shrines," in *ANRW*, Band II. 16. 1. Berlin: 1978, p. 1559.

[7]Ovid *Fasti* 6. 301-308; *Trist.*5.5.10. Cato *R.R.* 143.2. For the hearth see H.J. Rose, *Religion in Greece and Rome*, New York: 1959, p. 178.

[8]For Living Flame, "vivam flammam," see Ovid *Fasti* 6. 291. For Vesta see also Gerhard Radke, *Die Goetter Altitaliens, Fontes et Commentationes 3*, Muenster: 1965, pp. 320-324 and H. Hommel, *Vesta und die fruehroemische Religion*, *ANRW* I, 2, Berlin: 1972, pp. 397-420. For the State cult see Thomas Worsfold, *The History of the Vestal Virgins*, London: 1952.

[9]See Boyce, op. cit., no. 77 and no. 420.

[10]Michael Grant, *The Roman Forum*, New York: 1970, pp. 55-60.

[11]Ovid *Fasti* 295-398.

[12]The sanctity of the hearth fire seemed to be an ancient element of Greek household worship as well. Hestia, the Greek analog to Vesta, was also never completely anthropomorphized. In both Greek and Roman religion the hearth was versatile—it served both secular and non-secular functions.

[13]Two opposing theories have been formulated concerning the early history and evolution of the Lares in Roman religion. The first group holds that the Lares were originally agricultural deities and moved into the house from their early hegemony of the fields and crops. See Kurt Latte, *Roemische Religionsgeschicte,Handbuch der Altertumswiss.* V. 4. Munich: 1960, pp. 166-174; R.E.A. Palmer, *Roman Religion and Roman Empire, Five Essays*, The Haney Foundation Series 15, Philadelphia: 1974, pp. 114-115 and p. 117. The other concept argues that the Lares embodied the spirits of the dead ancestors of the family. See E. Samter, *Familienfeste der Griechen und Roemer*, Berlin: 1901, pp. 105-108. Perhaps this view was a Greek one which melded with the earlier Italic idea that the Lares came from the arable fields. See Margaret Waites, "The Nature of the Lares and Their Representation in Roman Art," *AJA*, 24 (1920), pp. 241-261.

[14]An inscription found recently at Tor Tignosa, outside Rome, further attests to this idea. See M. Guarducci, "Cippo latino arcaico con dedica ad Enea," *Bull. Com.* 76, *Bull. del Mus. della civilta Romana 19*, 1956-58, pp. 3-13. *Numen* was always recognized as being a kind of religious force which could be attached to objects and thereby increase their supernatural power.

[15]Virgil *Georg.* 3. 344. Martial 10. 61. 5.

[16]*Corpus Inscriptionum Latinarum* (afterwards CIL) III 3460. Ovid *Trist.* 4. 8. 22.

[17]Cato *R.R.* 143. 3.

[18]Plautus' *Aulularia* contains a prologue spoken by a Lar! In this passage is contained one of the best summations of their tutelary nature. *Aulularia* 1-5.

[19]A good description of the festival is given in W. Warde Fowler, *The Roman Festivals of the Period of the Republic,*London: 1899, pp. 279-80. See also Louise Holland, "The Shrine of the Lares Compitales," *TAPA*, 68 (1939), pp. 428-41. *Compita* were sacred spots located where four properties intersected or where four streets converged at right angles. Since Roman mensuration used squares and rectangles for city planning, many such spots existed in Roman towns. Pompeii's main east-west axis is provided with a street shrine at almost every *compitum.*

[20]Roads and travelers: CIL II 4320, CIL XIV 4547.

Soldiers and Military Camps: CIL III 3460

Games: CIL VI 36810

Imperial Residences: CIL VI 443, 445-449.

State: Ovid *Fasti* 5. 129.

[21]Tibullus 1. 10. 21-24. Horace *Carmina* 3. 23. 3-4.

Horace *Sat.* 2. 5. 12-14.

[22]For the *bulla* see Petronius, *Sat.* 60. 8.

[23]Boyce, op. cit., Plate 18, no. 1; Plate 24, nos. 1 & 2. Orr, dissertation, Corpus A, no. 3.

[24]Waites, op. cit., pp. 257ff. Georg Wissowa, *Religion und Kultus der Roemer,* Handbuch der altertumswiss., IV, 5, Munich: 1902, p. 172. For the Rhyton see Orr, *ANRW,* p. 1568, no. 67.

[25]Orr, *ANRW,* p. 1569, n. 74.

[26]Lillian M.Wilson, *The Clothing of the Ancient Romans,* Baltimore: 1938, pp. 55-56.

[27]W. Warde Fowler, *The Religious Experience of the Roman People,* London: 1933, pp. 73-74. Orr, *ANRW,* p. 1563, n. 28.

[28]Martial 8. 75. 1.

[29]Horace *Carmina* 2.4.15; 3. 23.19. The *Di Penates* were all the divinities worshipped at the hearth.

[30]Cicero *Rep.* 5.7. See also Orr, dissertation, pp. 42-43.

[31]Fowler, *Religious Experience,* p. 74. See also H.J. Rose, "On the Original Significance of the Genius." *CQ* 17, pp. 57-60.

[32]H.J. Rose, *Religion in Greece and Rome* New York: 1959, p. 193. Women were represented by their Juno. This concept also suggested the youth concept in the representation of procreative force.

[33]Orr, *ANRW,* p. 1570.

[34]Tibullus 1.7.49; 2.2.1.

[35]Ovid *Trist.* 3.13.17.

[36]Orr, *ANRW,* p. 1571.

[37]Street Shrines: Orr, dissertation, Plate XI, pp. 125-27. Also V. Spinnazola, *Pompei alla luce degli scavi di Via dell'abbondanza* 3 volumes. Rome: 1953, pp. 177ff. Domestic Numen: CILX 860.

[38]For example, the serpent in Greece was also the guardian of the house and an animal associated with good luck. They were also used as instruments through which the future could be read. See Martin P. Nilsson, *Greek Folk Religion,* New York: 1940, p. 71. Pliny mentions that snakes were kept as pets. See *N.H.* 29.72. He also distinguished between those which were poisonous (Aspides) and those which were non-poisonous (Dracones).

[39]Persius *in Georg.* 3. 417.

[40]Nilsson, p. 71. See also M. Nilsson, *The Minoan-Mycenaean Religion and its Survival in Greek Religion,* Lund: 1927, p. 281.

[41]Nilsson, *Greek Folk,* p. 71.

[42]Orr, *ANRW,* p. 1573.

[43]Ibid., pp. 1574-75.

[44]For example, certain representations, the Lares for instance, resemble those found elsewhere; see the images of the Lares and Genius shown on a street shrine altar found in Rome and now in the Palace of the Conservators, Rome, Italy.

[45]Orr, *ANRW,* p. 1585.

[46]Ibid., Plate One, Fig. one.

[47]Ibid., Plate One. Fig. two.

[48]Ibid., p. 1578.

[49]*Boyce,* Plate 30, Fig. four.

[50]Ibid., p. 18.

[51]Ibid., Number 77.

[52]Orr, *ANRW,* Plate Seven, Fig. fourteen, p. 1582.

[53]See Margherita Guarducci, "Dal gioco letterale all Crittographia Mistica," in *ANRW,* 16.2., Plate seven, Fig. eleven.

Bibliographic Note

Articles on Roman domestic religion can be found in the following standard handbooks: Latte, K., *Roemische Religionsgeschicte,* Handbuch der Altertumswiss. V 4 (Munchen: 1960); *Oxford Classical Dictionary,* 2nd ed., 1970; Wissowa, G., *Religion und Kultus der Roemer,* Handbuch der Altertumswiss. IV 5

(Munchen: 1912); De Marchi, A., *Il Culto privato di Roema antica* (Milan: 1896). Although out of date this monograph constitutes the only real separate study of the house cult; Ogilvie, R.M., *The Romans and their Gods in the Age of Augustus* (London: 1969); a concise little essay on domestic worship is included in this splendid study; Orr, D., "Roman Domestic Religion: The Evidence of the Household Shrines," in *Aufstieg und Niedergang der Roemischen Welt,* Band II.16.1. (Berlin: 1978), pp. 1557-91.

There exists at this time no serious study linking the Roman household cult with modern practices in Italy.

Acknowledgments

This essay is based on research done in Italy in 1966, 1970, and during the course of a Rome Prize Fellowship in Classics at the American Academy in Rome. Many fellows and scholars at that institution stimulated the author in his work there. Parts of this essay formed portions of the author's dissertation at the University of Maryland. The help provided by Professor Wilhelmina Jashemski is immeasurable; her constant encouragement made the author's labors an easy task.

IX

Popular Literature in Early Christianity: The Apocryphal New Testament

Popular figures, whether they are political heroes, entertainment stars or religious leaders, spontaneously generate the creation of an anthology of sensational anecdotes and supernatural attributes. During the lives of these persons, such apocryphal stories have some hope for verification, but as time moves on, the reality becomes increasingly elusive. When the cult is limited or ephemeral, as in the cases of Harry Houdini, Adolf Hitler, Elvis Presley or Jim Jones, questions of verification are not urgent, but in the rare cases that cults become major historical movements, the apocryphal literature is the center of significant controversy.

As Stephen Benko points out in "Popular Literature in Early Christianity: The Apocryphal New Testament," the books that have been excluded from the official Christian canon may not tell us much of Jesus or of Christian theology, but they may tell us a great deal about their early Christian audience. The audience is not unfamiliar to us today; it bears surprising resemblance to that of tabloid newspapers, where the high and the mighty are reduced to human level by exposing their shortcomings of character, where spiritual gifts are applied to commonplace prophecy, and where large movements in history are obscured by sensational headlines. But like the tabloids, the Apocryphal New Testament books provide entertaining reading and easy patterns for escapist fantasizing. They serve real social and psychological functions.

Benko's article first places the apocrypha into their proper historical context of emergent Christianity and discusses the characteristics and the social functions of the apocryphal testaments. Following an entertaining summary of some of the better-known books, Benko considers the apocrypha both as historical sources and as a continuing tradition in popular Christianity.

Stephen Benko is professor of Ancient History at California State University, Fresno. A half-dozen books and more than a score of articles in English, German and Hungarian deal with a variety of topics in Roman and early Christian history, in theology and in

Mariology. His most recent book (as editor) is The Catacombs and the Colosseum, The Roman Empire as the Setting of Primitive Christianity.

Popular Literature in Early Christianity: The Apocryphal New Testament

Stephen Benko

The Emergence of Christianity

According to accepted traditions the first Christian church was established in Jerusalem, somewhere around the year 33. Soon after that, small congregations were formed in other cities of the Roman empire mostly within the Jewish communities of such centers as Antioch, Alexandria and Rome. But then, very rapidly and particularly through the missionary activities of Paul, people of non-Jewish background were admitted to the fold and Christianity began its progress toward the status of a major religion. The progress was slow. During the first century A.D. there is not one single reference to Christians in the writings of Roman authors and it was only in the early part of the second century that the movement was given some attention. Even then it was referred to as a "disease" which should be cured (Pliny in 111 A.D.), a "pernicious superstition" (Tacitus in 115 A.D.) and a "mischievous superstition" (Suetonius around 120). Yet according to Pliny (*Letters* 10.96) at that time already many villages and cities of Asia Minor were "infested" with Christianity, which means that within less than a hundred years the new religion was firmly established. The number of Christians was still very small and relative to the total population of the Roman empire it remained small for a long time. While exact figures are not available and even estimates are difficult to make, it is possible that the total number of Christians in the city of Rome around 250 was not more than 20,000, in a population which was hovering around the one million mark. The relation may have been the same in other areas of the Mediterranean and a real and rapid growth of Christianity came only with the conversion of Constantine in the fourth century.

But Christianity was an unusually vigorous movement which demonstrated itself in prolific literary activity. Barely twenty years after the foundation of the first congregation Paul began to write his famous letters (around 50 A.D.) and this was followed by written accounts of the life and the works of Jesus when the end of the era of eye-witnesses drew near and the need was felt to preserve in writing

175

everything that could be remembered about Jesus. The so-called "post-apostolic" age created new types of authors, the "apostolic fathers," mostly reflecting on problems of everyday life and morals, were highly respected and often considered authoritative. The end of the first and the first part of the second centuries were the era of the "apostolic fathers" after which a distinguished line of Christian theologians began who systematized the Christian faith and expressed it in scholarly terms.

In spite of this solid appearance, however, the Christian Church was never a united movement. There was factionalism already among the disciples of Jesus and after Pentecost the "Hebrews" and the "Hellenists" (i.e. Jews who were natives of Judea, and those from the Diaspora whose mother tongue was Greek) spoke in different dialects, so to speak, and gradually drifted apart from each other. Peter and Paul had a serious theological clash and the letters of Paul are full of hints that many rival points of view contended for the allegiance of the Christians. Then in the third letter of John (v. 9ff) we read about a certain Diotrephes who did not acknowledge the authority of John (the author of the letter) and put out of the church those who were loyal to John's faction.

Clement (end of the first century A.D.) was written because of serious internal difficulties in the congregation of Corinth and the same letter makes references to difficulties among the members of the church of Rome. No less serious was the situation at Antioch, as the letters of Ignatius (second century A.D.) testify, and as the Christian church grew in members, more and more people began to advocate diverse views concerning their religion. One of the earliest was the interpretation of the person of Jesus: was he god or was he man and what was the relationship between the divine and the human in him? A sect called "Ebionites" maintained that Jesus was a man and not a god and this view became very popular later in the main church too, especially through the activities of the presbyter Arius from whom the movement was called Arianism. Theodotus in Rome, who was exiled by bishop Victor, held similar views. Then there were others, who claimed that Jesus was god and when he suffered god himself suffered. Because of this thesis they were called "Patripassians" (*Pater*—father; *passio*-suffering), or "Sabellians" from one of their leaders, Sabellius. These differences of opinion multiplied with each succeeding generation and much of the energy of the church was wasted in the endless Christological debates and speculations. These were useless debates, too, considering the fact that the New Testament itself is not interested in the question of who Jesus was or what was his nature but only in the fact of what he did and accomplished. Thus these theological discussions themselves represented a radical departure from the original spirit of Christianity.

But man has an inquisitive nature and as time went on Christians, too, began to ask more and more questions, not necessarily concerning the nature of Jesus or the relationship among the persons of the trinity, but also about matters relating to the history of the earliest period of the Christian movement which in the second century already appeared as the heroic age of the faith. There in the nearly mythical past lived the great saints of Christians, the family of Jesus, the apostles and others, about whom little or nothing has been handed down by either oral or written tradition and this lack of information has been filled in by pious inventions which became very popular and grew in numbers. This type of Christian literature is known as the *Apocryphal New Testament.*

The Apocryphal New Testament

The word "apocryphal" means "hidden" (in popular English usage today it also means "spurious"). "Apocryphal books" are those writings which claim to be equal to Biblical books but have not been included in the canon. There are apocryphal books of the Old Testament as a part of the Jewish religious literature and New Testament Apocrypha created by Christian writers. All apocryphal books resemble canonical writings, their authors usually ascribed them to biblical personalities and in the case of New Testament Apocrypha the format and style follow closely the four literary genre of the New Testament: gospels, acts, letters and revelations. What were the immediate reasons for the creation of the New Testament Apocrypha? The motives of the authors were not bad; most of the books were written with pious intentions within the official church body and they were meant as a devotional reading for Christians. The authors probably never realized the potential damages that their creations posing as historical realities may have caused in the minds of the readers. Looking for motivations behind the New Testament Apocrypha, we may find several: First of all, there was the desire to supplement the canonical gospels. None of the four gospels, and not even all four taken together, present a complete biography of Jesus. There are very wide gaps in our knowledge of the history of Jesus, e.g., the time between his birth and the beginning of his ministry is completely neglected in the gospel narratives and so also is the story of the forty days that he reportedly spent on earth between his resurrection and ascension. It is easy to understand that the curiosity of the Christians turned toward these unknown facts and sooner or later it was bound to happen that someone would make an attempt to fill in the gaps. The result was, of course, fiction, which had nothing to do with historical facts, but once these writings were in circulation it was unavoidable that some primitive believers would accept them as true facts, as indeed many of these tales became integral parts of the doctrinal structure of the Medieval Church. A similar process may be observed concerning interesting personalities of the New Testament narrative. We know very little about people who played an important role in the life of Jesus and who are mentioned several times in connection with him, e.g. Mary his mother, or Joseph, Mary's husband, or Nicodemus, or Joseph of Arimathea, or Pontius Pilate, to mention just a few. Very limited to our knowledge also are the apostles, including Paul and the Twelve. The missionary activities of the apostles and their end is also in the dark, and therefore pious imagination turned again toward these problems and attempted to provide the information which is missing in the New Testament.

Another motivation was the desire to provide the general Christian public with entertaining reading material that was free of the decadent characteristics of the contemporary pagan literature. The Christian Church discouraged its members from participation in pagan forms of amusements such as theater and circus which was crude and often cruel and even the use of such public establishments as the baths, which were promiscuous. The reading of pagan entertainment literature was also frowned upon, with good reasons as just a brief glance at one second century Roman novel will show: the "Metamorphoses" (or "Golden Ass") of Apuleius begins with the detailed description of a sexual encounter between Lucius and the slave girl Fotis, and the adventures of Lucius end with his conversion to the goddess Isis. Naturally the church could not encourage its members to read such material, but as soon as restrictions were imposed the need arose for something better and the gates were opened wide for Christian entertaining literature which appeared soon and offered the Christian readers the adventures of apostles in far away, exotic lands, and many similar subjects.

In addition to these, in themselves harmless motivations, the writings of New Testament apocryphal books was also determined by theological considerations. The aim may have been to popularize certain objects of faith, or perhaps to give written expression to an already existing popular belief. This theological motivation can be observed on both the "orthodox" and the "sectarian" level: in the orthodox literature we may find a definite promotion of Mariology; in Gnostic writings we may find attempts to popularize certain theories concerning the nature of Christ, promotion of ideas concerning sexual life, and similar sectarian views. (Gnosticism was a movement which often competed with Christianity during the second century. Unlike "orthodox" Christianity which was based on the historical figure of Jesus, Gnosticism was speculative and philosophical.) Indeed nothing was suited better for the diffusion of theological viewpoints than the apocryphal literature which except for the strictly secret writings was meant to be read by the masses and which was called by a modern writer the Sunday afternoon reading material of early Christians.

The general characteristics of these writings depend on their basic motivations. Those which are essentially "orthodox" in nature are more or less the extensions of canonical texts, i.e. they start their story with a longer or shorter reference to a New Testament event and they build their narrative upon it. The content is purely imaginary, full of alleged miracles which often border on the absurd and the ridiculous. Those which are the products of Gnosticism are often written in a language which is no longer clear to us—if it ever was meant to be clear at all. They imitate the style of the Apocalypse, but they use Gnostic vocabulary and terminology, which because of our still insufficient knowledge of Gnosticism makes difficult reading. Some of these books were at times considered "inspired," i.e. part of the canon and others were highly regarded as useful reading but ultimately by the process of elimination which established the New Testament canon they were all excluded from the list of authoritative writings.

In the following pages we take a random sampling of characteristic apocryphal writings. First, an example of a story dealing with the infancy of Jesus, and then an "Acts of the Apostles."

The Infancy Gospel of Thomas

This story about the childhood of Jesus is attributed to the apostle Thomas but it was in all probability written around the middle of the second century. It was especially popular in Egypt. The book is actually a collection of miracle stories which are told with very little connecting material. These are the main stories:

When Jesus was five years old, he played at a creek and made little sparrows out of clay. It was a Sabbath day and a Jew who saw him accused him to his father. (Jews were not permitted to do any kind of physical work on the Sabbath.) Joseph came and questioned Jesus, but he clapped his hands and the birds flew away. The son of Annas the scribe, stood by, and with the branch of a willow-tree destroyed the little pool that Jesus had made. When Jesus saw this, he became angry and said: "O you evil, ungodly, stupid man, what did this pool and the water hurt you? Now you will wither up like a tree!" The boy immediately died, and Jesus went quietly home. The boy's parents came and complained to Joseph: "That's the kind of boy you have!" After that Jesus went through the village and a boy pushed him on the shoulder. Jesus became angry and said: "You will not go on your way." This boy died, too, and his parents were very bitter toward Joseph. Joseph called Jesus to him and questioned him why he would do things like that. Jesus struck with blindness all those who complained about him. When Joseph saw what happened he grabbed the ears of Jesus and pulled them sorely; Jesus was very bitter. A teacher named Zacchaeus saw what happened and heard Jesus talking to his father, so he asked Joseph to let him take Jesus into his school where he would teach him knowledge and manners. He started to teach him the letters of the alphabet, but Jesus said to him: "You don't even know the Alpha according to its nature, how then can you teach the Beta to others?" Then he continued to explain to the teacher the mystical meaning of the two lines of the Alpha and the middle Line, running across the two, which go into each other. When Zacchaeus heard this, he asked Joseph to take Jesus out of the school. And as the Jews were talking with Zacchaeus, Jesus laughed at them and healed all those who were struck by him before. After that nobody dared to provoke him.

A few days later Jesus was playing with children on a housetop and one of the children fell on the street and died. The other children ran away, and when the parents of the dead boy arrived, they accused Jesus of having pushed the boy down from the housetop. Jesus went to the dead boy and asked him: "Did I push you down?" Immediately the boy woke up and vindicated Jesus. Another time a young man was chopping with an axe and split his foot; Jesus healed him. When he was six years old, his mother sent him to get water, but he broke the pitcher. So he spread out the garment he wore and brought water in it. In the time of sowing he went to help his father. He sowed one grain of wheat, reaped and thrashed it and made a hundred measure of it, which he distributed among the poor. Another time his father (who was a carpenter) was in the process of making a bed for a rich person, but one piece of wood was too short. Jesus made the wood longer. Now Joseph decided to try it again with the teachers and sent Jesus to another school. Jesus asked the teacher: "Tell me the power of the Alpha, and I will tell you the power of the Beta!" The teacher struck Jesus on the head, but Jesus cursed him and the teacher fell to the ground. Joseph was very sorry and told Mary: "Let not this boy go out of the house because everybody dies who provokes him!" After a while a new teacher took him to school with much fear, but instead of learning Jesus taught everybody. His teacher acknowledged the wisdom of Jesus on account of which Jesus was pleased, and as an appreciation healed the other teacher. One day James, brother of Jesus, was bitten by a snake and was going to die, but Jesus breathed upon the bite so that James was healed and the snake perished. Then Jesus performed two more miracles, by raising two dead, first a little girl and then a young man who died at the building of a house. The book ends with the story of the twelve year old Jesus in the Temple, written on the basis of Luke 2.41-52.

This is indeed a strange picture of Jesus that emerges from these stories. He is an arrogant wonder-child who takes pleasure in killing people and likes to demonstrate his magical powers. While this book does not add anything to our knowledge of the historical Jesus, it does throw some light on a certain class of Christians (were they the majority?) who produced and enjoyed such crude stories. They were basically pagans who were mostly impressed by two things concerning Jesus, one was his power and the other his knowledge.

They imagined a Jesus whose power was above the laws of nature and whose knowledge superseded anything and included even the future. The humanity of Jesus, which is a basic point of Christian theology, is very much neglected in this book. The question arises whether this is so because at a certain intellectual level people delight in miracle stories, or, was this neglect perhaps in line with the general trend among Christians who around this time began to make serious efforts to come closer to pagan ways of thinking? Since one of the strongest attacks by pagans was directed against the Christian teaching of incarnation (God *cannot* become man—the pagans stated), Christians, perhaps unconsciously but deliberately began to de-emphasize human characteristics of Jesus and began to talk more about his divinity.

There are several such "infancy gospels," many of them later creations. Well known is also the second century writing called *"The Protoevangelium of James."* This one deals with the birth and life of Mary, the mother of Jesus, and goes into often indelicate details to prove Mary's perpetual virginity, i.e. the thesis that the hymen of Mary was and remained intact before, during and after the birth of Jesus. The so-called *"Transitus Mariae"* literature, of which several versions exist, describes the death, burial, resurrection and assumption into heaven of Mary. Accounts of the life of Jesus, similar to the canonical gospels are also known to have existed. There was a *"Gospel of the Ebionites,"* a *"The Gospel of Peter"* and others. Of these only fragments remain in the works of the church fathers.

The Acts of John

Among the many apocryphal acts of the apostles this is the oldest, having been composed some time after 150 in Asia Minor. Its author is unknown. The first seventeen chapters are lost, and our resume therefore starts with chapter 18:

John was advised in a vision to go to Ephesus and he gladly obeyed. As they approached the city, the praetor of the city, Lycomedes, met him and falling down on his knees before him asked him to come and heal his wife who was stricken with palsy. Lycomedes said that he had seen a vision in which God manifested himself and told him that John would come from Miletus to restore the health of his wife, Cleopatra. Having heard this, John and his brethren who were with him went at once to Lycomedes' house where the praetor broke down in tears seeing his beautiful wife in such plight (as the story goes on, it becomes apparent that Cleopatra was already dead). John admonished him that instead of wailing he should pray to God, but Lycomedes fell to the ground and died. John prayed to God to help him in this situation, because the citizens of Ephesus would make him responsible for the death of Lycomedes. Already the Ephesians had come to the house, hearing that the praetor was dead, and John continued praying fervently asking Christ to raise Cleopatra. He touched the face of Cleopatra and commanded her to rise. At once she responded by saying, "I arise, Master! Save your handmaid!" The Ephesians were greatly impressed, but John led Cleopatra into the other bedchamber, where the corpse of Lycomedes lay. Seeing her husband dead, she bit her tongue and ground her teeth and after John prayed, she said quietly that she had only one desire, to die upon the body of her husband. John told her to go to her husband and tell him to arise to glorify God. She did that and Lycomedes was raised. Both asked John to stay with them, and as the others who were with him also urged him, John decided to stay (Ch. 18-25).

Lycomedes had a friend who was a good painter. He went to him and asked him to come and paint a picture of John. The first day the painter made an outline of John, and the next day he painted him with colors. Lycomedes was happy and hung the painting in his own bedchamber. He questioned him about this and when he discovered the painting with the garlands, and the altar and the lamp set before it he first thought that it was an image of one of Lycomedes' pagan gods. But Lycomedes assured him that he had nothing to do with paganism, and revealed to him that the painting was his image. John, who thus far had never seen his own face, could not believe it, until he was given a mirror and could compare the painting with his own image. Then he realized the similarity but he also remarked at once that a true image of a man could not be painted with material colors which only reflect shape and age, things that can be seen with the eye. Jesus knows the shapes and appearances of our souls, and he paints us all for himself. The colors, with which a person's real image should be formed are faith in God, fellowship, knowledge, kindness and all the colors that lead to Christ. Without this a physical image is imperfect; it is only a dead likeness of the dead (Ch. 26-29).

Brother Verus, who was serving John, received the commission to gather together all aged women in Ephesus, in order that John might heal them. He found out that among all women over the age of sixty, only four were in good physical health and thus John decided that the women should come next day to the theater. Already early in the morning they began to come to the theater and the proconsul himself hastened to take his seat. But a certain praetor, Andronicus, doubted John's ability and proposed that if John could really do such things he should come to the theater naked, holding nothing in his hands and refraining to utter the magic name. When all the women were brought into the theater, John came and addressed the crowd telling them to leave their sinful ways and then he healed all the diseased (Ch. 30-37).(There is a gap in the story here. From the following it appears that Andronicus was converted.)

Two days later was the birthday of the idol temple. Everybody went there clad in white but John put on black clothing and when they saw him they contemplated killing him. But he stood up and told them that if Artemis is really a goddess they should pray to her that John might die, or else John would pray to his God that the Ephesians should die. Now those of the people who had seen John raising up the dead cried to him and said: "Kill us not; we know that you can do it!" John answered: "The time has come that either you will be converted or I should die!" He prayed to God and immediately the altar of Artemis broke into pieces, likewise the images of the gods and all things dedicated in the temple fell. Half the temple collapsed and the priest himself was killed by falling beams. Some of the people tried to escape but others confessed faith in the God of John. John thanked Jesus in prayer and called the attention of the people to the fact that the power of Artemis had failed. The people, to show their good will, pulled down the rest of the temple and besought John for his further help. He said that it was only for the sake of the Ephesians that he had put off his journey to Smyrna. He would therefore remain in Ephesus until they were confirmed in the faith, because he was not perfectly assured concerning them. He stayed in the house of Andronicus. One of the men who had been converted was a relative of the priest who had been killed and he brought the corpse and laid it secretly in front of the door. After the discourse, prayer and the laying on of hands John was shown in spirit what had happened and he instructed the young man, the relative of the priest, to go to the corpse and tell him nothing more than this: "John the servant of God says to you, arise." The young man went outside in the company of many people and said this. He came back with the priest alive and then the priest also believed in Jesus and followed John (Ch. 38-47).

The next day John was instructed in a dream to walk three miles outside the gate and he obeyed the vision. There was a certain man who took to himself the wife of another man. His father admonished him, but he kicked his father and killed him. John, having seen what happened, noticed that this was why the Lord sent him to this way. The young man realized what he had done and he took a sickle that he had in his girdle and ran into the house to kill the woman and her former husband and then himself. But John met him on the way and made him stop. He asked the young man whether he would agree to abstain from the woman in case John would raise his father? The man agreed, and they went to the place where the father lay. Many passers-by had already stopped there and the young man repented of what he had done but John prayed that the old man might be raised. It happened and the old man said: "With my death I was released from many terrible things in life and the insults of my son, why, then did you call me back?" John answered: "If you are raised for the same end, it were better for you to die, but raise yourself to better things." They both went together into the city and before they reached the gate the old man believed.

The young man castrated himself and went to his wife and accused her of being the cause of his sins. Then he went to John and told him in the presence of the brethren what he had done, but John admonished him that he should not have done away with the place of sin but rather the thought which becomes active through the members. After these things the Smyrnaeans sent to John and asked him to come now to them (Ch. 48-55).

One day John was sitting and a partridge came and played before him in the dust. A priest, who heard John speaking, came by and found it unworthy that a man of John's stature should be amused by a partridge playing in the dust. John answered that it would be better for the priest to watch this partridge and cease to practice evil and shameful things; this partridge was an image of the condition of his own soul. The priest repented and became a disciple (Ch. 56-57).

John announced that he would have to go now to Ephesus. He left much money for distribution to the poor and then left for the journey in the company of several people who followed him with their families. On the first day they arrived (the story is told in "we" form) at a desert inn where there was only one bed. They left this to John, while the others slept on the floor. The bed was full of bugs and John could not sleep. In the middle of the night he was very annoyed and he said, "I tell you, O bugs, behave yourselves and leave your home for this night, be quiet somewhere, and do not disturb the servants of God!" Everybody laughed but soon they all fell asleep. Next morning, while John was still sleeping the others woke up and saw that a great number of bedbugs were standing and waiting before the door. They told John what they had seen and he addressed the bugs again, permitting them to return to their homes. At once they all ran to the beds, climbed up on the leg and disappeared in the joints. John remarked that an animal heard the voice of a man and obeyed, but when we hear the voice of God, we disobey (Ch. 58-61).

During their stay in Ephesus a man, whose name will be later revealed as Callimachus, fell in love with Drusiana, the wife of Andronicus. Since her conversion Drusiana had no sexual relation with her husband and even when he shut her up in a tomb and told her that either she would live with him or die, she would rather choose death. With such steadfastness she convinced her husband to live as she did.

Callimachus was told these things, but he did not give up, and continued to annoy Drusiana with his messages. From this Drusiana became sick and died. Andronicus mourned the death of his wife but when John learned the cause of her death he mourned even more. In the assembly John addressed the brethren, teaching them to leave temporal things in favor of the eternal ones. While he was speaking Callimachus bribed the steward of Andronicus whose name was Fortunatus, to open Drusiana's tomb. They both went to the tomb and Callimacus prepared to cohabit with her. They stripped the grave clothes from the corpse but before they could take the rest of the garments off, a serpent appeared and killed Fortunatus with a single bite. Callimachus fell on the floor and the serpent sat upon him. Next day, i.e. the third of Drusiana's death, John, Andronicus and the brethren came to the tomb to celebrate the Eucharist. They could not find the keys, but the doors were opened of themselves and as they entered they saw a beautiful youth smiling who told John that he should raise up Drusiana; then the beautiful youth went up to heaven. They saw Fortunatus and Callimachus on the floor and did not understand the situation until Andronicus went in and discovered the corpse of his wife half stripped. Then John commanded the serpent to go away and raised Callimachus. For an hour Callimachus could not speak but then he told them what had happened and he even disclosed that as he stripped the body of the grave clothes a beautiful youth appeared and covered the body with his mantle. Callimachus confessed his sin and was converted. John prayed to Christ and afterwards, at the request of Andronicus, he raised Drusiana too. Drusiana dressed herself and asked John that Fortunatus be raised also. Callimachus objected, but John reminded him that we should not repay evil for evil and he urged Drusiana to raise Fortunatus. Without delay she went to the body and prayed to Christ and commanded Fortunatus to rise. He did, but unrepented he ran out of the tomb. All those who remained celebrated the Eucharist (Ch. 85 contains an Eucharistic prayer) and then went to the house of Andronicus. Here it was revealed to John that Fortunatus died of blood-poisoning. One of the young men ran and found him dead for three hours. John said: "Here you have your child, Devil!" (Ch. 62-86).

Some of the brethren were perplexed because Drusiana told them that Jesus had appeared to her in the likeness of John and in that of a young man. Since these men were not yet firmly rooted in the faith John told them some of his experiences with Jesus. One day John and James his brother were at sea and Jesus came and called them. James saw him as a young child, but he appeared to John as a handsome man. As they went to the shore, Jesus helped them to land the ship and then he seemed to John to have thick beard but a rather bald head and to James to be a young man whose beard had just come. Often he would appear to John as a small man, then again as a tall man reaching unto heaven. His eyes were never closed but always open. Sometimes he would take John to his breast and his breast felt soft, but other times as hard as stone. One day he took them up to the mountain and as he prayed at a distance from the disciples, John crawled behind him and observed that he was not dressed at all; his feet were whiter than snow and the ground was lighted beneath them and his head reached to heaven. John was afraid and cried out and as Jesus turned around he appeared as a man of small stature. He pulled the beard of John and for thirty days so great was the pain at the part where he had pulled that John asked him: "Lord you pulled my beard in joke and it hurts like that, how much would I have suffered if you would have given me a beating?" Another time in Gethsemane John feigned sleep and saw that another man like Jesus talked to Jesus and said that the disciples did not yet believe. Jesus answered him that this was because they were men. Sometimes when John would touch the body of Jesus it would appear to be a solid body, another time as an immaterial substance. His footprint was never shown on the earth. Before he was taken by the Jews he gathered all his disciples and made them form a ring. He stood in the middle and while they all participated in a solemn dance Jesus sang a hymn and after each line the disciples answered "Amen." After the dance Jesus left and the disciples fled each in his own direction. John saw him suffer but could not stand it and he fled to the Mount of Olives. Here Jesus appeared to him in a cave and said that to the multitude he appeared as being crucified but he would speak to John what he should learn. Then he showed John a cross of light, around it a great multitude and above it Jesus not having any shape, just a voice. This voice said that a cross is sometimes called a word, or mind, or Jesus, or Christ, or door, or way, or bread, but these names are only toward men. In truth it is the limitation of all things and the harmony of wisdom. This is the cross which separates and unites all things, but it is not the cross of wood which can be seen neither is it Christ who is on that cross visible and which John will also see when he will get back down there. The multitude around the cross is of the lower nature but human nature needs to be taken up to the upper nature of Christ. Many other things yet Jesus said to John but those things cannot be uttered. After having finished his speech to John Jesus was taken up but not one of the multitudes noticed it. John laughed at the crowd since Jesus told him what was the truth. At this point John finished his recollection of his experiences with Jesus and urged those who listened to him not to worship in physical ways but with the disposition of the soul. It is not a man but God himself whom John preaches. Those who will abide in him will receive their souls indestructible. John finished his sermon and went away for a walk (Ch. 87-105).

Next day being the Lord's day all the brethren were gathered together and John preached a sermon to them, urging them all to remain established in the unchangeable, immaterial God Jesus Christ. He prayed to him and then they all partook of the bread of the holy Eucharist. After that John asked Verus to take two men and some shovels and come with him. He sent most people away from him and went out of the gate of the city. When they arrived at the tomb of a certain Christian man, John asked the man to dig a grave. When the grave was deep enough, John took off his garments and laid them at the bottom of the grave and lifting up his hands he prayed. He praised God for his marvelous works; he thanked him that he kept him for himself, untouched by intercourse with a woman. Three times John wanted to marry, each time Jesus prevented him; at the third time he even blinded him for two years. In the third year he opened not only his physical but also his mental eyes and John saw clearly what Jesus ordained for him. He thanked for all mercies of Jesus and then asked that as he was now coming to Jesus he might have a safe journey. May the fire, darkness, the devil, the powers, the places of the right, the places of the left and all means of Satan be restrained and may angels follow so that he might receive safely his reward. After this prayer John laid himself at the bottom of the grave and having greeted those who were around the grave, he gave up his soul. They brought a linen cloth and covered him with it. Next day they went out again, but they did not find his body, because it had been translated into heaven (Ch. 106-115).

The author of this book must have possessed considerable literary talents: his style flows smoothly, the stories are interesting and entertaining and even the incident with the bedbugs is not without a certain charm. There is only one crudely erotic story in the whole book, that of Drusiana—it looks as if in the second century, as in the twentieth, the author had to put in at least one erotic scene to make the book "sell." Of course we do not have anything historically reliable concerning the apostle John but otherwise the book is a mine of information concerning conditions in the Roman world and the Christian church in the second century. The experience with the bedbugs must have been shared with many travelers; the daily worship of Lycomedes in his private chambers before a garlanded image; pagans coming in white garments to celebrate the foundation of their temple—all these and many others appear like flashes on a movie screen bringing back everyday scenes from the life of a city in the second century. We hear much about early Christian practices. The book preserved for us an Eucharistic prayer (after the raising of Drusiana); we learn that on the third day after a funeral the Eucharist was celebrated at the tomb, and most interestingly we read in chapter 94 that liturgical dance, common in pagan religions, was also practiced by early Christians. Here too Jesus is more divine than human: he is so light that he does not leave footprints and his head reaches into heaven. By and large the book is even today entertaining reading and its popularity among early Christians is easy to understand.

There were many similar "acts of the apostles" produced by later Christians. Famous were *"The Acts of Peter," "The Acts of Paul," "The Acts of Thomas"* (who went to India, according to this book and still today is honored by Christians of India as the founder of their church), and many others. Several of the "Acts" survived and the interested student can obtain English translations of them with little effort. (Consult E. Hennecke—W. Schneemelcher: *New Testament Apocrypha.* Philadelphia: Westminster Press, 1964; or M.R. James, *The Apocryphal New Testament,* Oxford: University Press, 1955).

The letter format of the New Testament, cherished by the early church particularly on account of the many epistles of Paul, was also imitated by apocrypha writers who produced a number of alleged correspondences which never took place. As an example we might remember the *"Correspondences Between Seneca and Paul,"* a third century fabrication, the obvious purpose of which is to bolster the regard for Paul and his "school" by the authority of the first century great Stoic philosopher Seneca. There are also spurious letters of apostles; a spurious correspondence between the king of Edessa, Abgar, and Jesus (Abgar invites Jesus to escape the Jews by coming to Edessa); and a report of Pilate to Tiberus about the case of Jesus.

Finally, the book of Revelation was also imitated by later Christians in such writings as the Christian *"Sibylline Oracles"* containing apocalyptic visions, and, among others the *'Apocalypse of Peter"* and the *"Apocalypse of Paul."*

The Apocrypha as Historical Sources

We have already referred to the fact that the New Testament Apocrypha are valuable sources for the historian where one can gain insight into customs and social conditions of the age in which these books were written. The many anecdotes, folktales, and legends that are related here open for us the minds of the people and here the Christian historian also hears about the religious climate of the age and in particular about the ideals, the hopes and fears of the early Christians. They are then fairly reliable mirrors of popular piety both among pagans and Christians, while the many prayers, hymns and devotional practices mentioned and quoted in these writing enrich our knowledge of the history of Christian liturgy. The historian of art must be familiar with the apocryphal literature, otherwise many elements in medieval and renaissance art and architecture will remain obscure. Artists and poets often took their motifs from the Apocrypha, and the reader of Dante or the student of medieval cathedrals and their statuary cannot afford to be unfamiliar with these books. For the theologian and the student of religions the Apocrypha are indispensable. Many articles of faith which are today official doctrines of one or more Christian denominations found their first expression in popular piety represented by some apocryphal writing. Modern Mariology and the respect paid to Mary by many Christians is based partly on apocryphal material, e.g. the doctrine of Mary's "perpetual virginity" or her "assumption" were first written down in apocryphal books. But in other respects, too, many elements of popular Christian piety come from the Apocrypha: a deep sense for the unusual and the absurd, responsiveness for miracles, preoccupation with and fear of damnation and hell are, at least in part, the rather negative results of the works of these early Christian authors who originally may not have wanted to do anything else but entertain.

The historian, however, must raise yet another question: Is there anything in the Apocrypha that in any way would supplement our knowledge of the historical Jesus and his teaching, or the apostles and their teachings? And if the answer should be in the affirmative, how much is this material and how can it be distinguished from the merely fanciful? In connection with such questions we must remember first of all that the four canonical gospels were not the only narratives concerning the words and teachings of Jesus. Luke 1.1 reminds us that "many have undertaken to compile a narrative" about Jesus and John 21.25 says that in addition to what is in the gospel according to John "there are also many other things which Jesus did; were every one of them to be written, I suppose that the world itself could not contain the books that would be written." Thus the possibility always must be left open that a new and basically authentic material one day may come to light. It is also possible that some of our presently known apocryphal gospels preserved some sayings which actually may go back to Jesus, or that some of the apocryphal acts may have based their stories upon a tradition, either written or oral, that actually go back to apostolic times. We may also give this benefit of doubt to the Apocrypha, but at the same time we also must apply rigorous criteria as to what may be considered doubtful and what must be rejected as without a doubt false. When a saying appears to be tendentious or simply a variant of a canonical saying modified to suit the purposes of the book, or when an alleged event or miracle is evidently contrary to the spirit of the canonical books (e.g. Jesus or the apostles kill someone, or teach something that is contrary to the theology of the New Testament), we must consider the apocryphal text false. It is surprising how little will remain when the Apocrypha are tested by this method. And even that which would remain does not give us a deeper insight into the mind of Jesus and contributes little or nothing to our understanding of the New Testament. In this respect the contribution of the Apocrypha is rather negative: They present an opportunity to compare with them the canonical books, and they demonstrate that Christian faith and life is sufficiently expressed in the New Testament, which does not have to be enlarged or revised. The Apocrypha were only a by-product of early Christian life. At the same time when these tales were written the Christian Church produced the writings of the apostolic fathers and the early theologians, and then by the end of the second century the long line of distinguished Christian scholars and philosophers began with the serene figure of Irenaeus of Lyons. It was in their writings and not in the Apocrypha that the Christian genius revealed itself at its best.

Modern Apocrypha

The writing of apocryphal books has never really stopped because there were always pious Christians whose faith demanded signs and miracles. During the Middle Ages when new gospels and acts were no longer produced, the apocryphal mentality was hard at work creating legends of the saints, such as St. Francis of Assisi who walked on the water and preached to the birds. The best known collection of such miracle stories is the "Golden Legends" (*Legenda Aurea)* which was edited by a Dominican monk, Jacob of Viareggio (1230-1298). Like his predecessors of earlier times, the good monk collected any pious story he heard and made no attempt to scrutinze it. Many of his stories came from oral folk tradition and his book became the most popular reading material of simple Christians. In modern times, with the revival of fundamentalist type Christianity, a new crop of apocryphal writings appeared, practically all of them worthless forgeries, which take advantage of the piety of uncritical evangelicals. "The Unknown Life of Christ," "The Report of Pontius Pilate," "The Lost Books of the Bible" are just a few titles, but the list is much longer. Each time a "newly discovered" "secret" book about Jesus or the early church appears, some "sensational" material that church authorities had "hidden" for centuries "to keep the truth from the masses," one must always be suspicious that a new apocryphal book has surfaced.

Bibliography

The standard work is:
Edgar Hennecke—Wilhelm Schneemelcher: *New Testament Apocrypha.* English Translation edited by R. McL. Wilson. Philadelphia: Westminster Press. Two volumes, 1963, 1965.

The following books are also useful for reading the texts in English, German or Spanish translation:
M.R. James, *The Apocryphal New Testament.* New York: Oxford, 1955.
The Ante-Nicene Fathers, vols. VIII and X.
Michaelis, W., *Die Apokryphen Schriften zum Neuen Testament.* Bremen, 1958. (German).
A. de Santos Otero, *Los Evangelios Apocrifos.* 1956 (Spanish).

The following translations are listed for bibliographical purposes only:
Cowper, R. Harris, *The Apocryphal Gospels and Other Related Documents Relating to the History of Christ.* 2nd ed. 1867.
Excluded books of the New Testament. New York. Harpers, 1927.
Hone, William, *The Apocryphal Books of the New Testament. 1st edition 1820, several editions since. (For criticism see M.R. James, op. cit. pp. XIVff.)*
The Lost Books of the Bible and The Forgotten Books of Eden. Cleveland: The World Publishing Co. 1926.
Pick, Bernhard, *The Apocryphal Acts of Paul, Peter, John, Andrew and Thomas.* Chicago: Open Court Publishing Co. 1909.
Pick, Bernhard, *The Extra-Canonical Life of Christ.* New York and London: Funk & Wagnalls Co. 1963.

For the "modern apocrypha" a useful introduction is:

Edgar J. Goodspeed, *Strange New Gospels.* Chicago, Ill.: The University of Chicago Press, 1931.

General Literature:
Altaner, B., *Patrology.* New York: Herder & Herder, 1960.
Cross, F.L. *The Early Christian Fathers.* London, 1960.
Enslin, Morton S., "Along Highways and Byways," *Harvard Theol. Review,* 44 (1951), 67-92.
Findlay,Adam Fyfe, *Byways in Early Christian Literature.* Edinburgh, 1923.
Hervieux, Jacques, *What are Apocryphal Gospels?* London: Burns and Oates, 1960.
Jeremias, J., *Unknown Sayings of Jesus.* New York: Macmillan, 1957.
Milburn, R.L.P., *Early Christian Interpretations of History.* New York: Harpers, 1954. (pp. 161-192 on the "Transitus" literature.)
Robson, James, "Stories of Jesus and Mary." *The Muslim World* 40 (1950), 236-243.
Quasten, J., *Patrology.* Vol. 1, Westminster, Md.: The Newman Press, 1950.

X

Some Methodological Reflections on the Study of Medieval Popular Religion

To most persons the religion of the European Middle Ages is represented by the Gregorian chant, the cathedral at Chartres and the works of St. Thomas Aquinas. As Pierre Boglioni points out in this survey, the popular religion of the Middle Ages is part of the totality which is religious history, but it has too long been by-passed by study of that which is official religion, clerical, episcopal and monastic. The immense range of popular religion, especially the aspect that Boglioni defines as "religious life of the people," is carefully identified and categorized here as an aid to understanding the methodologies that are appropriate for further study. This survey of popular religion of the Middle Ages is not only of value to medievalists; it is also suggestive for students of contemporary religion, cults and psychology. With Boglioni's article American readers are also given a hint of the work done in popular culture by European scholars. In the bibliography prepared by Boglioni, as in those in the other articles, students of twentieth-century popular culture will find a number of leads to discovering historical perspectives on the contemporary world.

Pierre Boglioni is Director of the Institute of Medieval Studies at the University of Montreal, which publishes works on religious miracles and demonology, and sources for the study of popular religion of the Middle Ages.

Some Methodological Reflections on the Study
of Medieval Popular Religion

Pierre Boglioni

Recent publications on medieval popular religion.

Over the past few years historians of the Middle Ages have been showing increasing interest and more specific interest in popular religion, also sometimes called religion of the people, religion of the masses, religion of the layman, or religion of the ordinary Christian. Thus, Professor Raoul Manselli of Rome has just published an excellent and pertinent monograph on the subject.[1] In the last volume of Fliche and Martin's monumental *Histoire de l'Eglise*, for the first time a substantial section (authored by Etienne Delaruelle) is devoted to "The religious life of the Christian people."[2] After his death, friends of this great scholar published a sizeable volume which brought together all his contributions on popular piety.[3] In 1974 the 99th National Congress of French Learned Societies chose "popular piety" as the main theme of its meetings, while in 1975 the Fanjeaux (Toulouse) annual meetings dealing with the religious history of Southern France chose to study "Popular religion in Languedoc during the XIIIth and the beginning of the XIVth centuries."[4] In Montreal, there is a *Center for the Study of Popular Religions (CERP: Centre d'études des religions populaires),* where I work, along with other colleagues of the Institut d'études médiévales, in the sector concerned with the Middle Ages.[5]

To these specific studies may be added an extensive list of other studies of a more general character centering on Christian life in the Middle Ages, in which an explicit effort is made to encompass in their object the world of popular religion itself, especially those studies in the history of religious sociology conducted along the lines of research opened up by Gabriel LeBras.[6]

In any case it is quite evident that the interest in popular religion is deeply rooted in several major aspects of recent cultural evolution and that it is not a phenomenon limited only to the Middle Ages. The interest in renewed developments or techniques in historiography fostered through the collaboration between history and the social sciences (especially sociology); the renewal in theology, in ecclesiology, and even in pastoral studies in which the notion of the "people of God" increasingly preoccupies professionals of the various Christian denominations; the pressure exercised by Marxist historiography, as much interested in the masses as in the elite; the progressive secularization of the history of Christianity, more and more studied in the context of the general history of religions and outside any apologetic perspectives: all major factors contributing to establish, securely and undoubtedly for a long time to come, the phenomenon of *popular Christianity* as a concept to be dealt with by the historian, the theologian, the sociologist, and by the historian of religion and of culture in general.[7]

I would like on the basis of the first results of the vast movement I have briefly evoked to formulate some critical reactions, define more clearly the methodological problems that are now coming to the fore in much sharper focus, and indicate in general terms, albeit briefly, some of the methodological lines of inquiry that seem important.

The complexity of popular religion.

If we analyze a little more closely the objectives I have mentioned, one thing stands out: the almost endless variety of themes brought up by authors when they start speaking of popular religion. According to their interests and competence, they may include superstitions, major devotions to the Virgin, to saints and to relics, attendance at Sunday Mass or services, reception of the sacraments, religious theatre, brotherhoods and church-sponsored social groups, layman's manuals of devotions, the piety of Joan of Arc or Francis of Assisi, aberrations in religious feeling, mass heretical movements and the success of great jubilees or major indulgences.

It seems quite evident, in the face of such complexity, that the notion of *popular religion* is not a clearcut and distinct concept treated as a well-defined scientific discipline completely distinct from all others. Speaking in terms of formal logic, I would readily say that what we have here is an analogical concept, not a univocal one. The term itself may be kept because of its evocative power, but it should be clear, when it is used, that like other recent concepts of historiography—"the history of mentalities," "the history of sensitivities," "global history,"—it does not refer so much to a specific discipline as to a content of criss-crossing disciplines, not so much to a definite sector as to a whole of converging sectors.

Furthermore, as a result of earlier as well as of recent research, some sectors are now emerging in much sharper focus and it is possible to point out the disciplines feeding them or those nearest to them. I shall identify and characterize some of them, not so much to oppose them one to another as to bring out their particular emphasis and their specific contribution to the study of popular religion as a whole.

A first sector—one in fact that was identified and looked into a long time ago—is made up of the practices and beliefs formerly called superstitions, a word indicating the dominant religious authorities' negative reaction toward them, now simply included in the expression *religious folklore.*

Where medieval Christianity is concerned, this sector is made up of three main branches. First, we may consider true pagan survivals, still in operation during the early Middle Ages, and even as late as the XIth and XIIth centuries in some countries.[8] Next, we include pagan folklore, understanding here the substantial but scattered remnants of para-religious beliefs or practices living on outside the framework of any system whatsoever and referring either to some kind of animistic or cosmic religiosity, or to the religious framework of archaic social forms such as the patriarchal family or the autonomous and isolated village. I am thinking here especially of the various forms of magic, of pre-Christian or non-Christian charms, of beliefs linked with the astral bodies, of practices linked with illness and death, of customs relating to fertility and the agrarian cycle.[9] Finally, that of Christian folklore, including those elements of Christian origin which the people developed in an original way by themselves without any active influence on the part of the clergy. We may think here of the therapeutic or magical practices using sacramental materials (baptismal water, the consecrated host, the chrism of confirmation, holy water), of the spontaneous and unregulated forms of the cult of those numerous local healing saints, as well as of the local and peripheral forms of the sacramentals. We must also include in this category the widespread phenomenon of sorcery which must evidently be treated with the help of an appropriate methodology.[10] Naturally, in the study of these various branches, the most relevant disciplines are ethnology, anthropology and the comparative history of religions.

In the sector which could be called *parish life,* interests and disciplines are quite different. The common people are again those involved, but, in this instance, the goal is to find out what impact the obligations and values of the official church had on the masses and to verify this in the context that provides the clearest picture and framework of them, the parish.

The problems in this sector are extremely varied. The parish may first be studied in its socio-economic structure, especially as regards the aspects that are most closely related to a specifically religious dimension: for instance, the criteria and duties attendant on belonging to the Church, the Church council and wardens, the places and objects of the cult (their care and use), tithes and the reactions to them, religious brotherhoods and other social forms having a religious connection, excommunication and its practical effects.[11]

One branch in this sector which has been recently more and more studied is that of religious practice: here it is a question of verifying with the help of the most exact statistical and quantitative methods possible, at least the external adhesion of the people to Christian beliefs and practices, the number of those going to Mass on Sundays, of those going to communion and confession, of those who follow the liturgical calendar, who accept the church's norms concerning the main *rites de passage* (those surrounding baptism, confirmation, marriage and death). It must be said that research, mainly of the sociological kind, on this kind of problem is possible only for the later Middle Ages when church registers and archives become more numerous.[12]

Alongside the study of religious practice, there are also attempts to study the lower clergy: its training, culture, morality, mentality, pastoral methods and especially its preaching. The lower clergy, in fact, represent an essential link in the chain of transmission of official religion to the masses.[13]

Another important branch in this sector, the study of which is just starting to emerge, seems to be that of popular morality. In the final analysis, we know very little concerning the morality of the ordinary Christian, his scale of values, his attitudes concerning sexuality, personal property, aggressiveness or alcohol. Yet we have here a dimension which the historian of popular religion must, with the help of the sociologist, situate explicitly in the framework of his preoccupations.

As regards the history of this second sector, we are now much closer to a traditional history of Christianity. The historian will here be borrowing the sociologist's terms of analysis, his work hypotheses, and his methods of research, but he will need in addition a deep knowledge of theology, of canon law, and of local church legislation, because the history of parish life remains an absolutely unintelligible chapter if it is conceived outside the general history of the Church.

There is finally a third broad sector which should be considered as methodologically distinct from the others, and to which the name of *popular piety* could be given. As in the case of parish life, we are here again in a context where we must verify what impact official

Christian values had upon the masses, but in a framework, however, where the Church was not the source of the items in question, and where also she did not normally impose them as obligatory. The Church, here, in varying degrees according to time and place, was satisfied to control, orient and eventually to take them over, imposing certain adaptations. Popular piety, therefore, is a sector halfway between religious manifestations of a fundamentally popular origin and those other popular religious realities derived from a culture imposed by the Church. In this sector the creativity of the people was able to manifest itself in a relatively free climate and to produce massive phenomena of great richness.

This immense sector includes the history of the miraculous and the marvelous,the main cults of the Virgin, the angels, the saints and their relics, pilgrimages, indulgences, the various devotions to the humanity of Christ, private devotions, the small paraphernalia used in private or family devotions, such as scapulars, medals, pious images, etc. The researcher here must often follow leads that the traditional historians have more or less neglected, such as manuals of prayer and devotion, pious literature composed for the layman, statues of religious groups and brotherhoods, popular religious literature, popular translations of the Bible and of the apocryphal writings, innumerable forms of hagiographic documents. This sector becomes more diversified and more interesting as we near the end of the Middle Ages with the appearance of urbanization, of the Mendicant Orders, and of a certain lay culture and religious independence. It would seem that in this sector the historian's most useful discipline, along with sociology, is religious psychology.[14]

These three major sectors, without exhausting all relevant materials, have nevertheless been mainly examined by researchers on the religion of medieval people. Can they all be equally included under the heading of popular religion? We must recognize that there are shades of meaning and emphasis between the expressions *popular religion, popular religiosity* and *religious life of the people.*

"Popular religion" brings to mind first and foremost all those phenomena created and kept alive by the people independently of or notwithstanding explicit rules set up by the official church: this expression will be the one preferred by theologians and historians of religious folklore and of religions. "Popular religiosity" brings to mind on the other hand the inner make-up of the religion of the masses, those affective, imaginative and mental structures found underlying, in a more or less homogeneous state, all popular religious realities, whether or not they be of Christian origin: this will be the expression preferred by analysts of the history of religious psychology. "Religious life of the people" is undoubtedly the most comprehensive expression. It includes, on the same grounds and without distinction, all the sectors we have mentioned: outward manifestations as well as inner feelings, the practices and beliefs which the people have learned from their clergy as well as those which the people have developed spontaneously.

It seems clear that the last expression and global approach should be the ones preferred by the historian of Christianity and by the historian in general. If, indeed, the perspective is not one of a discipline, but one of the total history of a society,then it has to be conceded that all the aspects above-mentioned have effectively been a part of the religious life of the people. If we try to understand popular medieval religion from the viewpoint of the person practicing that religion—the peasant, the poor village woman, the merchant, the sailor—it is easy to see that all these elements were part of what that person considered to be religion: the sermons dished out to him by his pastor as well as the stories he was told by the pilgrim returning from Santiago, the sacraments he received as well as the talismans he wore, the prayers he learned in Church as well as the ancestral magic spells, the procession on the Feast of the Eucharist as well as the little pilgrimage he made to the local spring traditionally recognized for its rain-making power.

In the face of this complex world, the historian may provisionally isolate this or that element, to be treated with the help of various disciplines, to discover its origins, how firmly entrenched it was, its functions; but he will finally have to come back to the whole complex to examine all the various elements in their mutual relationships and to consider the final results they have produced.

Popular and non-popular religion.

This question may be asked: When we want to oppose popular religion to another type of religion, what does it oppose? The most simple answer and the classical one is to say that it is opposed to the official religion. As a sociologist recently wrote: "The concept of popular religion takes on a meaning in those societies where there are religious authorities functioning to ensure a strict regulation of orthodox tenets and practices: popular religion is then a religiosity—at the level of representations, affectivities and customs—lived out as something different from the official religion."[15]

The notion of differentiation is doubtless essential when searching for a definition of popular religion, but that of "official religion" seems to refer to a level of opposition which is much too vague and generic. Looking more closely into the matter, we see that the "official religion" presents itself under at least three rather different facets or poles, one of which may be described as judirico-pastoral, another as theologico-scientific, and the third as mystico-spiritual.

It can happen that the Church may propose or tolerate in her current legislation and pastoral criteria, religious practices which the theology of the times considers unacceptable, obsolete, too "popular" in character. Such was the case for the rite of ordeal, accepted in canon law, pastoral theology, and even in liturgy up to 1215, whereas as early as the IXth century a theologian, Agobard of Lyon, considered it unacceptable in the context of enlightened Christianity. Conversely, the popular devotion to the Immaculate Conception of the Virgin was included in liturgy and pastoral theology a long time before it was accepted by theologians. Similarly, mystical and spiritual religion may judge questionable religious expressions considered normal by both the theologians and the juridico-pastoral people. A typical example is the distrust shown by the *Imitation of Christ* toward pilgrimages.[16] In other words, just as we can say that popular religion is not a homogeneous whole, in the same way, the type of religion opposed to it cannot be thought of as being a monolithic, stable and unvarying block.

At this stage we could, had we the space, try to show how opposition between the popular and the non-popular plays itself out in the real world where the three poles we have spoken about actually exist, a problem well known to all theoreticians of folklore, which can be stated: Where is the popular to be found and how is it characterized? I shall indicate only briefly, without discussing them, the characteristics which seem most important in the case of medieval religion which concerns us here.

The popular is first of all that which is lay or secular as opposed to that which is clerical, episcopal or monastic. It is also the archaic as opposed to the new forms introduced by Christianity. It is that which is local, peripheral and particular as opposed to the centralized and the uniform. It is oral culture and group values as opposed to written culture and individual values. It is that which is affective, pragmatic, unconceptualized opposed to that which is intellectual, dogmatic, conceptualized. It is the charismatic and unforeseen as opposed to the institutionalized and the stable. It is often also the rural as opposed to the urban, the poor as opposed to the rich (although this is not that important in characterizing popular medieval religion), it is the ignorant person as opposed to the learned one.

Let me add, however, the following methodological remark which I believe to be of fundamental importance. All those opposed categories are valid insofar as they serve as epistemological instruments of analysis in identifying the popular, but they must not lead the historian of medieval religion to isolate the popular, to consider it as a separate block that can be studied by itself. Such an attitude would be irremediably wrong and would radically distort research. In fact, medieval popular religion is not a reality which is marginal, static or withdrawn unto itself. It is, on the contrary, in constant dialogue with official or learned religion, with which it shares a perpetual association, upon which it applies constant and enormous pressure, and which it has finally influenced as much as it has been influenced by it. It is not necessary to point out that, at the end of the Middle Ages, the over-emphasis of the popular components in medieval Christianity was one of the essential problems at stake between Catholics and Protestants.

In a perspective of this kind, the history of popular religion in the Middle Ages cannot be considered as "minute" history, as a minor sector barely useful enough to fill in the spare time of those scholars in quest of farfetched research subjects. It is on the contrary an essential part of the history of Christianity and of the history of Europe which current historiographers will no longer have a right to ignore.

Notes

[1]Raoul Manselli, *La religion populaire au moyen âge. Problèmes de méthode et d'histoire* (Montreal-Paris: 1975), p. 234. I am limiting myself here to the more recent publications and am perhaps showing some partiality in favor of French, French-Canadian, and Italian literature because of my background and training.

[2]In E. Delaruelle, E.R. Labande, P. Ourliac, *L'Eglise au temps du Grand Schisme et de la crise conciliaire (1378-1449)*, II (Paris: 1964), pp. 601-879 (Fliche-Martin, *Histoire de l'Eglise depuis les originies jusqu'à nos jours, vol. 14/2)*.

[3]Etienne Delaruelle, *La piété populaire au moyen âge*. Avant-propos de P. Wolff, Introd. de R. Manselli et A. Vauchez (Torino: 1975), pp. XXVIII-563.

[4]The Proceedings have just been published: *La religion populaire en Languedoc du XIIIe à la moitié du XIVe siècle* (Toulouse: 1976), p. 472.— "Popular Belief and Practice" was also the theme of the ninth Summer meeting (held at Fitzwilliam College, Cambridge) and the tenth Winter meeting of the Ecclesiastical History Society (England), the Proceedings of which have been published: G.J. Cuming, D. Baker, ed., *Popular Belief and Practice* (Cambridge University Press: 1972), XII-321 pp. (*Studies in Church History,* 8).

[5]Address: 2715 Cote Ste-Catherine, Montreal, Canada, H3T 186. Among its activities may be mentioned the annual Colloquia held since 1970, the Proceedings of which have been regularly published.

[6]Among G. Le Bras' extensive production, see especially his latest work: *L'église et le village* (Paris: 1976) 289 pp., and two other of his works considered classics: *Introduction a l'histoire de la pratique religieuse en France,* 2 vols. (Paris: 1942-1945) and *Etudes de sociologie religieuse,* 2 vols. (Paris: 1955-1956).

[7]It is impossible to indicate here, even summarily, the convergence of opinions on the subject. See the special number of *Social Compass,* XIX/4 (1972) on *Popular Religiosity;* the special number of *La Maison-Dieu,* 122 (1975) on *Religion populaire et réforme liturgique,* which updates the question where France is concerned; popular religion will be dealt with in one of the next issues of *Archives de sciences sociales des religions.*

[8]Unfortunately there is nothing in recent bibliography which compares with the systematic,

albeit somewhat outdated work of Paul Sebillot, *Le paganisme contemporain chez les peuples celto-latins* (Paris: 1908), XXVI-378 pp.

[9]Reflections on method are found in Jacques Le Goff, "Culture cléricale et traditions folkloriques dans la civilisation mérovingienne," in *Annales. E.S.C.*, 22 (1967), pp. 780-791 and "Folklore et culture ecclésiastique: saint Marcel de Paris et le dragon," in *Studi C. Barbagallo*, II (Naples: 1970), pp. 53-90. For the period immediately following the Middle Ages, the work of Keith Thomas has already become a classic: *Religion and the Decline of Magic. Studies in Popular Beliefs in Sixteenth- and Seventeenth-Century England* (London: 1971), 853 pp. In the latter are found abundant materials even for the Middle Ages.

[10]Among recent studies, some of which often greatly transform the state of the whole question, see Richard Kieckhefer, *European Witch Trials: Their Foundations in Popular and Learned Culture, 1300-1500* (London: 1976), X-181 pp.; Norman Cohn, *Europe's Inner Demons. An Enquiry Inspired by the Great Witch-Hunt* (Sussex Univ. Press: 1975), XVI-302 pp.; Jeffrey Burton Russel, *Witchcraft in the Middle Ages* (Ithaca and London: 1972), XII-394 pp.; should also be mentioned the works of Alan Macfarlane, Carlo Ginzburg, H.C. Erik Midelfort, William E. Monter and others.

[11]See for example Paul Adam, *La vie paroissiale en France au XIVe siècle* (Paris: 1964), 328 pp., and G. Le Bras' study referred to in note 6; there is much information on life in a medieval parish, but in a very anthropological perspective in Emmanuel Le Roy Ladurie, *Montaillou, village occitan* (Paris: 19750), 642 pp.

[12]In this perspective see the monumental work of Jacques Toussaert, *Le sentiment religieux en Flandre à la fin du moyen âge* (Paris: 1963), 886 pp.

[13]See for example Peter Heath, *The English Parish Clergy on the Eve of the Reformation* (London-Toronto: 1969), XIII-249 pp.

[14]See note 3 and among the recent studies which I personally consider to be models, that of Jonathan Sumption, *Pilgrimage. An Image of Mediaeval Religion* (London: 1975), 391 pp.

[15]J. Maître, art. "La religion popularire," in *Encyclopaedia Universalis,* vol. 14 (Paris: 1972), p. 35.

[16]Imit., I, 23.4. This criticism meets with those of Chaucer, Langland, Nicolas de Clamanges, and others.

XI

Synchronic vs Diachronic Popular Culture Studies
And the Old English Elegy

One aim of this collection has been to inform the study of recent and current popular culture with the insights and perspectives of scholarship from students of earlier culture. Tim D.P. Lally in his essay takes a skeptical view of much contemporary theory and methodology and proposes several concepts that may help to resolve some confusion. Although Lally accepts, along with many of today's writers, the narrowed definition of popular culture as leisure activities and their associated artifacts, he rejects as false and unproductive the usual division of leisure culture into folk, popular, mass and elite. This division not only leads to the questionable categorization of individual artifacts and activities, but implies that individual persons cannot or do not participate in more than one kind of leisure culture. Moreover, it restricts "popularity" to a synchronic phenomenon, that is, to a given time and place. This, Lally argues, denies the diachronic history of an artifact, and produces such hairsplitting absurdities as forbidding the consideration of Homeric epics as popular culture because they are not best-sellers synchronically, or the immensely popular King Tut treasures museum-exhibition because it is in art museums and represents royal culture.

Furthermore, synchronic popularity should not necessarily be interpreted as reflecting the values of its audience; the audience is always in part the creation of the artist. This fictive audience may subscribe to an art form for leisure without subscribing to its content in total. In addition, when viewed diachronically, certain "unpopular" cultural items may be waiting for popularizing mediation as the Greek Homer waited for Chapman, or as the Latin Bible waited for Luther. Lally's speculative case in point is the Old English elegy, where J.R.R. Tolkien's medievalism has tilled the ground, and where new translations of elegies may seed a new popularity.

This is a lively essay, filled with challenge and controversy, and is particularly applicable to the subsequent essays on literary topics

202   5000 Years Of Popular Culture

by Jankofsky and Hayes. Ultimately it addresses major concerns of all interpreters of the human cultural heritage of how to fashion new bottles for fine old wines.

Tim D.P. Lally is a member of the English Department at Bowling Green State University who has written several articles on aspects of medieval literature and on the teaching of literature and writing in today's university.

Synchronic vs Diachronic Popular Culture Studies
And the Old English Elegy

Tim D.P. Lally

The exact state of theory in popular culture studies is difficult to discern. Although some attempts to define popular culture tend to leave the question open, it is probably fair to assert that the most commonly used theory defines popular culture as the leisure activities which the working or middle classes of industrial society enjoy.[1] Popular culture is what you do when you are not working or politicking or going to religious meetings, and it is particularly those things you do which a large number of people like yourself also enjoy. The difficulties which surround any popular culture theory are legion, not the least of which is continuity: what is popular today is very often passe tomorrow. Popular culture viewed over a decade or even fewer years offers a bewildering variety of phenomena for study and reflection; surely this plethora of evidence is one cause for the high incidence of what I would term *synchronic* popular culture studies. I use this term advisedly, in that the problem is as much with cultural contexts as it is with a given time-frame. For instance, MacDonald's "'The Foreigner' in Juvenile Series Fiction, 1900-1945" covers several decades of popular fiction which the author claims projects "the picture of a detached and self-assured America."[2] The study makes no attempt to put this literature into a cultural context—to correlate this fiction with other kinds of fiction or entertainment that the same audiences might also have enjoyed, or to assess or speculate about how this more or less static picture of America could appeal to audiences whose other experience included two world wars and a depression. MacDonald's essay is similar to obscure antiquarian studies about out-of-the-way places now largely forgotten—work of interest to the narrow specialist (which of course has genuine though limited value) but not to the historian whose interest is to discover and interpret significant evidence and ideas. In a case like R. Serge Denisoff's "Death Songs and Teenage Roles," an interesting idea is mentioned but never closely examined: "Coffin songs...may have...lessened the dysfunctional psychological costs of passage for the adolescent."[3] This notion offers a perspective on the songs which claims for them an importance beyond mere synchronic popularity; Denisoff's study does not quite achieve the status of a *diachronic* popular culture study which it might if this larger cultural context were examined and coffin songs of great popularity related to other sorts of experience which were enabling in the same way for adolescents.

Lest my attitude seen unduly harsh, let me acknowledge that we owe much to antiquarians and that they should be encouraged in their work—they have and will preserve evidence which others once thought worthless but now find valuable. We owe the existence of many medieval English manuscripts to antiquarians who saved them during the dissolution of the monasteries in the sixteenth century. (About some poems in one Anglo-Saxon manuscript, more later.) The contemporary popular culture scholarly endeavor will be instrumental in preserving and cataloging the records and artifacts of commonplace leisure activities of industrial society. But the developement of a theory or theories about this mass of evidence and about popular culture in general is necessary; otherwise we will have a storehouse without a proper set of keys.

Theorists have taken some pains to distinguish popular culture from other forms of culture—elite, mass and folk cultures usually round out the paradigm.[4] These distinctions are not very convincing, at least to me, because they do not take into account the fact that one person may participate in all sorts of cultural activity. Indeed, it could be argued reasonably (though this is not the place to do so) that the complete citizen of a given society would be able to enjoy all forms of culture (perhaps this is what a liberal education really provides). In this regard we need popular culture studies of a demographic nature which demonstrate the range of cultural activity of all or some part of the United States. It is possible—though perhaps not politically practicable—that a few questions on the census forms would provide at least a rough estimate of our total national cultural profile. My assumption is that people get as much of and as various a cultural experience as possible; the limitations are not so much personal as institutional or questions of access. For instance, there are the recent popular exhibits at museums: grave goods from the People's Republic of China and from Egypt, and a new and popular exhibit about Pompeii in Boston. Under the leadership of Thomas Hoving, New York's sleepy Metropolitan Museum has become the city's number one tourist attraction. This is not to say that many, indeed most of those who enjoy the museums do not also watch their fair share of TV, follow professional sports, listen to the Top Fifty songs, and read sensational novels with zeal.

Perhaps part of our difficulty in using the paradigm of

elite/popular/mass/folk culture is that we have to tinker with it every time we use it—we define and redefine these four pigeon-holes so that we can sort things out to suit ourselves. It is not embarrassing to say that our paradigm of culture looks like a Rube Goldberg cartoon if we recall that Thomas S. Kuhn, in his seminal works *The Copernical Revolution* and *The Structure of Scientific Revolutions,* reminds us that the paradigm provided by a Ptolemaic idea of the universe was an embarrassment to scientists long before the Copernican paradigm gained its popularity.[5] Although I cannot claim Copernican insight (nor is popular cuture theory so grand a conception), I do suggest that we consider a new paradigm by which we first view all culture as one expression of a given society's leisure needs and opportunities, and then distinguish degrees of popularity along two axes: synchronic and diachronic. The optimal study generated by this paradigm would attempt to be precise about popularity and to see the phenomenon under consideration in *both* a synchronic and a diachronic context.

For instance one calculation which such a paradigm could provide would contrast two cultural phenomena which can be proven highly popular in quite different ways: a highly synchronic popular phenomenon such as the film *Star Wars* or the novel *Uncle Tom's Cabin,* and a highly diachronic popular phenomenon such as Homer's *Odyssey* or the Bible. It is quite possible that more people attended movie houses to view *Star Wars* for a certain period of time than read the *Odyssey* in that same span. Yet I think it is reasonable to assume that the total readership of Homer's poem since it was written down (it would probably be exponentially larger if we include all its audiences for oral delivery) will equal or even exceed the audience of the movie. Not only that, but these two phenomena have different futures: I assume that *Star Wars* will drop out and claim *per se* only antiquarian interest as a strictly synchronic cultural phenomenon, while the *Odyssey* will continue to draw a steady if unspectacular audience. This example suggests others, for instance, a play of Shakespeare compared to the once-popular TV show *Gunsmoke.*

Another aspect of popular culture studies in which we could improve is the question of audience. It is profitless to read an analysis of popular culture in which the scholar attempts to discover the character of the audience which does in fact enjoy that certain form of leisure. For a hypothetical example or two, you do not have to be a racist to laugh at a racist like Archie Bunker, any more than you have to be demonic to be fascinated with Milton's Satan in *Paradise Lost.* It is true in both cases that your taste—your preference for certain kinds of culture—must include some provision for representations of evil in various settings (Queens Borough and Hell respectively). Although you do not have to be evil yourself, you have to recognize evil and accept representations of it in your leisure activities.

But in any case it is impossible to prove that the writers who created Archie Bunker or the John Milton who created a memorable Satan sized up a specific real audience. In a recent seminal article, Walter Ong's "The Writer's Audience Is Always a Fiction," literary study has been freed from a useless notion about audience and provided with a potentially powerful one.[6] To simplify Ong's idea, in addition to other aspects of the work of art, the author creates a possible audience for his work which is implicit in it. As readers, it then follows, part of our act of attention is to identify this audience, or as much of it as we can, although we do not necessarily have to identify *with* it. In so far as we can accommodate our taste—our own culture—to this fictive audience, we can enjoy the work of art. Such identification and accommodation does not necessarily imply approval of the values implicit in the work of art. For instance, it is entirely possible that someone may have sat through all nine hours of the recent TV marathon narrative *Holocaust* and still maintained anti-Semitic values, although it was plain (at least to this observer) that the fictive audience was supposed to be pro-Semitic. Be that as it may, the notion that literary works, and by extension all works of art, large and small, contain an implicit fictive audience as an integral part of their structure, possesses great potential for cultural studies, including popular ones.

On the basis of a fictive audience we may sketch out a few differences between a synchronic and a diachronic popular culture phenomenon. For instance, a synchronic phenomenon will have a fictive audience with topical or contemporary features—an interest in World War II, or the Trojan War. A diachronic phenomenon will have a fictive audience that includes both a topical and an aesthetic feature which expands the topical feature to typical or mythic proportions. (Here I postulate Brecht's notion that the mythic is the typical.) In other words, the diachronic cultural phenomenon contains a fictive audience which, while focused on a topic, perceives this topic in some larger context or contexts— philosophical, moral, social, intellectual, political, religious and so forth. It is possible to speculate that there may be some direct connection between the complexity of the contextual relations of a diachronic phenomenon and its popularity—why Homer is more popular than Pindar, why Dickens more than Henry James, why T.S. Eliot more than Ezra Pound, could so be explained. These works of durable popularity might be described by the Latin word *altus*, which means both high and deep. If in the case of a synchronic phenomenon the contextual relations are weak, then the attraction of the fictive audience will be directly related to the currency and novelty of its topic. If, as in the case of *Gunsmoke,* the contextual relation was with a simple law-and-order morality, the topic of cowboy life will soon be stale, and another will be sought to replace it. The cowboy will be replaced by the policeman, although the contextual relation may still be to a simple law-and-order morality. In this case, the diachronic study of TV shows will reveal an interesting similarity between the synchronic cowboy and cop shows—a shared feature in both fictive audiences, a link between two decades of TV programming. And of course, from this point, some popular culture studies would begin to make inferences about the morality of the TV audience, as if the fictive and the real audiences were identical, which would be a serious error. Only an aesthete like John Ruskin would hazard the notion that if you tell me what you like I will tell you who you are; it is an interesting weapon in polemics, one of Ruskin's special skills to be certain, but it is not useful in careful scholarly studies. Some connections can be made, of course, between a fictive and a real audience, but these connections are difficult to identify and require vast interdisciplinary skill which we have yet to develop.

In the case of the largely synchronic phenomena which appear on TV, we need to be very aware of the features of even the least distinguished program's fictive audience because they tell us a good deal about the mediators. Analysis of fictive audiences can reveal with some precision the attitudes of the mediators. There is already some provocative theoretical thinking on the role of the mediators in mass media—those in charge of writing and producing the TV, radio and film programs, although much the same could probably be perceived about the editors and writers of the newspapers and magazines.[7] One must recognize that, in the case of print media, the real audience is always much more independent than with film, radio and TV. There is a vastly larger selection of reading material than there is of visual stuff; the reader is much more in charge of his cultural schedule than the viewer, or will be so until the cost of video production and portable video recorders lowers considerably.

Even so, given the pressures which are applied to TV programming, and taking into account Ong's insight about the fictive audience, a rather interesting picture of the TV audience begins to come into focus. This image contrasts with the cliche of the TV viewer as a mindless automaton, since it suggests a sophisticated awareness for many viewers. Since the preoccupations of the mediators will be reflected in the fictive audiences they create for their shows, and since the mediators will be preoccupied to some degree with meeting the demands of the powerful corporations which support the entertainment industry through advertisements, the TV audience is able to identify the values of the powerful members of their society (the ruling class, if you will) through the fictive audiences of the TV shows. There is an operation here analogous to allegory. That the ruling class might like the real TV audience to *identify with*—to become—the fictive audience is probably true, since the real audience would become much more manageable. But there is no evidence which demonstrates that the real audience has given up its own variety of identities for the fictive one. This does not exclude the possibility that the TV shows are a means—perhaps a principal one—by which the ruling class and the ruled classes communicate. If this is true, the official ratings of TV show popularity provide a kind of response to the messages contained in the fictive audience.

In this case, diachronic studies of TV would focus on a wide selection of synchronic successes—all public order shows, all situation comedies, all quiz shows, all news shows, etc. We could begin to trace out this indirect means of communication, showing what the powerful wanted to communicate and to some degree which part of their message the TV audience accepted.

An assumption that lurks behind any argument for including, say, Shakespeare in the popular culture camp is that his plays enjoyed initial synchronic success. Shakespeare, it is well known, was a successful businessman as well as an accomplished artist. Similar assumptions apply to Dickens; for poems composed in an oral-formulaic tradition (Homer's epics and *Beowulf,* for example) there is growing evidence that poetic composing ability is popular rather than 'elite' in those societies where it thrives.[8] Yet a good number of diachronic popular works had a rather modest beginning: John Donne's poetry, *Moby Dick,* the paintings of the Impressionists, and of course anything interesting you reclaim from a gravesite—no one in China or Egypt was supposed to stroll through the tombs of the wealthy to enjoy the magnificent artwork!

Although the causes for the eventual diachronic success of these slow-starters are complex and deserve full treatment elsewhere, it seems obvious that in every case a so-called elite not only discovered the artwork but also promoted its popularity rather than keeping the treasures to themselves. While the specialists in literature, art and archaeology can tell us much about metaphor or brush-stroke or the construction of a jade funeral gown, it is the specialists in popular culture who can explain why twentieth-century audiences were able to recognize the fictive audiences of these works; such a task probably requires expertise in the subject to which the work belongs as well as in the theory or theories of popular culture, which are still evolving.

These questions lead me at last to the Old English elegy, the diachronic popularity of which has not reached the level of Donne's poetry or King Tut's sarcophagus. The Old English elegy is still largely if not exclusively in the hands of an elite, although it need not remain an elitist artwork. Interest in Old Engish poetry has grown with the Industrial Revolution, first through the efforts of antiquarians and independently interested amateurs, then of academics. During the nineteenth and early twentieth centuries Old English poetry was studied largely by German scholars who established its place in linguistic history and used it indiscriminately to support a now discarded theory about a 'Germanic' antiquity for northwest Europe.

However, since the 1930s, when *Lord of the Rings* author J.R.R. Tolkien launched the literary criticism of *Beowulf* there has been an Anglo-American industry aimed at a full literary appreciation of Old English poetry. Part of this production has been a steady flow of translations into Modern English of nearly all the poems; the best of the translators is probably Burton Raffel, whose work is readily available in paperback editions. A survey of the criticism of the elegies—nine lyric poems in a manuscript called *The Exeter Book*— up through 1970 showed three-fourths of all entries date after 1930.[9] Although this sort of popularity hardly ranks with the major phenomena in popular culture—synchronic or diachronic—it shows an increasing interest in the poems and may augur well for a wider readership.

The elegies are poems which contrast past and present conditions; they show awareness of the transitory nature of earthly splendor, joy and security; and they present as a central feature a pattern of loss and consolation.[10] The most famous—and most studied—is *The Wanderer*: an exiled speaker's awareness develops in the poem from a concern with himself alone to a reflective wisdom embracing all this transitory life, but never achieving specific Christian knowledge of salvation.[11] Obviously there are attractions for the modern audience in the fictive audience of this poem, which would include interests that could be characterized as alienation, loss of homeland, psychological crisis, loneliness and wisdom achieved almost solely through reflection. That there is a modern "Literature of Exile" which focuses on the objective and subjective aspects of the exilic condition has been well demonstrated in a recent special issue of *Mosaic*.[12] That alienation is a fundamental aspect of the modern condition is by now axiomatic: witness the writings of Marx, the existentialists and Riesman. Some excellent reflections on the American variety of alienation are in Philip Slater's study, in which he identifies three human desires that are deeply and uniquely frustrated by American culture: the desire for community; the desire for engagement with social environment; and the desire for dependence (sharing social responsibility).[13] This concatenation of observations suggests a general predisposition in our culture for appreciation of an elegy like *The Wanderer*. Because I have earlier defined culture as an expression of a society's leisure needs and opportunities, and have now accounted for its needs, I turn to the opportunities.

One limit to opportunity for anyone to appreciate *The Wanderer* is that the usual environment for doing so is the academy—university or college courses in literature. Other forms of poetry once similarly imprisoned have jumped the walls; to keep excellent poetry in the academy is like keeping King Tut's tomb hidden away, only to be seen by those enrolled in a course in archeology. The problem lies, then, with the mediators.

One answer to this problem lies in the example offered by the front-runner in diachronic popular culture, the Bible, whose influence is due in no small part to its translators—Jerome, Luther, the scholars appointed by King James. Another answer can be found in a tradition of translation of Homer which postulates that every generation will translate it anew as an act of interpretation (rather like remaking an old movie). Old English poetry resembles both the Bible and Homer's epics, a remarkable possibility for translation. Both Homer's epics and Old English poetry are formulaic in character, while the poetry shares with Old Testament poetry a system of parallelism or (as Old English scholars call it) 'variation' in which ideas rather than words are rhymed.[14] This double relation to two kinds of poetry already well-translated promises a translatable structure for Old English poetry—and for the elegies—that should invite a wide interest by poets who could in turn produce many versions for a rich reading variety.

Old English elegies will probably never rival the leaders of diachronic popular culture—Shakespeare and the rest. But it is reasonable to predict, given the similar interests of the fictive audience of the elegies and of contemporary American culture, that such highly translatable poetry might be able to attract over the next quarter century as many readers as persons who attend one well-regarded stock-car race or perhaps a couple of pancake derbies. The refrain from one elegy called *Deor*, the name of the *scop* or poet who reports the loss of his post as court-poet but whose abiding wise patience seems to augur well for his regaining it, goes like this: Þaes *ofereode; thisses swa maeg.* Which may be freely translated: other hardships have passed by; so might this one. There is a durable wisdom, expression of courage (in the older sense of great heart as well as the more recent notion of grace under pressure), and a dignity wrought out of loneliness which could speak profoundly to any modern person. We are probably at a place with regard to the Old English elegies that Homer was when Chapman created the first popular Englishing of the ancient Greek poet; Chapman started a tradition which is still viable, and his translation spoke to Keats over the distance of two centuries, whose sonnet still bears eloquent testament to Chapman's feat. Perhaps Old English poetry has found its Chapman in Raffel, or will soon in another translator. That would be a welcome event in popular culture.

Notes

[1]See esssays by Bigsby, Williams, Barbu, Burke, Kress, Hodge and Craig in *Approaches to Popular Culture,* ed. by C.W.E. Bigsby (London: Arnold, and Bowling Green, Ohio: Bowling Green University Popular Press, 1976); see essays by Browne and Rollin in *Theories and Methodologies in Popular Culture,* ed. by Ray B. Browne, et al (Bowling Green University Popular Press); and see essays by Browne and Nye in *The Popular Culture Reader* ed. by Jack Nachbar and John L. Wright (Bowling Green University Popular Press, 1977).

[2]J. Frederick MacDonald, " 'The Foreigner' in Juvenile Series Fiction, 1900-1945," *Popular Culture Reader,* pp. 125-139.

[3]R. Serge Denisoff, "Death Songs and Teenage Roles," *Popular Culture Reader,* pp. 116-124.

[4]Ray B. Browne, "Popular Culture: Notes Toward a Definition," *Popular Culture Reader,* pp. 1-9; Russel B. Nye, "Notes for a Rationale for Popular Culture," *Popular Culture Reader,* 10-16.

[5]T.S. Kuhn, *The Copernican Revolution: Planetary Astronomy in the Development of Western Thought* (Cambridge: Harvard University Press, 1957), and *The Structure of Scientific Revolutions* (International Encyclopedia of Unified Science, Vol. II, No. 2) (Chicago: Univ. of Chicago Press, 1962; 2d enlarged edition, 1970).

[6]Walter J. Ong, S.J., "The Writer's Audience is Always a Fiction," *PMLA,* 90 (1975), 9-21.

[7]Raymond Williams, "Communications as Cultural Science," *Approaches to Popular Culture,* pp. 27-38, and Stuart Hood, "The Dilemma of the Communicators," *Approaches to Popular Culture,* pp. 201-212.

[8]*The Making of Homeric Verse: The Collected Papers of Milman Parry,* ed. by Adam Parry (Oxford: Clarendon, 1970); Albert B. Lord, *The Singer of Tales* (1960; rpt. New York: Athenaeum, 1965); Jeff Opland, *"Scop* and *Imbongi:* Anglo-Saxon and Bantu Oral Poets," *English Studies in Africa* 14 (1971), 161-78, and *"Imbongi Nezibongo:* The Xhosa Tribal Poet and Contemporary Poetic Tradition, *PMLA,* 90 (1975), 185-208; F.P. Magoun, Jr. "Oral-Formulaic Character of Anglo-Saxon Poetry," *Speculum,* 28 (1953), 446-467; and S.B. Greenfield, "The Formulaic Expression of the Theme of 'Exile' in Anglo-Saxon Poetry," *Speculum,* 30 (1955), 200-206.

[9]W.B. Knapp, "Bibliography of the Criticism of the Old English Elegies," *Comitatus,* 2 (1971), 71-90.

[10]S.B. Greenfield, *A Critical History of Old English Literature* (New York: New York University Press, 1968), pp. 213-214.

[11]Greenfield, *Critical History,* pp. 216-218.

[12]"The Literature of Exile," *Mosaic,* 8 (1975), special issue edited by R.G. Collins and John Wortley; essays by various hands.

[13]Philip Slater, *The Pursuit of Loneliness: American Culture at the Breaking Point* (Boston: Beacon, 1970), p. 5. I thank Pham Le for bringing this book to my attention.

[14]Ruth apRoberts, "Old Testament Poetry: The Translatable Structure," *PMLA,* 92 (1977), 987-1004.

Bibliographic Essay

There are many excellent translations of the Old English elegies including Burton Raffel, *Poems from the Old English* (Lincoln: Univ. of Nebraska Press, 1960); J. Duncan Spaeth, *Old English Poetry: Translations into Alliterative Verse* (1921; rpt. New York: Gordian, 1967); Keven Crossley-Holland and Bruce Mitchell, *The Battle of Maldon and Other Old English Poems* (London: Macmillan, 1965); Michael Alexander, *The Earliest English Poems* (Berkeley: Univ. of California Press, 1970); Charles W. Kennedy, *Old English Elegies* (Princeton: Princeton University Press, 1936) and *An Anthology of Old English Poetry* (New York: Oxford, 1960).

For the study of the culture of Anglo-Saxon England, the best place to start is G.A. Lester, *The Anglo-Saxons: How They Lived and Worked* (Chester Springs, Pa.: Dufour, 1976). Subsequently one should read Peter Hunter Blair, *An Introduction to Anglo-Saxon England* (Cambridge: Cambridge University Press, 1956) and Dorothy Whitelock, *The Beginnings of English Society* (Hammondsworth: Pelican, 1963).

For non-literary remains of Anglo-Saxon culture see R.L.S. Bruce-Mitford, *The Sutton Hoo Ship Burial: A Handbook* (London: British Museum, 1968) and *The Archaeology of Anglo Saxon England*, ed. by David M. Wilson (London: Methuen, 1976).

For the standard texts of all Old English poetry (though not in translation) see *The Anglo-Saxon Poetic Records*, 6 vols., ed. by George P. Krapp and Elliott V.K. Dobie (New York: Columbia, 1931-1953).

For annual coverage of all aspects of the culture, see the annual survey *Anglo-Saxon England*, published by Cambridge University Press. For literary studies, see the annual bibliography in the *Old English Newsletter*, published by SUNY-Binghampton. In the summer of 1978 the University of Toronto published S.B. Greenfield and Fred C. Robinson, *A Bibliography of Publicatons on Old English Literature from the Beginnings through 1972*, an exhaustive checklist which will include translations.

XII

Entertainment, Edification, and Popular Education in the *South English Legendary*

Violent stories of cowboys, detectives and spies have dominated much of modern popular entertainment. While these stories have rarely demonstrated reasonable ways of life, they have shown glamorous ways of facing death. In Jankofsky's study of a medieval anthology of saints' legends we are shown popular tales of Christian heroes and heroines that were designed to set forth patterns for life and for death. They are true instances of popular culture because as Jankofsky points out, these are "Englishings" of Latin sources, with many entertaining additions that were designed to enthrall the audiences to whom the legends would have been read. Students of popular culture of more recent times will find Jankofsky's identification of characteristics that mark the popularization of cultivated materials (by simplification, expansion and concretization) useful. The article begins with another aspect of popular culture: the rapid assimilation of news events into popular legend, in this case the execution of Sir Thomas More.

Klaus P. Jankofsky is an Associate Professor of English and Assistant Dean of the Graduate School at the University of Minnesota, Duluth. His particular interests are in the literature, iconography and psychology of death in Medieval England and Europe.

213

Entertainment, Edification and Popular Education in the *South English Legendary*

Klaus P. Jankofsky

In *The Lyfe of Syr Thomas More* an anonymous author known to us only by his initials Ro: Ba: tells the episode of a man from Winchester suffering from severe bouts of depression who had repeatedly sought help from More and who now comes to More's execution to speak to him one more time:

'Maister More, doe you knowe me? I pray you, for our Lordes sake, help me. I am as ill troubled as I ever was.' Sir Thomas aunswered, 'I remember thee full well. Goe thy waies in peace, and pray for me, and I will not faile to pray for thee.'[1]

It is intriguing to speculate if More,"God's servant first," was conscious of his being on the way to sainthood and of his possible role as an intercessor on behalf of the physical and spiritual ills of men. What we do know with certainty is that the men who wrote biographies of More—Roper and Harpsfield among the better known—approached their subject as a saint's life, as a model for our self-criticism and our encouragement. Their primary purpose was not to write history, says Helen White, but to compose a devotional work for the edification of their readers.[2] In that sense they continue a medieval tradition, observable even in the English historical chronicles from the 12th to the 15th century, of combining elements of historiography with legendary narration. Similarly, we find in the greatest of the early Middle English collections of saints' lives, in the so-called *South English Legendary,* a great deal of biographical and historical-political information about the English saints in particular, for example in the "Life of St. Thomas a Becket." That and an astonishing amount of "Englishing" of the predominantly Latin sources and materials, their adaptation to an unlearned, English audience, to its familiarity with national history, custom and events, and to its knowledge of local traditions, relics and shrines takes these legends beyond mere stimulation for the edification of the faithful and lends them, to a certain degree, the character of historical documentation.

214

What the lengthy biographies of More and the predominantly short narratives in the *South English Legendary*[3] further have in common is their presentation of a completeness and a fulfillment in the lives of saints and martyrs which can be used as a model and a standard of comparison to one's own life; these stories can be seen as complete lives from which values and guidelines can be derived for more complete living. In that perspective even the seemingly diversified collection of narratives of the *South English Legendary* reveals its underlying coherence and unity.

It is the purpose of this paper to identify the principal features that characterize the *South English Legendary* (and distinguish it from Jacobus de Voragine's *Legenda aurea*), to point out some of its typical elements of entertainment and edification, and to suggest that the lessons to be derived from these lives may well be among those factors which perhaps in the long run account for the "typically English" Christian acceptance of suffering and death which we find documented especially in the public executions for political and religious reasons in the 16th and 17th centuries in England. The belief in ultimate values, the concept of the morally responsible individual personality with freedom of choice in his conscience, the obligation of proper self-fulfillment, trust in God, and a certain cheerfulness in facing the end of one's own earthly existence are the components of an apparently then widespread and pervasive attitude to life and death.[4] They are also the qualities that we find demonstrated in the simple narratives of the *South English Legendary*. The focus of this paper then is on what appears to be a continuity of thought and feeling in the face of suffering and death which extends from the 13th century to the beginnings of what we call the modern world.

The *South English Legendary* as we read it now in modern editions probably never existed as such. In its earliest preserved form, MS Laud 108 in the Bodleian Library, Oxford, it consists of a random arrangement of 64 lives in a mixture of calendar vs. hierarchical order.[5] The latest edition of the collection in the EETS series contains 90 items, among them *sanctorale* materials, the legends proper, including short lives of Pontius Pilate and Judas Iscariot, and *temporale* materials, the accounts of liturgical events throughout the church year, such as the Circumcision, Epiphany, Easter, the Assumption of the Virgin, All Saints, All Souls.[6]

Without going into the very complex history of the textual tradition of the *South English Legendary* in this paper, it seems certain that the collection originated in the latter part of the 13th century (ca. 1270-1285; Görlach, p. 78) in the Southwest of England, possibly in Worcester, whose cathedral library seems to have been

well equipped for the production of a comprehensive work such as
the *South English Legendary*. As sources for the *South English
Legendary* compilation we must consider a *legenda* close to Sarum
Use, some *summa*, a copy of the *Legenda aurea* of the Dominican
bishop of Genua, Jacobus de Voragine, some text of native saints for
the longer legends, e.g. Thomas a Becket, a copy of a *temporale*
collection in English, general knowledge of the Bible, and perhaps a
calendar of the church year.[7]

The purpose of the collection obviously was the instruction of
the laity in matters of the faith. What is surprising, however, is that
any missionary zeal is missing, that there is no hierarchy of virtues,
and more importantly, that the technique of presentation is not that
of the sermon, particularly of the hell-fire and brimstone type about
the Four Last Things,—Heaven, Hell, Purgatory and Death. Rather,
the audience is presented with a straightforward story that can be
understood at first hearing, without unnecessary digressions, and
without any specifically didactic finger-pointing moral. The
narratives are written in a basically dignified, elevated seven stress
line in rhyming couplets. The principles that characterize the
composition of the entire *South English Legendary*—despite a very
complex textual tradition of more than 50 extant manuscripts
attesting to its popularity—are the following:

1) a *simplification* of complicated theological-dogmatic problems
and hagiographic traditions;
2) an explanatory, interpretive, and didactic *expansion* of subject
matter in view of the audience's knowledge and powers of
imagination;
3) a process of *concretization* through the enlivening creation of
dialogues and scenes where the sources may have plain third-person
narrative; in other words *dramatization*.

Like any good public speaker, the original author aimed at
entertaining his audience as well as providing them with food for
thought, doing so by frequently intervening in the course of his
narrative to address his audience directly:

—Why do you sit so still, why don't you say 'Amen'—

This is how he jolts his listeners when they seem to be spell-bound by some
of St. Peter's exploits in his struggle with Simon the Magician. Or he adds
his own commentary to the story and relates a point to the listeners' own
experience, as when he tells of St. Swithin at whose exhumation the cadaver
was found smelling sweet, a phenomenon starkly in contrast with the

experience of their own senses. Periodically, ironical-clever remarks accentuate the narrative, having the effect of refreshing breaks in an otherwise relentless account of tortures, suffering and pain. Often the downfall of an antagonist or the demise of an executioner is accompanied by comments that are reminiscent of the grim humor we find in the Middle English romances, especially when they tell of mutilations, dismemberment and disfiguration of enemies, giants or monsters.

When Simon Magus crashes down from the roof of the temple in his illfated attempt at flying, the narrator comments:

Wat is nou sire wilde gos woder hadde he itho3t
His fetheren were alle to feble is art ne halp him no3t
He fel doun to is owe kunde as he moste nede
Hail min ape wat wolde he ther him com sone is mede

423-426

And the torturer who had beheaded St. Alban had no reason to boast of his deed, for when his eyes popped out thereupon, the narrator remarks

He mi3te segge wanne he comth hom war her comth the blynde (90)

Besides the momentum of the stories themselves, these remarks help to articulate the narrative avoiding monotony, to provide some humorous relief (not necessarily "funny" in our perception, as when the apocryphal, oedipal Judas steals not only the apples from his father's orchard, but rips off the pears as well), and to firmly anchor the narratives in a universe in which ultimately good is rewarded and evil punished.

Together with the bidding prayers at the conclusion of each life authorial comments such as "there he ended his life as he well deserved it" (regarding the suicide of Pilate), or "And his soul to heaven went" speaking of a saint, provide an immediate bond between speaker and audience and tie the narratives more firmly to the common concern, the saving of souls.

The very unifying and unified presentation as a story of the often discrepant hagiographic traditions concerning a particular saint must be considered an especial achievement that provides the pleasurable satisfaction of curiosity about men and women of the past, a certain amount of exotic information, of adventures, and vicarious participation in the joys, pains, anguish and ultimate triumph of the saints. The entertainment value of these legends as romances of Christian adventure is established by the *South English Legendary* itself in the Prologue entitled "Banna Sanctorum." Here an extended simile establishes a bond between the content and the listeners' experience on two levels: that of the cycle of the natural seasons and the new fruit—Christendom—that is brought forth, the seed of Christianity that was sown and is watered by the blood of the martyrs; and the sphere of medieval warfare and battle with the saints as the knightly champions and battle companions of Christ, the leader and King, and the prophets and patriarchs as the avant-garde, and the followers of Christ now, all Christians, as the rear-guard whose duty it is to prevent Christ's victory from being undone.

At the end of the extended comparison which takes up 60 lines, the narrator contrasts his *true stories* with those *false stories* that people like to listen to in the narratives of fights and battles as found in the secular entertainment literature of the day:

Men wilneth muche to hure telle of bataille of kynge
And of kni3tes that hardy were that muchedel is lesynge
Wo so wilneth much to hure tales of suche thinge
Hardi batailles he may hure here that nis no lesinge
Of apostles & martirs that hardy kni3tes were
That studeuast were in bataille & ne fleide no3t for fere
That soffrede that luther men al quik hare lymes totere
Telle ichelle bi reuwe of ham as hare dai valth in the 3ere

                                                                    59-66

More important than these items that have to do with narrative presentation and setting is the entirely new tone and atmosphere in the *South English Legendary*. The mood of compassion and warm human participation in the description of the lives of the saints, disciples, apostles, confessors, virgins and martyrs which permeates the entire collection is the result of a more "realistic" and purposely heightened depiction of the sufferings and joys of the protagonists and of the direct appeal to the emotions and empathy of the audience. This is the area where, to my mind, the truly important contribution of the *South English Legendary* to English literature and more so to the emotional history of a country or a people lies.

Two examples must suffice here, one randomly taken from the life of St. Juliana, the other from the life of St. Thomas a Becket.[8]

In contrast to Latin texts which describe Saint Juliana's martyrdom in only a few terse sentences,[9] the *South English Legendary* depicts in detail how the keenly sharpened blades of the iron wheel against which St. Juliana is stretched penetrate deep into her naked flesh, so that it is cut to pieces. So deep enter the revolving blades that the bones are slit and the marrow forced out:

A weol of ire swuthe strang byuore hure hy caste
Al were the uelien aboute with rasors ystiked uaste
That weol hi turnde al aboute the maide therby hi sette
Dupe wode in hure naked fleiss the rasors kene iwette
That tho hure uless was al to torne so deope wode, gnowe
That the bones hy to slitte and the marrou out drowe
That marrou sprang al about, so ouercome heo was

141-47

The intensity of the pain is then depicted by the remark that she almost gave up the ghost, that yet she spoke always of Christ's even greater suffering, and by the joyful words of the "evil men" who see her so close to death:

That heo almest 3af the gost & no wonder it nas
Of al that me drou hure tendre limes hy nere enes sore
Ac euere sede that Jesu Christ tholede for hure more
Glad were tho the luther men that so ney the dethe hure seie

148-51

Afterwards we read that an angel with naked sword came down from heaven and destroyed the wheel. But before that, this interception is anticipated by the narrator with the remark, "Ac oure Louerd is wille nas it no3t that heo ssolde deie." (152)

In this explanatory note we perceive the attitude of the narrator who here, as elsewhere, puts this single case into a more general context, an order in which the sufferings of the saints stem ultimately from God's will; all these hostile judges, prefects, kings, torturers and executioners we encounter in the legends seek to overcome a human being—whom when all other methods fail they kill by the sword—yet in reality they eventually have to deal with God himself. The saints and especially the martyrs are witnesses, tools, ultimately, of the Divine will.

In the case of St. Juliana, after different torture methods with fire and liquid lead have been to no avail in trying to overcome the saint, the Latin account of the *Legenda aurea*[10] says only: *Tunc iusit eam decollari.*

The *South English Legendary,* in contrast, creates movement and dramatization by using direct speech and emotional gestures. The judge shouts,

Heo nessel me wraththi namore ichelle pleie other game
Com vorth he sede mi manquellare led this hore fram me
And smite of hure heued withoute toun that iche neuere eft hure ne se
Glad was this holy maide tho heo weste hure ende
For heo weste after hure tormens woder heo ssolde wende

Heo thonkede uaste Iesu Crist that wolde after hure sende
Go blieue heo sede to the quellare & bring me of this bende

184-190

After a humorous interlude with the under-devil Belial whom
she had castigated earlier in prison and who now is telling the
executioners from a safe distance "to speed it up," the *South English
Legendary* continues:

Tho this maide com to thulke stude as heo ssolde biheued be
To oure Louerd heo bad hure orison & sat adoun akneo
The quellare as heo bad hure beden drou is swerd kene
He smot of hure heued fram hure body that it fel in the grene

203-206

The gesture of kneeling down and praying, the sharpness of the
sword, the head tumbling onto the grass, these are all additions
which are characteristic of the overall depiction of martyrdoms in
the *South English Legendary*. They are meant to increase the
emotional reaction of the audience to the saints' suffering.
Emphatic exclamations on the part of the narrator such as "O Lord,
great was the pain," or "it was pity to see" and numerous similar
expressions punctuate the narratives, providing greater human
interest and inviting vicarious participation in the agony of the
saints.[11]

On the other hand, the equally numerous narrative formulas
such as "with joy and bliss," "with great honor," "as right was to
do," and finally the closing bidding prayers help to establish an
equilibrium between the depiction of pain and the final glorious
outcome of the various conflicts. It is this overall balance of the
appeal to emotional involvement and the counterpoint of a calm,
reassuring, consoling and comforting outlook which is typical of
this work.

In its attempt to make the invisible visible, to show the concrete
presence of the supernatural (and miraculous) in the here and now
the *South English Legendary* resorts to a heightening of emotion
through a "realistic"—one might be tempted to say, an
exaggeratedly naturalistic—depiction of physical lacerations of the
body. That this "realism" can be both historically true and symbolic
at the same time becomes evident in the account of the death of that
other most famous of English saints, Thomas a Becket.

The life of Thomas Becket is one of the longer biographical *vitae*
of the collection, probably the most accomplished from a literary
and artistic point of view. Drawn into Becket's political conflict with
Henry II is his own struggle with the world, his secular office, his

ecclesiastical responsibilities and the fate of his soul, a conflict finally culminating in the inevitable murder in the cathedral and thus solved in martyrdom.

Becket's death is seen as an *imitatio Christi,* once by Becket himself in the course of the narrative, and once by the narrator. In the dying scene, the parallelism to Christ's death is established in a threefold way: first, the monks flee in fear, a parallel to the biblical "when men smite the shepherd, the sheep will flee"; next the murderers utter a boastful speech reviling him, and finally, Robert de Brok returns to the slain man to scrape the brain out of the open skull in a last gesture of brutality, thus inflicting the fifth wound in analogy to the five wounds of Christ.

The *South English Legendary's* account interrupts the chronological flow of events describing the archbishop's murder to give an explanation of the typological significance of certain details. It sees the blood and brain which surround the temples of the prostrate primate realistically and symbolically at the same time:

With thulke strok he smot al of the scolle and eke the croune
That the brain orn abrod in the pauement thare doune
The wite brain was ymeng with the rede blod Bere
The colour was Bell uair to seo thei it rulich were
Al round it orn aboute is heued as it were a diademe
Al round there aboute lay war of me tok gret 3eme
For wanne me peint an halwe 3e ne seoth no3t eleued
That ther nis ipeint a round al about is heued
That is icluped diademe and me say thare a uair cas
Bi the diademe of is heued that he halwe was

2161-2170

The naturalistic, gory details of blood mixed with brain are interpreted in traditional hagiographic color symbolism—red for martyrdom and white for innocence—and as the attribute of sainthood, the halo or nimbus. At the same time, the seemingly horrifying and repulsive spectacle is valued as beautiful (fair to see, a fair instance). This aesthetic judgment, strange as it may seem to us, points to the murder's spiritual dimension: precious is in the sight of the Lord the death of his saints.[12]

This is, of course, the ultimate meaning of the often hyperbolic depiction of suffering and torture encountered in hagiography and especially in the *South English Legendary.*

Something else can be noted here, and again this is representative of the entire *South English Legendary:* the picture of the bloodied head or body can be related to what is called in art-historical terms an "imago pietatis" or "Andachtsbild," a picture whose contemplation is to induce in the onlooker an emotional empathy, an increase of devotion, a heightened awareness of suffering, and a more intense feeling for the preciousness of the blood ultimately shed for the onlooker's spiritual benefit and salvation.[13] In other words, to serve as the starting point for an interiorizing process, the edification of the individual; this kind of edification must be interpreted as more than a pious shiver or a more or less pleasant sensation as the use of the term since the 18th century suggests, but edification in the medieval sense of the word— awareness of the potential sanctity of the body as the temple of the divine persons and the membership of the individual in the mystical body of Christ and his Church, and also an incitement to the betterment of the self.

In this context it should be pointed out that this individual interiorizing process can—and often does—take place in a public setting. With few exceptions, mainly in the case of hermits, do death and suffering occur without spectators, whether hostile or friendly. In that sense the audience (both the original spectators and the audience who hears/reads these lives) can bear witness to the inner convictions and qualities which the saints and martyrs manifest with their *physis*. It is thus both a teaching and a learning how to die.

Thus, two conclusions can be drawn from a study of the lives of the saints in this work: physical suffering is subordinated to a greater purpose, it is meritorious; and it is "the end that qualifies all," in the words of John Donne. This latter aspect may not be so obvious in the legends themselves, mainly because the hagiographic schema assures the reader/listener from the very beginning of the proper outcome; however, in the realities of lived life it is important as the relevant descriptions and comments in historical documents and chronicles of the Middle English period show.[14] For the audience to whom the lives of the saints were presented as life models and exemplary performances in the face of severest adversities, the behavior at the hour of death observable in their own contemporaries became a standard of judgment of ultimate convictions, beliefs, loyalties and absolute morals.[15]

It would be rash to postulate a direct and immediate influence of the lessons of the legends on actual behavior, but the cumulative effect of this part of religious instruction, together with other teachings of the Church and certain legal and political realities in the 15th and 16th centuries cannot help but be felt in the overwhelming acclaim with which a book such as Foxe's *Book of Martyrs*[16] was greeted about two hundred years after the effectiveness of the *South English Legendary* is supposed to have ceased.[17]

It is really not surprising to see—beyond the rejection of miracles as lies and the repudiation of the Catholic Church as a corrupt institution—the survival and a new culmination of the hagiographic scheme in the depiction of the lives and deaths of the new Protestant martyrs.[18] The very fact that thousands died during the political and religious persecutions of the 16th and 17th centuries in a way reminiscent of the early Christian persecutions and that their deaths and sufferings were described in a way reminiscent of the earlier hagiographic tradition attests to the inner continuity of certain modes of perception and expression.

The publicness of English men's and women's deaths—we read that sometimes tens of thousands would attend executions—and the publicity their dying speeches received can be explained by more than a perverse sensationalism or vulgar curiosity.[19] The spectacle of the executions was also edification: "...for the more public the death be, the more profitable it shall be to many"—profitable does not mean here the possible preventive effect on potential criminals, that concept is alien to that time—"the more profitable it shall be to many; and the more glorious, in the sight of all who shall see it."[20] "Profitable" can here be defined in terms of an edifying spectacle which demonstrates *ad oculos* certain Christian virtues, repentance, humility, steadfastness and ultimate trust on the threshold of life and death in the face of eternity, even in the case of persons who have forfeited their lives by the laws and rules of earthly powers and who by their deaths bring about a certain atonement.

The lessons to be learned from the stories of the saints seem to have been enacted in reality. That these deaths are characterized by steadfastness, Christian humility, patience, and not infrequently by a certain cheerfulness, even gallows humor, seems to be a typically English phenomenon.

"Our condemned persons do go so cheerfully to their deaths, for our nation is free, stout, haughty, and prodigal of life and blood.... In no place shall you see malefactors go more constantly, more assuredly, and with less lamentation to their death than in England."[21]

"It is the full acceptance of death coming out of the full acceptance of life," writes one scholar about the Elizabethans.[22]

One is reminded of the illuminations in an early 14th century manuscript of the *Legenda aurea* (Huntington Library HM 3027) which show the various executioners and their victims with finely differentiated grins and smiles respectively on their lips, while the kings, judges, and prefects gesture in anger and wrath. Could it be that so many attended the executions to see if the riddle of the Christian paradox of death both as the wages of sin and the entrance to everlasting life seemed about to be solved by those on the threshold?

The teaching of the *South English Legendary* (as all Christian education in general) is "popular" in the widest sense of the word since it addresses itself to all men; in its aim to present in a simplified, it is true, but nevertheless unified, form and not without grace an explanation of the structure and meaning of man's life on a popularizing level, and in its attempts to instill in its audience an awareness of the individual soul's way back to its Creator, it can be seen as a preparation for more complete living. That, I think, was in essence the original concept of the purpose and scope of the *South English Legendary.*

The saints and martyrs, here as elsewhere, were the outstanding, specially noted people who belonged to both worlds, this and the other, by virtue of their origins and their achievements. As such they were thought to play the role of mediators. The veneration they found paid tribute to this. Are we surprised then to read in Ro: Ba:'s story that after Thomas More's execution our melancholy man from Winchester never suffered from his affliction again?

Notes

[1] E.V. Hitchcock-P.E. Hallett, eds. *The Lyfe of Syr Thomas More, Sometymes Lord Chancellor of England by Ro: Ba:* (EETS OS 222, London: OUP, 1950), pp. 260-261. "This poore man was greivouslie vexed with verie vehement and greivous tentations of desperation...."

[2] H.C. White, *Tudor Books of Saints and Martyrs* (Madison: Univ. of Wisconsin Press, 1963), p. 124.

[3] Except for "Edmund of Canterbury" and "Thomas a Becket" even relatively long legends, such as "St. Brendan" (734 lines) can be read or related orally in less than an hour, often much less.

[4] See W. Farnham, "Tragic Prodigality of Life," *Essays in Criticism,* second series, Univ. of Calif. Publications in English IV (1934), pp. 185-198; Th. Finkenstaedt, "Galgenliteratur. Zur Auffassung des Todes im England des 16. und 17. Jahrhunderts," *DVJS* 34 (1960), pp. 527-553; L.B. Smith, "English Treason Trials and Confessions in the Sixteenth Century," *Journal of the History of Ideas* 15 (1954), pp. 471-498; L.B. Wright, *Middle Class Culture in Elizabethan England* (Chapel Hill, N.C.: Univ. of North Carolina Press, 1935).

[5] For the history of the relationship between extant manuscripts and their description and evaluation, see M. Goerlach, *The Textual Tradition of the 'South English Legendary'* (Univ. of Leeds: Leeds Texts and Monographs, New Series 6, 1974), p. 90.

[6] Ch. d'Evelyn-A.J. Mill, eds., *The South English Legendary* (3 vols., EETS OS 235, 236, 244, London: OUP, 1956-59). All quotations from this work are taken from this edition.

[7] Goerlach, p. 78, p. 29, *et passim.*

[8] See also "St. Valentine" (39 f.), "St. Peter" (473-475), "St. Lawrence" (145-154), "St. Bartholomew" (243-246), "St. Denys" (127-130), "St. Quentin" (87-112), "St. Clement" (112-114), "St. Oswald the Bishop" (90-93).

[9] See for instance the relevant passages in her life in B. Mombritius *Sanctuarium seu Vitae Sanctorum* (ed. by two monks of Solesmes, Paris, 1910), vol. II, pp. 77-78; and J. Bolland, ed. *Acta Sanctorum* (Antwerp, 1684), Februarius II, p. 877.

[10]T. Graesse, ed., *Legenda aurea Jacobi a Voragine* (Vratislaviae, 1890³), p. 178.

[11]The first to pay special attention to this aspect of the *South English Legendary* was Th. Wolpers, *Die englische Heiligenlegende des Mittelalters* (Tuebingen: Niemeyer, 1964); see esp. pp. 235-237, 246ff.

[12]For an interpretation of these lines in the larger context of medieval English modes of perception, see my "A View into the Grave: 'A Disputacion betwyx by Body and Wormes' in British Museum MS ADD. 37049," TAIUS 7 (1974), 137-159.

[13]Wolpers, pp. 30 ff. *et passim.*

[14]See my *Darstellungen von Tod und Sterben in mittelenglischer Zeit.*Untersuchung literarischer Texte und historischer Quellen (Duluth, 1970), esp. chapter 4.

[15]For the 16th and 17th centuries, see the references listed above in note 4.

[16]Also known by its original title *Actes and Monvments* (4th edition, London, 1583).

[17]Goerlach, p. 31, p. 62.

[18]In this context the part of the prefatory materials entitled "The Vtilitie of the Story" is of great interest, not the least because of Foxe's use of similar terminology as the "Banna Sanctorum" prologue of the *South English Legendary*:

I see no cause why the Martyrs of our time deserue any lesse commendation, then the other in the primitiue churche, whiche assuredly are inferiour unto them in no poynt of prayse; whether we view the number of them that suffered, or greatness of theyr torments, or theyr constancie in dying, or also consider the fruite that they brought to the amendment of posteritie, and encrease of the Gospell. They did water the truth with theyr bloud, that was newly springing up: so these by theyr dethes restored it agayne, beyng sore decayed and fallen downe. They standing in the forwarde of the battell, did receaue the first encounter and violence of theyr enemies, and taught us by that means to ouercome such tyranny: These with like courage agayne like ould beaten souldiours did winne the field in the rereward of the battayle. They like famous husbandmen of the world did sow the fields of the Church, that first lay unmanured and wast: these with fatness of theyr bloud did cause it to battell and fructifie. Would to God the fruite might be speedely gathered into the barne, whiche onely remayneth behinde to come.

[19]Finkenstaedt, p. 533.

[20]R. Pitcairn, ed. *Criminal Trials and other Proceedings before the High Justiciary in Scotland* (Edinburgh, 1883, vol. II, p. 447); quoted by Finkenstaedt, p. 533.

[21]Farnham, p. 188; also Finkenstaedt, pp. 545-46, quoting from a different source, F.J. Furnivall, ed., Harrison, *Description of England* (New Shakespeare Society, 1881, ff), vol. II, p. 447; slightly modernized by me.

[22]Farnham, p. 194.

XIII

Gothic Love and Death:
Francois Villon and the City of Paris

Some of the most profitable areas of study in popular culture are the points of intersection with other cultures. Joseph J. Hayes' article weaves together several of these intersections in the period when the middle ages were waning, just before the invention of movable type printing. The elite culture at this time was moving from the countryside to the city, and its courtly literature of love was losing its relevance along with the change of setting. In addition, a whole new audience for literature was developing in the city, something that had not existed since the fall of Rome a thousand years before. Hayes states that the Parisian poet Francois Villon occupies a pivotal position between old and new literary styles and between old and new reading audiences. Like Klaus Jankofsky in the previous article, Hayes finds that attitudes toward death and dying tell us much about the values held by the audience and by the society at large. In the poetry of Villon, as in the popular Dance of Death woodcuts of the day, we observe death acting as a democratizing force that lowers the status of the medieval elite.

Joseph J. Hayes is Professor of English and Comparative Literature at California State University, Fullerton. He is interested in the mutually affecting influences of aristocratic and popular culture in medieval art and literature.

Gothic Love and Death:
Francois Villon and the City of Paris

Joseph J. Hayes

In the popular imagination one literary figure from the close of
the Middle Ages towers above all others—Francois Villon. Later
ages have made much of his death-defying scrapes, underworld
connections and grotesque cynicism. For the poets of l9th-century
France he was the archetype of the romantic Bohemian. Robert
Louis Stevenson described him as the "sorriest figure on the rolls of
fame." Our own, more cynical, age takes his phrase "I laugh
through tears," for our ironic motto. Whatever model his life may
provide for the imagination of an era, the art of Villon has not lost its
popular appeal since the appearance of the first printed edition of
his works in 1489, for he is perhaps the first widely-known *city* poet
of the Western world. In fact, Villon's art, forged out of the union of
"courtly" and "popular" literary traditions, marks the first
important appearance of an *urban* imagination in medieval letters.

My argument is threefold. First I wish to place Villon within the
context of medieval poetic practice, particularly the conditions and
themes of court poetry. Secondly, I present a discussion of Villon's
particular view of the city of Paris as a *locus* for the transaction of
amatory and commercial ventures. Finally I wish to suggest that
the fusion of popular and courtly elements in Villon's *Testament* is
accomplished by inverting the usual *eros/thanatos*
conflict,wherein *eros* (the life principle) is seen as separating and
dividing, and *thanatos*(the death instinct) is seen as uniting and
equalizing.

I. The Country

The literary context of Villon's *oeuvre* is important because
"poetry" in late Gothic Europe was nominally a court art and Villon
was an independent poet. His peers and predecessors, the medieval
court poets (Guillaume de Machaut, Eustache Deschamps, Othe de
Graunson), were often no more than entertainers for the king, and,
of course, social inferiors. For these court poets, writing lyrics could
only be an avocation and not a vocation. Their livelihood depended

on a noble person, who might influence them in the subject matter, style and form of their work. Indeed the principal and sometimes sole means of social intercourse between the bourgeois poet and the court audience was the presentation and reading of poetry.

At best the system of patronage could encourage innovative and creative writing. More often, however, it could prohibit experimentation in subjects and styles objectionable to the patron. The interests of the medieval court poet, then, were inevitably those of the court circle, and politically and culturally conservative.

In the early Middle Ages the court itself was usually located in the countryside and the *locus* for most court poetry is the idealized bucolic setting, frequently modelled after descriptions of the golden age. In this pastoral setting the conventional contest between the lover-poet's hopeless ardor and the lady's cold aloofness (her *danger*) is displayed within the narrow confines of the court perspective. Literary love at court may be described as a series of small skirmishes between the poet and his lady, in which death—of the heart or the body—lurks decorously at the periphery of the erotic play. Moreover, this attitude was thought exclusive to the court circle and was a mark of nobility. As Johan Huizinga sums it up: "Life [at court] is regulated like a noble game. Only a small aristocratic group can come up to the standard of this artistic game.... The aspiration to realize a dream of beauty in the forms of social life bears as a *vitium originis* the stamp of aristocratic exclusiveness."[1]

To state the case somewhat briefly, the tension between the lovelorn poet and the responsive lady turns *eros* into the process of separation and stratification. The court circle makes itself separate from the commons by giving elaborate conventions to literary love. Moreover, men and women in the court circle are seen as irreconcilable in erotic warfare, with man subjected to woman as sinner is subjected to saint. At the basis of the conflict are the wish for and hopelessness of achieving redemption through erotic union.

So pervasive is the medieval tradition of an erotic contest of wills in a bucolic setting that its features are retained even after the courts become more closely associated with the cities and, thus, a wider audience. While the themes and subjects of the lyric may not have changed radically in the late Middle Ages, the growing association of the court with an urban center did bring about an expansion in the audience for literature. The increasing economic and social power of the cities' magnates and the emergence of a *commercant* class eager to imitate genteel customs extended the reach of poetry outside the narrow confines of the court.[2] Paradoxically, though, the interest of a city audience in amorous poetry of the old bucolic manner did not decline, but rather increased, probably because of aristocratic prestige. Increasingly, then, love poetry at the close of the Middle Ages, although reaching a wider audience, was in danger of becoming standardized and rigid, arid in themes and attitudes. The expression of feeling and emotion, reduced to the contest between ardor and ladylike hauteur (*danger*) risked being formulated merely as a set of bald literary conventions.

The important contribution of Francois Villon to literary culture was the revolt against this static, old bucolic ideal. In his poetic will, *The Testament,* the penniless rogue and sometime scholar replaces the old style with a new one, by the fusion of "popular" and "courtly" elements, to provide a new, *urban* style.

By "courtly" I am referring to the concerns, mannerisms and fashions of the aristocratic, bucolic ideal. It is formal and discreet in its address, indirect in its reference to the object of erotic urban union and conventional in its language. The court poet is expected to exhibit courtesy (court manners) and never to provoke or chastise.

The term "popular" in medieval culture is more difficult to define. Indeed we should not think of courtly and popular concerns as mutually exclusive. For the purpose of discussion, I am construing the term "popular" as a free and unfettered mode of address (i.e., *un*courtly) whose subjects and themes are not drawn from aristocratic circles. The popular poet may address whomever he wishes as he wishes; he may use informal and obscene language. Most importantly, his audience is not clearly defined. He may write to "all the ladies" or to "fellow drunks" or to no one in particular. If the court poet is formal and discreet in his address, Villon is slangy and reproachful. If the court poet refers only indirectly to erotic union, Villon brags of sexual contests, both his own and others'. If the court poet only alludes to unnamed ladies and allegorical personages, Villon celebrates the whores of Paris by name and invokes the likes of Pity and Death to bring pestilence on women who have mistreated him. What is important to understand here is that Villon acted as a reformer or reinterpreter of the courtly traditions themselves. He did not create his poetry *de novo,* but stayed with the externals of courtly form, which he wed to popular elements.

Villon's major innovations are twofold: 1) the presentation of a new kind of poetic persona, and 2) an original approach to the theme of love. He continued writing with the forms and genres of the courtly style, using the moral *ballade* and the lover's *complainte* as well as some of the familiar themes, but created a new persona out of the popular traditions of the drinking songs, *sotes chansons* and mocking poems.[3] Thus he solved the problem of finding a voice for his poetry by uniting a *picaro* persona with an aristocratic form. In so doing he created a revitalized poetry with a distinct style. This amalgam of the courtly and the popular has come to represent what we call a *city* poetry, in much the same manner that urban "aristocrats"—the cities' magnates—mingled courtly manners and commercial practices.

This new style is sardonic and cynical rather than romantic and idealizing. In blending the courtly with the popular modes, Villon made the formerly exclusive material of the bucolic court accessible to the city, and so, in turn, accessible to the widest audience. The freedom to develop this new style surely comes directly from Villon's freedom from the constraints of patronage.

His second innovation, the treatment of the theme of love, moves Villon securely into this new, urban tradition. In place of pining lovers and cold maidens, there are whores and pimps, in brothels and taverns, to populate the world of *The Testament*. In fact, Villon conceives of the city as a place principally inhabited by gamblers, counterfeiters, jesters, itinerant musicians, wandering players and drunks:

> Keep well away from such trash
> Plough, scythe the fields and meadows
> Groom and feed horses and mules
> Even if you can't read or write
> You can live pretty well if you go easy.[4]

Paris and its low life become the sole context for the expression of love. Thus Villon's art is best understood through his view of fifteenth-century Paris and its special milieu.

II. The City

For Villon, as for all medieval Christians, the universe contained two metaphors for the urban center—the City of God and the City of Man. Dante adds a third, or infernal city, Dis. It is a perverse place, made of an ever-narrowing funnel: I AM THE WAY TO THE CITY OF WOE. / I AM THE WAY TO A FORESAKEN PEOPLE. / I AM THE WAY INTO ETERNAL SORROW (*Inferno*, III).[5] It was the goal of every Christian to reach a celestial city: in life to achieve the earthly cathedral and the sacred city of Jerusalem, at the end of life's pilgrimage to pass out of the earthly city to the Heavenly Jerusalem.

Compared with the overwhelming light of the celestial city, the city of man was a dark shade, a meager and imperfect inversion of the Great Jerusalem. Since it was a secular city, and a place of sin, medieval literature often singled it out as the appropriate stage for lust, and contrasted the love of man unfavorably with the love of God. In the moral literature of the period human love is consistently depicted as sickly, fleeting and subject to death, whereas divine love is unchanging and eternal. As a man of his age, and a city poet, Villon seizes as his central image the fact that human love alone is irrevocably associated with death and decay.

In the celestial city, *eros* is ultimately transformed into *agape*. In the medieval city of man, *eros* leads only to *thanatos*. In the heavenly city human love is widened into spirituality; in the earthly city human live is narrowed into nothingness. What unites the celestial and earthly cities, then, is the nexus of love and death. In response to the paradox of love (celestial) achieved by death in the City of God, medieval man posits the certainty of love (human) leading inexorably to death and decay in the city of man. In the literature of the Middle Ages the obsession with death and its inextricable union with love becomes almost a mania at the end of the Gothic age:

> Since the thirteenth century, the popular preaching of the mendicant orders had made the eternal admonition to remember death swell into a sombre chorus ringing throughout the world. Towards the fifteenth century a new means of inculcating the awful thought into all minds has added to the words of the preacher, namely the popular woodcut. These two means of expression, sermons and woodcuts...could only represent death in a simple and striking form...the sense of the perishable nature of all things.[6]
>
> Nowhere else were all the images tending to evoke the horror of death assembled so strikingly as in the churchyard of the Innocents at Paris. There the medieval soul, fond of a religious shudder, could take its fill of the horrible.... Day after day, crowds of people walked under the cloisters, looking at the figures and reading the simple verses, which reminded them of the approaching end...it was a public lounge and a rendezvous. Shops were established before the charnal-houses and prostitutes strolled the under the cloisters.... To such an extent had the horrible come familiar.[7]

In line with this growing emphasis on the *physical* aspects of death in the waning Middle Ages Villon transforms the idealizing formal description of love in the court lyric into a physical and concrete representation of it. For Villon death is more than a convention. We might say that in Villon's work death is the *only* reality. But since death has only a decorous place in the bucolic setting of court poetry, Villon had to move the poetic *locus* from the court to the city. I would suggest that with an increased sense of realism and physicality in late medieval art comes an inevitable shift of scene to the city.[8]

If the union of love and death in the Heavenly City is to be found in the image of Christ's passion, where is it to be found in the secular city? In the human body and our attachment to it, matter which will compose and vanish. Only through the flesh can sensual love be made known, only through the flesh can we find the manifestion of death in the city of man. Thus Villon focuses on the flesh in *The Testament* through three important themes—*commerce, deception* and *metamorphosis.*

Perhaps nowhere is Villon's attitude toward love made clearer than in the *Ballade for Fat Margot.* In this poem the commerce of love is the central theme, and two differing styles are used to develop it. Villon alternates the language and style of court poetry with the slangy idiom of low-life Paris. The first stanza is composed by alternating lines in the two styles for comic effect:

> Because I love and gladly serve this woman
> Must you call me degenerate and a fool?
> She has something for the nicest taste
> For her love I strap on shield and dagger
> When clients come I run and get a pot
> And go for wine taking care to be quiet
> I offer them water, cheese, bread, and fruit
> If they pay well I tell them *"Bene stat*
> Stop in again the next time you feel horny
> In this whorehouse where we hold our state."
>
> (II. 1591-1600)

The old courtly ideals of gallantry and the heroic quest are turned inside out to become the service of a pimp to his whore and heroic expeditions to get wine and food for the lady/prostitute's clients/knights. The quest of love—a staple of medieval love poetry—is here reduced to a mercantile quest, the pursuit of greed by means of the lowest occupations. Ironically, Villon is not the noble lover striving valiantly for his chaste lady's love, but an amatory entrepreneur who offers her to other men. Her love is not sought as his exclusive property, but is offered to as wide an audience as possible. The milieu for exchange is Margot's bed; Villon acts as doorkeeper. Like an earnest member of the local chamber of commerce, Villon invites the clients to return during the next rutting season.[9] The pursuit of filth and the flight from honor are the principal occupation, but he concludes that at least it is a living, if a dishonorable one:

> Wind, hail, frost, my bread's all baked
> I'm a lecher, she's a lecher to match
> Like one of us better? We're a pair
> Like unto like, bad rat bad cat

On filth we dote, filth is our lot
Now we run from honor and honor runs from us
In this whorehouse where we hold our state.

(II. 1621-1627)

The manner in which people use each other in their attachment to
the flesh—openly and cynically—is an important part of Villon's
commercial metaphor.

The Testament's larger theme of death and fleshly decay
subsumes the metaphor of commercialism. In the *Lament of the
Belle Heaulmiere* ("the old lady's longing for the days of her youth"),
Villon presents the prostitute's, rather than the pimp's, view of
bordello life. La belle Heaulmiere is Fat Margot grown old. At the
center of her lament she contrasts the way she was—"my beauty
used to give me [great power] over merchants, clerks and
churchmen"—with her present state:

The forehead lined the hair gray
The eyebrows all fallen out, the eyes clouded
Which threw those bright glances
That felled many a poor devil
The nose hooked far from beauty
The ears hairy and lopping down
The cheeks washed out, dead and pasty
The chin furrowed, the lips just skin.

(II. 509-516)

This catalogue of the ravages of time concludes with this
observation, an echo of the late medieval cry, *momento mori!*:

This is what human beauty comes to
The arms short, the hands shriveled
The shoulders all hunched up
The breasts? Shrunk in again
The buttocks gone the way of the tits
The quim? aagh! As for the thighs
They aren't thighs now but sticks
Speckled all over like sausages.

(II. 517-524)

If the sale of flesh provides Margot and Francois with a living, the
decay of the flesh and its diminishing economic power are the
themes of la belle Heaulmiere. Her lament is for "human beauty's
end," but her subsidiary theme is the end of human love. The change
from youth to old age signifies for the old woman the loss of power
which only her (evanescent) beauty had given her:

Ah, cruel, arrogant old age
Why have you beaten me down so soon?
What holds me back from striking myself
From killing myself with a blow?

(II. 457-460)

The poem's concluding vision of the *poures vielles sotes* ("poor old fools") who are squatting on their haunches around the hemp-stalk fire summarizes the course of human beauty—youthful love flares up, burns brightly and briefly, and dies out quickly. The fate of la belle Heaulmiere is the fate of everywoman. If Margot's brothel is, in a sense, a metaphor for the world where flesh is bought and sold, so too we must see in the old prostitute's fate that all the world comes to her fate: "But so it goes with one and all," she says. The courtly lady and the daughter of joy are both prone to decay of the flesh. La belle Heaulmiere advises both to enjoy their youth. To the refrain, "love must find a place of virtue," la belle Heaulmiere points out that age and poverty work to corrupt virtue, that honesty is the luxury of youth and wealth.

Villon urges the theme of death's inevitable corruption of love more directly in his *Ballade to his Girlfriend*. Here he depicts in grotesque detail the physical decay that come in old age, urging Martha to put aside her pride. One of the conventions of the theme of *carpe diem* is the use of witty and indirect arguments. Villon breaks all these conventions by arguing with her directly, reproaching her with the cry: "See what you've done to me!" As a serious man, who frequently mingled sexual and financial commerce, and who values the women of the streets above all others, the courtly lady's *danger* is an exasperating affectation, to be mocked by time's harsh treatment:

A time is coming that will wither
Tarnish and wilt your blossoming flower
I'll laugh if my mouth will open that far
But by then it would look queer
I'll be old, you ugly, sapped of color
So drink deep while yet flows the river
Don't lead everyone into this despair
Save a poor man before he sinks under.

(II. 958-965)

In sum, the placement of human love within the larger perspective of the decay of the flesh emphasizes two common and related themes of the late Middle Ages, the mutability of the world and the deception of women. Specifically, Villon sees woman's deception as a result of her inability to envision the end of life. Were

Villon's women to feel, as he does, the link between copulation and death, they would not reserve themselves "for later."

In the most famous and enigmatic of Villon's lyrics, the *Ballade of the Ladies of Bygone Times,* there is a haunting sense of the evanescence of the flesh and the transitoriness of earthly love which all critics find difficult to describe. To his usual themes of the commercialism and deception of human love, he adds a third theme, the concept of metamorphosis. Although the ballade's subject is once again the decay of the human flesh, the poem's range touches on many different kinds of love, from the profane to the mythological to the divine.

Most of the women in the poem undergo a transformation in love which allows them to transcend the decay of the body through myth or legend. Each of the dead women is the subject of a famous love legend. There are two prostitutes (Flora and Thais), a woman who dies injured for love (Echo), a queen who used and destroyed her lovers (Jeanne de Navarre), three heroines of the *chanson de geste* (Beatrice, Alice and Berthe), a woman who died for love of God and country (Jeanne d'Arc), another who became victim of the conflict between spiritual and human love (Heloise), and the only woman to transcend death through love (the Virgin).

The enigma of Villon's haunting refrain—*Mais ou sont les neiges d'antan?"*—reminds us that the decay of the flesh is eternal, but that the legend of love may survive beyond death. Death, the shadow of the infinite, is the common lover of all these women— saint, sinner and princess alike. Only human love, which decays with the flesh, may live on in poetry, and thus achieve a literary metamorphosis. Since all must reach the same end only the fleshly pleasure of youth and the memory of love after death will be eternal. Perhaps this is why Villon's answer to the question, "where?" is another question:

> Prince you may not ask this week
> Where they are nor this year
> That I won't tell you back the refrain
> But where are the snows are last winter?

$$\text{(II. 353-356)}$$

III. EROS/THANATOS

The interlocking circles of Villon's Paris—university, tavern, prison and church—neatly hold everyone within the same precincts and contain their common struggles. Paris is its own universe and all its citizens share a common fate.[10] At court, the poet's role was to idealize and flatter his subjects, and the mark of his artistry was the separating and exclusive quality of the work. I wish to suggest that the city poet, in contrast to the court poet in his bucolic setting, makes all persons equal. His role is to show us more of what we have in common than how we differ. If we are not equal in the society of this world, we are all equal in the society of death.

The figure of Death leads us in the *danse macabre,* joining the hands of emperors with those of peasants:

> I know that the poor and the rich
> The wise and the foolish, the priests and the laymen
> The nobles, the serfs, the generous, the mean
> Small and great, handsome and ugly
> Ladies in upturned collars
> No matter what their rank
> Whether in kerchiefs or *bourrelets*
> Death seizes them without exception.
> (II. 305-312)

This image of death is one of the most important features of the late Gothic imagination throughout France. As Norman O. Brown has said, "the dance of life [is] the whole story of our wanderings; in a labyrinth of error, the labyrinth of this world."[11] As a manifestation of the error of life, which is the error of the flesh, sexual love represents the consummate original error, the fall and the act of making unequal: "The woman penetrated is the labyrinth.... Every coitus repeats the fall; brings death, birth, into the world."[12] As Villon sees it, the city of the world is the body of the world. The decay of each body prefigures the decay of the race.

To the extent that the courtly, bucolic ideal of love denies the existence of death, except at the periphery of the erotic play, it attempts to elevate the court beyond the grip of *thanatos.* The bucolic setting suggests the pre-lapsarian *etas prima.* This may account for the coy treatmet of themes of sexual fulfillment and death in court poetry. Villon changed this convention, however, by placing *thanatos* at the very center of *eros,* and in so doing, changed the bucolic ideal of separation into the urban ideal of equalization.

Psychologists tell us that *eros* is the instinct to make "whole," whereas *thanatos* is divisive and destructive. I think that we must reverse this metaphor if we are to understand the popular mind of the Middle Ages. We must see that contrary to accepted theory love is what stratifies, divides, separates, drives asunder; is insecure and uncertain, a shadow of higher love, as it is codified in the court literature of Gothic Europe. Only when human love is finally described as subject to the death of the flesh is it possible to have "wholeness." The city is the post-lapsarian state, the *locus* for observing the human condition. The city channels energy toward death or money, which is the same thing.[13] At the waning of the Middle Ages, the poetic metropolis cannot be called the *erotopolis;* it is rather the *necropolis.*

By inverting the common metaphorical relationship between *eros* and *thanatos* Villon made possible a new kind of writing, wherein the identification of the self and the body—ordinarily reserved only for popular verse—can be combined with courtly subjects and themes. The late medieval obsession with the vision of death finds vivid representation in the works of Villon, paradoxically bringing new life to late medieval culture. No longer is the world of the self kept separate from the world as inhabited—a courtly rather than a popular sentiment—but that very self becomes itself, its own state: "The real apocalypse comes not with the vision of a city or a kingdom which would be external, but with the identification of the city and the kingdom with one's own body."[15] For the popular mind in art, at the dawn of the European Renaissance, *eros* was the way to separation from self, *thanatos* the road to union and equality. This transformative vision of Francois Villon signals the shift of culture from the rural court to the more egalitarian city.

Notes

[1]Johan Huizinga, *The Waning of the Middle Ages* (1924; rpt. Garden City, N.Y.: Doubleday, 1954), pp. 39-40.

[2]Gervase Mathew, *The Court of Richard II* (London: John Murray, 1968), pp. 53, 107.

[3]Villon's *ballade*, "Des contres verites," is written entirely in the style *per antiphrasim.* The "Epitre a Marie d'Orleans" is a *royal panegyric.* The "Ballade a s'amye" is a *lover's complainte,* as is the "Ballade de la Belle Heaulmiere."

[4]The standard French edition of the works is that of Auguste Longnon—Lucien Foulet, *Francois Villon, Oeuvres* (Paris: H. Champion, 1967). All translations into English are taken from the facing-page edition of Galway Kinnell, *The Poems of Francois Villon* (Boston: Houghton Mifflin, 1977). The passage here is lines 1709-1712.

[5]*The Inferno,* tr. John Ciardi (New York: New American Library, 1954), p. 42.

[6]Huizinga, p. 146.

[7]Ibid., pp. 148-49.

[8]Eugene Robison Swigart, "Three Poets of the City: Theocritus, Villon and Beaudelaire," Diss. SUNY Buffalo, 1972, pp. 32, 151.

[9]David Kuhn, *La poetique de Francois Villon* (Paris: Armand Colin, 1967), p. 30.

[10]See St. Augustine, *City of God,* 18.2: "The city of man, for all the width of its expansion throughout the world and for all the depth of its differences in this place and that, is a single community. The simple truth is that the bond of common nature makes all human beings one." Compare Norman O. Brown, *Love's Body* (New York: Random House, 1966), p. 40: "For the true form of unification—which can be found either in psychoanalysis or in Christianity, in Freud or Pope John, or Karl Marx—is: 'we are all members of one body'."

[11]*Love's Body,* p. 40.

[12]Ibid., p. 48.

[13]"The dehumanization of man is his alienation of his own body. He thus acquires a

soul...but the soul is located in things. Money is the world's soul. And gold...is the death of the Body.... What then is a city? A city reflects the new masculine aggressive psychology of revolt against the female principles of dependence and nature" [Norman O. Brown, *Life Against Death* Middletown, Conn.: Wesleyan University Press, 1959), pp. 281-282]. Thus Villon's bequests of worthless coins, or goods which he does not possess, lifts from him the onus of money's corrupting influence: *radix malorum omnium cupiditas.*

[14]Northrop Frye, *Fearful Symmetry: A Study of William Blake* (Boston: Beacon Press, 1947), p. 431.

XIV

Social Themes in Urban Broadsides of Renaissance England

With Frederick O. Waage's article we cross the Gutenberg divide, for he is dealing with printed popular sources. Yet Waage argues persuasively that the broadside ballads operated in an oral tradition, not that much different from the manuscript designs of the South English Legendary or from the songsheets distributed among youth groups today. Printed only to be memorized and sung to popular tunes, these ballads are throwaway culture, like so much later popular culture. The throwaway character and the anonymous authorship combine to make much of the methodology of popular culture studies akin to the archaeologist's fitting together of incomplete jigsaws, and yet, emerging from both, we can discern patterns of culture. Waage's article opens with the ballad of an audacious, somewhat irreverent type of woman that we will recognize as not too far from television's Maude; *other ballads cited will anticipate the journalistic sensationalism of tabloids and* True Detective Mysteries; *but at the same time, we are aware of narrative styles and character types reaching back to the Middle Ages. Folklorists will readily identify type-motifs among the broadside ballads. Themes from previous articles, such as the concepts of death, of the city and of moral education are easily discerned, and a theme that is latent throughout this collection, that of woman, becomes salient here.*

Frederick O. Wagge is an Assistant Professor of English at East Tennessee State University.

Social Themes in Urban Broadsides of Renaissance England

Frederick O. Waage

In the early seventeenth-century broadside ballad of the "Wanton Wife of Bath,"[1] the Wife, of Chaucerian renown, comes to heaven to seek admittance. As all the saints, companions and precursors of Christ, from Solomon to Mary Magdalen, deny her admittance for her sins; she scolds back at them, pointing to *their* sins, which she does not share:

"Who knocketh there?" quote Judith then, "with such shrill sounding Notes?"
"This fine minks surely cannot hear," quoth she, "for cutting throats."

Good Lord! how Judith blush'd for shame, when she heard her say no.
(Rox., VII, 215)

Even Christ's pardon and admission of her, after she has abashed His heavenly company, is motivated by the presumptuous parable she teaches him:

"Do thou forgive me now," quoth she, "most lewdly I did live;
But yet the loving Father did his Prodigal son forgive."
(Rox., VII, 215)

The Wife is "bad," as a common scold, a "froward wife," yet she has nationalistic literary connotations that make her ambivalently heroic. Although her ballad is mainly matter of amusement, her behavior at heaven's gate is definitely subversive of conventional piety, Anglican or Puritan; as a pure, self-confessed scold, she is somehow more admirable than the hypocritical saints. She forces them to become humanized, identified by their sins. The scold makes heaven her own sitting room.

The Wanton Wife is one of many ambivalent social types, caught in ambivalent dramatic situations, who flourished in London printed broadside ballads of the sixteenth and seventeenth centuries. They were created at a crucial time and place in a culture that was transforming through the growth of urban society, and through religious and social conflict. Many broadsides, such as this

242

one, of the time, bring together in unholy union the sacred and the profane, the social and spiritual realms of man's and woman's being. They evoke the self-contradictoriness of traditional world views. Precisely because of their "ephemeral" nature, they are more expressive of Renaissance culture than "literary" creations, written to endure, stylized by aesthetic or intellectual structures.

The texts of printed broadsides were prosodically organized to fit new or ancient tunes, known by heart, referred to on the broadsheets by title only: "To the tune of——". The themes, ideas, histories contained in urban broadsides were mostly chosen to be of immediate, local, topical interest, to the widest possible audience. They were thus often inherently reductive and "democratic"—so universal in appeal at their moment in time that they did not exclude hearers and understanders for religious or social reasons.[2]

Crucially a broadside is printed yet not meant to be printed. Once the buyer has memorized the words, the folio broadsheet can be thrown away.[3] Its fragility and disposability explain why most broadsides of Tudor and Stuart times exist in one or a few copies only. The broadsides are the architect's plans, not the building itself—directions for the creation of a *purely oral* experience. Urban ballad-writers wrote to be heard, not read. Individual, not "collective"[4] creators, many of whose names are known to us, they had definable artistic identities, yet were uninhibited by the possibility of permanence that could give form and topical irrelevance to the books of their contemporaries, the "serious" professional musicians and lyricists, such as Morley and Campion. In many ways the broadsides are the "White House Tapes" of Renaissance literature; their survival was not intended. They are "truer" than sanctioned literature. They capture the proverbial experiential human reality of their time.

Most studies of broadsides have considered only those of the Restoration and after; the idea of the "Other Victorians" is more titillating today than that of the "Other Elizabethans."[5] Although there are extensive and well-known library collections of broadsides, the growing interest in popular culture has not resulted in their editing or reprinting to any significant degree. In fact the best accessible Renaissance collection, which is source of most of the texts discussed below, remains that of the "Roxburghe Ballads," made by the Ballad Society in the 1870s and 80s. A deeper reason than the cost of book production today lies behind contemporary lack of interest in reprinting earlier broadsides: we discount their value because we don't know how to read—or "hear" —them. We hear their conventionality, not their radicalism and uniqueness. The "Wanton Wife of Bath" is jocular, grating, lacks the "lyric purity" and mystery that we tend to associate, as a mark of "value," with the Child ballads, for example. The song we call "Greensleeves" today is really just one of many lyrics set to the tune which took its name from that particularly admirable one, and survived through many others. Our identification of particular words with particular music is significant: we don't credit the broadsides' words, since their music is mostly lost to us, or at a remove from the words; and the words themselves do not possess the sophistication and complexity associated with literary Renaissance poetry.

London broadsides are generally "external"—their themes are on the surface, satiric of, rather than compassionate toward, what they represent. The primal duality in many is that of the reaffirmation and denial of commonly held beliefs about how people should behave toward each other as God-fearing Christians. The Wanton Wife of Bath is one of many ballad-shrews. Her name makes her conventional. But the scene her ballad dramatizes creates the social paradox of her preaching to the Fathers with reason. The ballad writer is not naive; he is playing with her assumed conventionality, not subverting our response to it by placing it in an "impossible" situation. Of course, he could not do this unless there were a powerful consensus of non-paradoxical broadside expression.

This pious orthodoxy is most evident in the religious broadsides, yet even in these the most ritual bewailings of sin hold surprises. A most common genre of religious broadsides is the complaint of the sinner against the evil world. The speaker is strongly individuated in religious broadsides. As heard, rather than seen, the singer "becomes" the sinner, and his identity, rather than his credo, is what the hearer fixes attention on, and derives his truth from. Thus, in "The Sorrowful Lamentation of a Penitent Sinner" (Rox., VIII, 99), we have unexceptional supplication:

I am afraid of Thee, O Lord, because thou didst me beat,
But yet I know that Jesus Christ will for my soul entreat.

But the individuation can lead to an irreverent source of faith:

But do not beat me overmuch, my loving Father sweet,
Lest that this frail land wicked flesh should from sweet Jesus fleet.

This sounds more like a threat than a submission; moreover, our "Father" becomes, through the repetitions of "beat," almost a human father, threatened by his beaten offspring—a situation of the "prodigal son" ballads described below.

The "recantation of an ill-led life" is often the form taken by a sinner's self-complaint. Through its topical circumstance, as well as individuation of the speaker, it ties the ballad-singer to the life of the hearer. Franklin's Tyburn farewell is representative:

> Oh, let my ending of my loathed breath
> Make all men care to shun eternall death![6]

The ballad-singer, as at one with the condemned sinner, of course tends to make him more of a physical presence than a moral abstraction. The more truths the singer-sinner utters, the more he gains a human sympathy from his hearers at odds with his abstract moral status. Perhaps even more than in the complexities of a dramatic homiletic tragedy, the repentant ballad-villain's monologue—as one condemned, fulfilling law, and pardoned, fulfilling grace—makes him an individual hero, transcending categories and the very homiletic reason for his speech:

> Though my life eternall fire did merit,
> Yet God in mercy hath receiv'd my spirit.
> Farwell, my countrey, by whose iustice I
> For mine vniust and bloody action dye! (B-L.B., 87)

The autobiographical penitent, like the famous Luke Hutton, is more interesting for his texture of life than for his spiritual role. As exemplary sinner, he provocatively turns the world upside-down. With twelve fellows, whom he calls his twelve apostles, Luke robs from the rich. To keep him out of trouble, he is given a sinecure, a job as a jailor, in which condition he is captured and imprisoned. His kinfolk bewail that he "should hazzard life and lands" rather than that he should sin. His lawless life is ordered by ceremony: born on St. Luke's day, he celebrates ; "In honor of my Birth-day then / I rob'd in bravery nineteen men."[7] Underlying the many conventional words of warning against his vices are the amorally appealing patterns of the events of his immediate life. The ballad's role is twofold: it separates, through its "I" voice, doctrine and experience, what Luke is and what he believes.

The anonymous author of "A Godly Ballad" (Rox., III, 198), strings together pious commonplaces to make us aware of passing time and desirous of harvesting "grapes of grace." Yet the hearer becomes aware that beside the conventional moral conclusions from mutability (in complement, not contradiction) is a non-Christian vision of unredeemed mutability:

Men for the most part do rejoice
    When sons to them are born,
Whose weeping eyes bewail their woes,
    Our sinfulnesse to scorn;
They are the messengers of death,
    Our time is passing fast. . . .(Rox., III, 198)

That newborn babies' cries are for their fathers' sins is a pretty exaggerated conceit of devout pessimism. That babies are "messengers of death," in body and spirit, is "true," but goes against conventional iconography of nativity as hope. Some of the paradox in this ballad may be attributed to its female authorship. The anonymity of broadsides allows them to be extremely personal, since the authorial voice cannot be traced. But it is also the literal voice of the ballad's singer. When the ballad lyricist injects his or her own persona into a ballad, it becomes, when sung, the voice and personality of the singer before you. The authoress of "A Godly Ballad" ends her ballad by singing about it, when it is still in progress, as though piety were merchandise:

This have I done to please your will,
    Now let me have my hire;
I have bewray'd my want of skil
    In doing your desire.
The weakness of a woman's wit
    Is not through Nature's fault,
But lack of education fit
    Makes Nature oft to halt. (Rox., III, 199)

The voice of the singer addressing "you" the hearer directly creates a "meta-ballad"; confused pietistic verses become demonstrations of a social paradox. This paradox is that education, conventionally human "art" added to nature, is something within and *prior to* fulfilled nature. The ballad-singer (author) draws an unacceptably feminist sociology therefrom: that women are by implication naturally wise or skilled; the deprivation of education necessary to fulfill this inherent wisdom is against nature. The spiritual truth of female inferiority is socially a falsehood.

    The ballads discussed above have evoked a disparity between religious and secular "reality." The aesthetic analogue of this difference is that between the extremely individual and the extremely formulaic—formulaic social types like the suicidal maiden and the shrewish wife, or formulaic verbal constructs like the impossible prophecy or the dialogue of gossips. The formulae of the "Godly Ballad" were vividly invaded by the individual voice of the writer (singer). Ballads overtly concerned with secular

matters—social morality, family life, love, money—tend even more
strongly to interject the singer's uniqueness into formulae. Each of
the countless topical news ballads of murders, rapes, abductions
makes a song of a unique event that is also an instance, for
reflection, of the failure of the assumed social order.

Most frequent, grievous and fascinating are the broadsides of
hostility and violence between members of urban middle-class or
working-class families. The ubiquitous tune of "Fortune My Foe"
makes a timeless exemplum of "Anne Wallens Lamentation. For the
Murthering of her husband John Wallen a Turner in Cowlane neere
Smithfield; done by his owne wife, on Satterday the 22 of June, 1616,
who was burnt in Smithfield the first of July following" (Rox., I, 85).
As usual, the author has given to the vividness of his Anne Wallen's
tale of what happened a gloss of confessional rhetoric: "My dearest
husband did I wound to death, / And was the cause he lost his
sweetest breath" (Rox., I, 86). Embedded in the imposed meaning is
the graphic and brilliant dialogue-verse, where "Anne" tells how
she cursed out her husband for coming home late and drunk from
bar-hopping. In argument "He then arose and strooke me on the
eare," whereat Anne got (with unthought symbolism) one of his own
tools:

> Amongst his intrailes I this Chissell threw,
> Where as his Caule came out, for which I rue,
> What has thou don, I prethee looke quoth he,
> Thou hast thy wish, for thou hast killed me. (Rox., 86).

John lives only until the next day: "Wives be warned, example
take by me." "Anne's" moral meaning is "don't kill your husband";
her reported experience is of a "natural" emotional response of
defense, with a morally appropriate weapon, to violence and attack.
The primal social crime of creating death where there should be
divine love—between the married couple—is given, in the ballad,
emotional (non-moral) causes by the criminal herself. Anne reponds
to her husband's violation of the household order with immoderate
words; he makes the fatal (and unjustified in household
government) response of blows to her words. It is Anne's equivalent
physical response that produces death. Emotionally her action is
the equivalent of his. But the broadside's *moral* gloss experiences
only the death. The narrator's psychological meaning includes the
circumstances of the death; Anne, as persona, has to accept the
meaninglessness of her circumstances to be able to lament her
unjustified murder. The broadside's hearers would experience
conflicting senses of murder—as sin, and as understandable action.

When a domestic tale is not of an actual, topical event, but one the writer has fabricated, using a formulaic plot, there are other possibilities for doubleness of meaning. "The Husband who met with his match" (Rox., III, 224) has a version of the January and May motif: an older miser marries a series of ancient wives, who quickly die, leaving him their money. Then he imprudently marries a young woman, canny, who starts spending his money so profligately that it drives him to his grave, leaving her with his inheritance to use in attracting young suitors. The "tamer tamed" formula here, within this plot, involves a cynical poetic justice, of cupidity, and only when the miser "fails" to an act of sexual, versus financial, cupidity. Also it emphasizes the strong tendency of all social ballads to covertly vindicate their women. The dramatic focus which most breaks the formulaic mold is the third of the "old" wives, "not above fifty at most," who, on their marriage night, starts removing all her false "comely" attributes (like her husband's desires, they are non-living):

> Two rowes of white teeth she tooke out of her mouth,
> And put 'em straight into a little round boxe;
> A glasse eye likewise she pull'd out of her head,
> Which made the man feare that his wife had got knocks.
>
> (Rox., III, 278-279)

(Naturally her appearance doesn't faze him; he only fears she has syphilis.) In sequence the lady removes her false hair and her wooden leg. Even when she has removed most of what makes her human, she ("to revive him") throws him ironically the keys to her treasure, and this "...made him to love her, so both went to bed, / Where he did embrace her: what would you have more?"

By creating this artificial lady, and saying "What would you have more?" the balladeer has established a symbolic social world of social materialism, which denies even simple sexuality as meaningful. His view of the world is about the same as the miser's, whom the formulaic story-line is directed toward chastising morally; thus he subtly discredits his own moral. The miser wasn't evil, he was just not clever enough.

Social relationships in broadsides are often expressed in consciousness of the difference between urban and rural life. London city is a universe whose laws contradict, or pose impossible challenges to, life governed by Christian belief. How can "rural" innocence be preserved in the city? The heroine of "A Fayre Portion for a Fayre Maid" (Rox., I, 365) by Martin Parker, one of the most prominent and prolific Jacobean balladeers, is one of many rural maids new to the city. The ballad's subtitle is

> The thriftie Mayd of Worstershire
> Who lives at London for a Marke a yeare;
> This Marke was her old mother's gift,
> Shee teacheth all Mayds how to shift.

This maid lives richly off the gifts that her suitors, from all walks of urban life, give her; like an amoral, single Penelope, she keeps her suitors in hope but unfulfilled. Her virtue becomes coin, yet is preserved by the men who buy their own fantasies of its loss:

> Though I am but a silly wench,
>   of countrey education,
> Yet I am woo'd by Dutch and French,
>   and almost every nation:
> Both Spaniards and Italians sweare
>   that with their hearts they love me deare:
> *Yet I have but a marke a yeare,*
>   *and that my mother gave me.* (Rox., I, 366)

Since this maid loves riches, scorns her rural kin, wants her country sister to come and try her method, she is a very tarnished mirror of modesty. The twin of her story of virtue preserved in the diabolical city is that of the maiden who falls, gets pregnant by a man unknown, and then must try to restore social morality by finding a husband after the fact: "Pitty the state of a teeming maid / that never was wife, yet must be a mother" (Rox., III, 47). The dramatic "I" in this broadside of the "Witty Western Lasse" tells no adventures. Her monologue concerns her state of mind, how to choose action to cope, deserted by her lover, with both survival and the scorn and disinterest of the "world." Her condition is social, not moral. Her salvation also is to go to London:

> Obscurely Ile lye, where none shall descry me:
>   And when I am eased of my paine
>   And cruell gripings in my belly,
> I for a maid will passe
>   And need not cry, alack, a welly! (Rox., III, 48-49)

In the second half of the western lass's ballad she tells her plans: she will use the amoral jungle of the city as a paradoxical restorative for her virtue. Once delivered of the baby (its fate is not her concern):

> Some trades-man there I will deceive,

> by my modesty and carriage,
> And I will so my self behave
> as by some trick to get a marriage. (Rox., III, 49)

And if marriage doesn't work, she will live merrily with whatever men are willing. She recognizes her planned course as "odious," but since it is forced on her, she will be merry in it. It is hard to know whether this amoral confession is meant to be experienced with irony, as critical of her resolve. It seems unlikely since the value she presents is an elevated freedom from subjection to your own emotions, particularly despair. Importantly, the first part of the ballad presents her sympathetic woefulness as a deserted and betrayed girl; the second part, on the broadsheet's reverse side, details her cynical aims for survival in London. As pitifully deceived and pitilessly deceiving, country innocent and London wench, the lass's double self is conveyed by the separate but equal sides of the broadsheet. Complementing the disposability of broadsides such as this one is their inconclusiveness; in social ballads, the second part and side is an answer to the first, e.g. the speeches of the wooer and the wooed. There is no "third side," no resolved answer. The broadsheet has a structure of dialectic, not logic.

"The Userer and the Spendthrift" (Rox., I, 129) is a good example of the use of this irresolution. Money's power, we have seen, is an essential leveller of virtue. The motto of this broadside is "What the father gathereth by the Rake, the Sonne doth scatter with the forke." The first part (side) is the father's monologue-ditty in praise of his gold. The second is the prodigal son's description and lament of his spending it. The first is headed by a woodcut of the father raking in gold, the second of the son raking it out. Though each one's monologue ends with a morally appropriate warning against the practice which defines him, the broadside's deeper pattern is one of inevitable action and reaction, getting and spending being as fixed and inevitable patterns as the seasons. The spendthrift is a "prodigal son" whose life-course is a governing motif for many male broadside protagonists, as that of the defiled virgin is for females. The prodigal likewise violates accepted social order.

"A Warning to Youth" is a powerful late sixteenth-century ballad telling the life of a London merchant's prodigal son who goes wild upon his father's death (Rox., III, 36). He establishes a harem of mistresses richly dressed in male attire. His insatiable lust is for sexual novelty. He sells this establishment and travels "into countries strange," "strange women for to know." In Antwerp he meets, courts, inebriates with wine, and ravishes, a widow's beauteous virginal daughter. Pregnant, she becomes a type of the "western lass," but unlike her, she does not identify with and merrily accept fate:

> "This babe that breedeth in my wombe,"
> quoth she, "shall nere be borne,
> Nor call'd a bastard by such wives
>   that hold such loves in scorn...." (Rox., III, 39)

"Ill Fame" is her bane, more than lost virtue; but she symbolically destroys her child by killing herself drinking burning wine. Her mother's widow's curse "miraculously" succeeds in rotting away the prodigal's limbs, burning out his mouth. But, concluding with "take heed," the ballad-writer yet uses the instance of Richard III and Queen Margaret to parallel the power of the widow's curse. This meeting of the prodigal and the wronged maid and widow is eternally perpetuable, made more so by the historical analogy with royalty (Richard III as the ur-seducer). The ballad's warning is subsidiary to the "inevitability" of the dramatic meeting of prodigal and victim, and the sensuous scene of seduction.

Betrayal of the uncorruptibly innocent by the unrepentant guilty as motif also involves the common theme of betrayal of parents by children, breaking the lines of life. In "A Most Excellent New ballad of an Olde Man and His Wife" (Rox., II, 348), the old couple, impoverished, are on pilgrimage to their gallant son's new house. Although the balladeer writes in the third person, he intensely individuates the couple:

> They sate them on the green,
> Their shoos and hose to trim,
> And put clean bands about their necke,
> Against they should enter in. (Rox., III, 349)

But despite their desperate pleas ("I bore thee in this womb, / These breasts did nourish thee") the son casts them off emotionlessly: "The world is not now as when I was borne, / All things are grown more deare." But the son's own children, seeing how successful he was with his parents, decide to do the same with him. Like his parents before, he pleads, but " 'Speake not to us' quote they, / 'For thou the death shalt dye!' " (Rox., III, 351); and they take his gold. But their cousin, hearing of this, comes "with a great club, / In dead time of the night," and kills them, takes the gold, until he himself is captured and killed. On one level this is a genealogy of divine retribution (like the prodigal's miraculous overthrow before). In its more direct sung experience, it is a microcosmic family-society's inherited, self-created "law" of self-destruction, with no divine import. The son creates a value-system, and his children uphold it. Like John Wallen, the turner, this son establishes the "natural" circumstances of his own destruction; the ballad chronicles the results of a willed choice.

Our patterns of conflicting religious and secular order can conclude with a companion ballad to "The Wanton Wife of Bath": "The Devil and the Scold" (Rox., II, 366). The writer prepared his broadside to be experienced purely orally, for he or she begins:

> Give eare, my loving countrey-men
> that still desire newes,
> Nor passe not while you hear it sung,
> or else the song peruse....

The song has a secular morality: learn of the scold how to "gull the world." But the scold it evokes is so evil that she is determined to contrary her husband in everything:

> Bade he, "Wife go to church,
> and take the fairest pew."
> Shee'd goe unto an alehouse,
> and drinke, lye downe, and spew....(Rox., II, 369)

The Devil, enticed by her contrariety, makes a deal with the husband to get the scold to go with him to hell. Then in the working of a folk ballad that was widespread and apparently timeless, in shape of a horse, he seduces her to mount him, but she refuses to dismount, drives him where she will, torments him as though he was in hell, even marks his ear as her property. In the end, desperate, he bears her back to the husband as too evil even for hell to handle. The writer is so opposed to scolds that he even rejects them as customers: "But, honest men and wives, / buy these before you go." This scold is both social villain, in this comic mold, and collective cultural heroine. She is "redeemed" by the power of her vice.

All the broadsides I have discussed in some way or other present a "double vision" of social reality; they make truth more difficult to accept collectively. And they represent only a tiny fraction of the entire rich diversity of subjects and themes sung of in the streets of sixteenth and seventeenth London. As ambiguous and influential works of art and shapers of cultural history, on the divide between oral and written expression, many being essentially written down versions of common folk ballads, the broadsides deserve much more currency among students of popular culture than they have yet received.

Notes

[1] *The Roxburghe Ballads,* ed. W. Chappell and J.W. Ebsworth (Hertford, England, 1890), VII, 212-16. All citations from other ballads printed in this series are identified "Rox.," with volume and page number.

[2] Many broadsides are versions of elegant writings by non-"popular" authors. Marlowe's "Come live with me and be my love..." and Raleigh's reply to it, for example, were printed on opposing sides of a broadsheet. The balladeers took all of London and English life as their subject, and often they reported events with amazing rapidity. For example, generally the accounting of a hanging or other execution (with woodcut picture of the "victim") was on the streets the day before the event took place. Further, there were many genuine folk songs and ballads taken down from someone's memory and redistributed by this printed word.

[3] The titular woodcuts in broadsides pose a challenge to the idea that they were not perceived in their time as having inherent aesthetic value or form as printed material. Increasingly, standard interchangeable blocks were replaced by blocks carved for a specific broadsheet. When Samuel Pepys collected broadsides, he appreciated their aesthetics with the sophisticated interest in naivete with which one might collect bumper stickers today.

[4] Martin Parker, Lawrence Price, William Elderton were some of the prominent broadside creators. The theory of "collective"origin of *traditional* ballads, although of some importance in past debates has now generally been discredited and is tenable only in the light of some known or unknown individual presenting his unsigned work "as though it were" collective, that is the work of various hands and voices. This self-representation as "vox populi" is potentially subversive, as the persuasive pamphlet literature preceding the English Revolution was to demonstrate strongly.

[5] The connection between "popular" and Elizabethan and Jacobean writing, and the skeptical innovations of science and social theory of the time has not been sufficiently investigated. My forthcoming article in the *Huntington Library Quarterly,* "Touching the Compass: Empiricism in Popular Scientific Writing of Bacon's Time," approaches the subject. The "Other Elizabethans" were, in one sense, the mass of artisans and "empiricks" who, like the broadside writers, were judging experience by cause and effect, not by dogma.

[7] Of course, criminals like Luke Hutton and Gamaliel Ratsey were celebrated in print in other forms than the broadside ballad; the main difference between a ballad and a confessional pamphlet is the immediacy of the sinner's voice.

Bibliographical Note

Broadside ballads have been incredibly neglected in 20th century scholarship. Still comprehensive is Hyder E. Rollins' article, "The Black-Letter Broadside Ballad," *PMLA*, 1919, 258-336. The two books of any comprehensive note are Leslie Shepard's *The Broadside Ballad* (London, 1962), and Claude M. Simpson's *The British Broadside Ballad and its Music* (New Brunswick, N.J., 1966). Neither of these books, rich in information though they are, discusses broadsides in any depth as literary works, for social or psychological content. Shepard's book has a good bibliography, including the main printed collections of broadsides accessible, *The Roxburgh Ballads* (see note one), reprinted in 1966 by the AMS

Press, and Hyder E. Rollins' collections, of which the most vast is *The Pepys Ballads,* 8 vols. (Harvard, 1929-32). An earlier volume, which should be a model for any future studies of ballads and broadsides is Charles R. Baskervill's *The Elizabethan Jig.*

XV

The Role of the Masses in Shaping the Reformation

Unquestionably the invention of movable-type printing was one of the factors that made possible the Lutheran Reformation, for without widely-distributed Bibles, the concept of "every man his own priest" was empty words. And unquestionably the Reformation was one of the main factors in increasing literacy in the modern world. Yet, as Peter J. Klassen points out in this article, literacy was not a requisite for choosing sides in the early Reformation. Cartoons, ballads, sermons, political oratory and lively discussions constituted as much or more of the media of influence upon the popular movement of the Reformation as the printed word.

In the previous two articles an aspect of popular culture has emerged that is the main topic of Klassen's "The Role of the Masses in Shaping the Reformation." This is the concept of the populace as social entity and historical force. As was remarked in Schroeder's introductory essay to this volume, modern marxist scholars have emphasized this aspect of popular culture and Klassen discusses marxist contributions to the issue that he is addressing. The issue is one of causation: was Protestantism furthered only by action of established political powers, or was it the result of a mass movement? Klassen sets forth the prevalent answers to the question and thereupon tests the matter by close and exhaustive attention to the records of many German cities and towns. What develops from the evidence is a complicated and dynamic pattern of causes and influences, for which simplistic or ideological explanations are inadequate. One brief instance brings curious echoes of Marchese's article of the classical city of some sixteen centuries earlier: in the city of Rottweil in 1529, the populace was leaning so heavily toward Lutheranism that the council invited the peasants from the surrounding villages to help resolve the issue. They were strongly in favor of the old religion, and thus rustic villagers helped established townsmen to win a majority for Catholicism.

Peter J. Klassen is a Professor of History and has served as Dean of the School of Social Sciences at California State University, Fresno. He is author of The Economics of Anabaptism, 1525-1560, Church and State in Reformation Europe *and numerous journal articles.*

Erflerūg, der schendlichen
Sünde der jenigen/die durch das Concilium/
Interim/vñ Adiaphora/von Christo zum Antichrist fallen / aus diesen
Prophetischen gemelde/des z. Eliae seliger gedechtnis/D. M. Luth. genomen.
Durch Matth. Fla. Illyr.

1545.

The gullible masses of Germany, symbolized by the pig, are warned not to be tricked by the papacy into deserting Luther by accepting a compromise with the pope.

The Role of the Masses in Shaping the Reformation

Peter J. Klassen

Few assumptions concerning the Reformation in the Empire have been so unhesitatingly asserted and so widely accepted as the view that political establishments determined local responses to the Reformation. Generations of historians have perpetuated the view that the Reformation was "imposed from above."[1] Many scholars speak of the "magisterial" Reformation in which the magistracy is regarded as the decisive factor. Government officials are seen as those who shape policy and implement it; the citizenry as a whole is of little consequence. The magistracy, whether in the person of a territorial prince, city councils or territorial ecclesiastical princes, was sufficiently powerful to determine which religious changes, if any, would be adopted in a particular city or territory. A typical expression of this viewpoint is found in the Reformation volume of the *New Cambridge Modern History:* "...the Reformation maintained itself wherever the lay power (princes or magistrates) favored it; it could not survive where the authorities decided to suppress it."[2] Similarly, a prominent American Reformation specialist has written: "Only one comment may be made safely: people became Protestant (at least outwardly) whenever their ruler commanded them to do so."[3] Such conclusions continue to characterize a large part of Reformation historiography.

Many contemporary Reformation historians take this assumption for granted. If there is any doubt, a quick reference to "cuius regio, eius religio" is surely more than adequate to persuade the hesitant. Owen Chadwick, in his Pelican *History of the Reformation* regards the decisive role of the temporal power as beyond serious question. "Throughout the Empire, from Hamburg in the North to Zurich or Geneva in the south, the cities easily accepted the new doctrine and their councils easily undertook the reform and supervision of the parishes."[4] The questions of why city councils undertook such action, or what role the citizenry played in decision-making,however, are left unanswered.

Other historians have depicted the Peasants Revolt as a major turning point as far as the significance of popular opinion is concerned. Under the leadership of Thomas Muentzer and other champions of the peasants, thousands of the poor rose against their oppressors, usually the local landlord. The poorly-led and ill-equipped armies of the peasants proved no match for the military forces of the lords, and soon the revolt was drowned in a sea of blood. Some historians have argued that the bitterly disappointed peasants now turned against Luther and his reformation. They had learned that the will of the masses counted for little. Similar conclusions have been expressed by various Marxist historians. One of the recent writings of a historians' "collective" in the German Democratic Republic depicted Luther as having provided an opportunity for the exploited peasants and the town laborers to rise against their oppressors, but by 1523 the "peasant-plebeian masses"[5] were being deserted by him, for he had drawn ever closer to the territorial princes and the emerging capitalistic bourgeoisie. When the populace learned that Luther's religious reformation could not be used to effect a social revolution, Luther and his reformation lost their popular appeal.[6] A new champion of the exploited poor appeared: Thomas Muentzer now led what the late Soviet historian M.M. Smirin described as a "people's reformation."[7] Then, with Muentzer's defeat, according to the German Marxist Alfred Meusel, the reformation movement was narrowed to "a reformation of the princes."[8]

Such sentiments are, of course, by no means limited to Marxist historians. Widely-used textbooks have perpetuated the idea that, after the Peasants Revolt, Lutheranism ceased to have "broad class support."[9] Similarly, James MacKinnon spoke for many when he wrote that with the defeat of the peasants, "Lutheranism ceased to be a popular creed,"[10] while one of the most prominent historians writing today contends that after the Peasants Revolt, the "Magisterial Reformation in Germany stood with the princes and patricians."[11]

The early Lutheran movement has, of course, always been recognized as having gained broad popular support. Cardinal Aleander's frequent references to the popular clamor for Luther are a fair indication of the alarm felt by many contemporaries. But such support has not generally been regarded as a decisive factor in shaping Reformation policies. Recently an increasing number of scholars has come to insist that townsmen and peasants have been underestimated as participants in the drama of that age. Studies such as those of Bernd Moeller, [12] Franz Lau,[13] Helmar Junghans,[14] Gerhard Seebass,[15] and others have supplied an overdue corrective. Further examination of archival sources is needed to determine the extent to which popular opinion actually forced the hand of the magistrate, and why the populace acted as it did. In numerous instances, the magistracy vigorously opposed the Reformation, yet it was introduced and established. Popular pressure was often a decisive factor, both before and after the Peasants Revolt. Obviously, the administrative machinery of the political establishment was used, as the vehicle for change, but such action was often the result of coercing the magistrates. In some instances, where magistrates refused to respond to popular pressure, they were summarily removed from office.

Instances of popular pressure prevailing over the wishes of the magistracy are numerous. At the same time, they are clearly not universal, and so generalizations about the decisive role of the peasants or the townsmen are dangerous—just as sweeping assertions about the all-powerful role of the magistrates are inaccurate. It must be remembered that the Germany of Reformation times was composed of scores of political entities, such as independent principalities, imperial free cities and ecclesiastical territories. Political structures varied from substantially democratic to virtually absolute, from essentially independent to the largely subordinate. No formula fits all situations in this mosaic, and no uniform policy of responding to the challenge of the Reformation is to be found. But two conclusions can be safely made: towns and territories did not become Protestant or remain Catholic simply because their princes or town councils told them to do so, nor did the populace respond only to any one specific stimulus.

Some indication of the significance of popular opinion is suggested by the extensive efforts put forth to shape that opinion. Avalanches of pamphlets and broadsides were often loosed upon communities (see illustrations), while persuasive orators addressed crowds in city squares and elsewhere. Often the popular movements generated their own forms of expression and expansion, as is demonstrated by the numerous ballads and folksongs which swept the crowds along.[16] Illiteracy was not so great a barrier to propaganda efforts as might be expected, for the cartoons of the broadsides often told the story as compellingly as any treatise could. Beyond that, public orators, or readers, to assembled throngs, further mitigated the problems of illiteracy, while the emotions generated by the songs of the time needed no written expression. Clearly the masses were subject to manipulation by many elements, but that did not mean that their aroused sentiments, however biased or ill-informed, were inconsequential in shaping events. The 16th century towns and villages were often swayed by crowds who were aroused, and in their excitement were determined to control their destiny.

Revolutionary pamphleteers urged that tyrants, like mad dogs, should be killed.

The widespread image of the "bloodthirsty Turks" spread terror among the masses

Propagandists attacked the papacy as the source of innumerable
evils which reated a "rule of the devil"

Ulrich von Hutten, the volatile humanist, is confident that his "truth" will triumph over the pope

Hutten calls on the peasants to join him and Luther in a war against the papacy

wider die rew
bischen vnd mordisch
en rotten der an/
deren baw/
ren.

Mart . Luther
Wittemberg.

.1 5 2 5.

Luther's savage denunciation of the rebelling peasants

It must not be assumed, however, that the victory of popular pressure necessarily meant the triumph of pro-Reformation forces, either before or after the Peasants War. On more than one occasion, the retention of the traditional faith represented a victory for the sentiments of the citizens. The imperial free city of Rottweil presents an interesting case study for the conflict of popular movements. Here the Reformation made substantial inroads so that at the Diet of Nuernberg in 1524 the cardinal legate Campeggio warned that Rottweil was "lutheranissimo."[17] Nonetheless, when a pro-reformation communication from Constance was delivered to the city council, the council threw the messenger in the tower.[18] As tensions mounted, the council tried to preserve peace by expelling leaders of both sides. Yet such a measure failed to stop the agitation, and the city divided into two hostile factions. In July and August 1529 civil strife threatened to break out into the open, for champions of both positions held public rallies, and numbered their supporters in the hundreds. Archduke Ferdinand warned the city that unless decisive action were taken the imperial Hofgericht would be transferred from Rottweil, thus depriving the city of a significant source of income and prestige.[19] But such economic pressure did not quiet the populace. Finally the council invited the peasants in the surrounding villages, which were under Rottweil's jurisdiction, to come into the city to help resolve the issue. These peasants did not share the widespread feeling of anti-clericalism and were strongly in favor of the old religion; consequently that faith now enjoyed a clear majority position. Thus reinforced, the council ordered those who refused to support the traditional faith to leave the city. As a result, 60-100 families left the city.[20] Rottweil, in response to pressures of the majority of the townsmen and peasants, had remained Catholic. Emperor Charles, in gratitude for this action, suspended the city's imperial financial dues for fifteen years.[21]

In several other imperial free cities such as Bachau, the Reformation movement never gained a significant following, so that no popular pressure was necessary to retain the old faith. Sometimes, as in Heilbronn in the 1520s, strong popular agitation for, and vigorous public defence of, both Catholic and Lutheran positions neutralized the power of the citizenry and allowed the city council to direct affairs, but only until one side gained a convincing majority.[22] In other centers, such as Rottenburg on the Neckar, strong popular support kept the city Catholic.

Many of the northern towns similarly adapted their religious practices to popular pressure. In Osnabrueck, a Hansa town as well as the seat of an archbishop, champions of both positions carried their cases to the citizenry by means of public debates. A contemporary chronicler noted that Lutheran teachings gained strong support and were introduced into all the churches except the cathedral, and that this was done "without the approval of spiritual or secular authorities."[3]

A reluctant council continued its struggle, but gradually pressures from the "common people"[24] forced the authorities to changes they had been unable to prevent. At least to participants in the struggle, the outcome demonstrated the very real power of the citizenry, quite apart from the wishes of the authorities.

The decisive role played by the "common man" (*der gemeine Mann*[25]) is also illustrated in the case of Goslar. Despite repeated attempts to maintain the traditional position, the city council in 1528 admitted that refusal to bow to public clamor would mean the outbreak of revolt.[26] The resolute opposition by the burgermeister led to his being forced from office, and the Reformation movement, pushed by the "miner and the common man,"[27] compelled the magistrates to bow to the popular will. A similar trend of events occurred in Bremen, Soest, Luneburg and Herford; in each instance, the city councils resisted change, but were compelled to permit the introduction of Lutheranism when pressure from the populace proved too strong.

Few towns so clearly demonstrated the power of an aroused populace as did Luebeck.[28] Here champions of the Lutheran position often interrupted religious services by singing the widely-recognized symbol of Reformation zeal, "Ach Gott, vom Himmel sieh darein." A determined council, however, vigorously resisted change, so that tensions between it and the citizenry steadily mounted. After several confrontations, matters reached a crisis on December 10, 1529. A crowd assembled on the city square and demanded that the council appoint Lutheran ministers. The council refused, and when a spokesman for the populace asked those who were prepared to "live and die according to God's Word,"[29] to raise their hands, members of the throng did so. The council was forced to capitulate; two Lutheran preachers were appointed.

But even this retreat proved inadequate, for the citizens soon demanded that the mass be abolished throughout the city. Again the council resisted. The townsmen were warned that to carry out such a policy would have dire consequences; besides, why not await decisions of the imperial diet?[30] Once again the citizens refused. A beleaguered council finally yielded, and agreed that a formal Reformation should be introduced. Johann Bugenhagen was accordingly invited to direct the Reformation of the city.

In the city of Halle, ecclesiastical and political rulers cooperated to prevent the introduction of the Reformation, but their efforts failed. The city was under the jurisdiction of the Archbishop Albrecht of Hohenzollern, who attempted, from his residence in the Moritzburg, to direct the affairs of the city. With the defeat of the peasants in 1525 the archbishop was able to consolidate his position, but only temporarily. Lutheran tendencies again asserted themselves, and Albrecht responded by removing some of the council members. At the same time, he enlisted the support of his brother, Elector Joachim I of Brandenburg. These two were joined in an alliance with Duke George of Saxony, Duke Erich of Braunschweig-Kalenberg and Heinrich of Braunschweig-Wolfenbuettel. Despite such a formidable alliance, Archbishop Albrecht could not halt the growth of Lutheranism in his city. When the citizens elected pro-Lutherans to the city council, Albrecht declared that he would rather have "a small Christian, obedient council than a large one composed of opponents of the old religion,"[31] and banished those councillors who supported Lutheranism. This was in 1539; two years later he had to admit that he had lost the struggle. Now, he was prepared to strike a bargain: if the city would accept new taxes, he would withdraw his opposition to religious change. The council presented this proposal to the citizens, and found the townsmen ready to accept an added financial burden in exchange for religious self-determination. Accordingly, the archbishop was given his added revenue, while the people were permitted to have their new religion.[32] Albrecht soon left the city and ensconced himself in the more hospitable environment of his archiepiscopal seat in Mainz.

Developments in some of the small territorial and city states were often complicated by the influence of more powerful neighboring states. Thus when the Reformation gained some support in Hildesheim, bishop and council opposed the change. A determined minority of the city thereupon approached the ardently Lutheran Philip of Hesse, and enlisted his support.[33] Faced with the threat of intervention by Philip and his allies, the city council decided to bow to the inevitable and introduce the Reformation. An external threat had proved decisive—and such tactics were by no means unusual, and were used both by Catholics and Protestants. When the small county of Ortenburg, an independent principality but surrounded by Bavarian territory, adopted Lutheranism, the duke of Bavaria used military force to restore the old religion.[34] Similar tactics were used by a resolutely Lutheran prince in the case of Gnoien[35] when duke Johann Albrecht used military force to introduce the new religious order. Not infrequently, however, developments in the smaller principalities were determined by internal factors. In the county of Baden, the local lord, Heinrich

Flackenstein, was vigorously and successfully resisted when he attempted to prevent religious changes in Weiningen.[36]

In Ortenau, Count Wilhelm von Fuerstenberg found that the new teachings could not be regulated or stopped by his decree.[37] Again when authorities in the county of Lippe tried to halt the growth of Lutheranism, they found themselves unable to cope with the situation and had to yield to popular pressure.[38] On the other hand, official policy in the county of Haag favored Lutheranism, but a determined populace forced the retention of the old faith.[39] Similarly, in many of the large and important cities, such as Strassburg, Nuernberg and Augsburg, councils adopted the Reformation because of "pressure from the populace."[40]

At the same time, powerful rulers, as in Bavaria, the two Saxonies, and Hesse, were often the decisive element in either maintaining the old religion or establishing the new. Such instances demonstrated effective political organization, or, not infrequently, a lack of popular support for the Reformation. Historians have too often forgotten the substantial number of people in the Empire who had no desire to change the religious system.

The refusal of the populace simply to be a passive bystander while the political establishment decided official religious policies is further demonstrated by the various efforts put forth to worship in accordance with specific beliefs. Frequently a persistent pro-Catholic segment of the population went to considerable lengths to maintain the old religion, and was fully prepared to accept the added inconvenience of going to a nearby village or town in order to hear the traditional mass. Thus when the Reformation was introduced in Frankfurt, parishioners who remained faithful to the old religion went to mass in nearby Bockenheim.[41] And when the Reformation was introduced into Tuebingen, adherents of the traditional position went to mass in neighboring Lustnau. Similarly, when Lutheranism triumphed in Schwaebisch Hall, many townsmen made the added effort to go to mass in a nearby church.[42]

Neither Catholics nor Protestants were prepared simply to bow to official policies. Thus when George, Duke of Saxony, vigorously opposed Lutheranism, some of his subjects such as the peasants of Annaberg and/or the townsmen of Leipzig undertook journeys of several hours' duration in order to worship as they wished.[43] Even expulsion of some offenders did not bring a uniform religious policy. Ironically, in electoral Saxony, Frederick could see no reason why he should dispose of his relics and thus deprive himself of an important source of revenue. Only reluctantly did he yield to popular demands and remove the relics.

Conditions in the peasant parishes around Ulm (but within the territorial jurisdiction of the city) are a good indication of continued devotion to Catholic practices, even in areas which had vigorous pro-Reformation forces. When the city council learned of numerous parishioners who went to mass in nearby villages, an extensive survey was ordered. Some of those interrogated declared openly that they could not give up their old faith,[44] no matter what the personal or economic consequences. An examination of the court records demonstrates that Protestants had no monopoly on a willingness to suffer for their faith. Nor were these adherents of the traditional position content to accept the decisions of the city council. Clearly, both Catholics and those who became Protestants were often united in their belief that religious faith was not simply to be based on decisions reached by the political authorities.

Towns, whether imperial free cities or territorial cities, afford especially many instances of decision-making by non-magisterial elements in the population. The imperial free city of Reutlingen presents an unusually clear picture of the power of the populace as opposed to that of the magistracy, and may serve as a case study. Here Matthaeus Alber, the champion of Luther's teachings, gained a significant following. By 1523 the situation had become sufficiently alarming to unite the Bishop of Constance, the Swabian League and Archduke Ferdinand in their determination to prevent the growth of heresy.

In September 1523 the Hapsburg authorities in Stuttgart[45] warned Reutlingen that unless appropriate action were taken, Wuerttemberg would implement an economic boycott of the city.[46] The city council responded by denying the charge of heresy, but at the same time, professed a readiness to take corrective action, should any proof of the allegations be forthcoming.

When Archduke Ferdinand reiterated the charges,[47] and, in addition, the Swabian League warned of the danger of heresy, the city council determined to clear itself of the charge. Alber would be sacrificed for the well-being of the city. The council requested the Bishop of Constance to hold a hearing in Reutlingen; the Bishop agreed to send his vicar, Dr. Johannes Ramming. Aware of the popular support enjoyed by Alber, the city council tried to counteract this potential threat by appealing to the guilds for support. The guilds, however, refused this request. In a memorable meeting in the town square, they insisted that the council change its position. There would be no hearing for Alber unless a similar process were initiated against "the small and the great councils, or the entire citizenry (Gemeinde)."[48]

Faced by the solid opposition of the citizenry, the city council reversed its position. Popular pressure had proved stronger than the will of the council. At the insistence of the assembled citizens, the burgermeister and council were forced to join the citizenry in a common vow to "remain with the pure word of God."[49] Popular agitation carried the day against formidable political pressure.

Archduke Ferdinand was not to be easily dissuaded, and on September 18, 1524, ordered all his subjects in Wuerttemberg to have no contact or business dealings with Reutlingen.[50] Yet even so drastic a measure failed to alter the determination of the Reutlingen citizenry. Even the threatened military intervention of the Swabian League moved the city only to adopt a more conciliatory position, but not to abandon its Lutheranism.[51]

Variations of the Reutlingen procedure are to be found in numerous other centers of Reformation activity. In the important imperial free city of Ulm, Lutheranism gained an early following, so that by 1522, the city council was arresting and imprisoning those suspected of holding to the new teachings.[52] The city fathers were convinced that the peace and order of the city were threatened[53] by a movement which drew its support from the "common man."[54] After several years of efforts to halt a movement which many viewed as being potentially seditious as well as heretical, the city council finally submitted to pressure, and referred the issue to the citizenry. Almost 2000 citizens were entitled to vote on the matter; 87% supported a Lutheran position. Faced with such a decisive verdict, the council moved to implement the wishes of the citizenry. In Constance, popular sentiment early became a decisive—and coercive—factor. When an imperial representative attempted to proclaim the edict against Luther, a crowd gathered on the marketplace and prevented his doing so. When a local priest, Johann Wanner, became a champion of Luther, Bishop Hugo of Constance in 1524 tried to remove him from his position and bar him from further priestly activities. The city council tried to comply, but finally had to admit that they could not control events; Wanner continued to preach.[55]

Other centers experienced similar popular pressures. In Coburg, pressure from the citizenry had become so strong by 1524 that the city council decided to yield.[56] In Muehlhausen, the monk Heinrich Pfeiffer launched an incendiary attack on the religious establishment, and gained an enthusiastic following as early as 1523. When the council tried to take action against him, a threatening crowd persuaded the authorities to desist. The Archbishop of Mainz urged action, and the council again tried to devise an arrangement which would avoid radical change. The crowd responded by presenting the council with a series of demands

(July 3, 1523). Faced with a determined citizenry, the council capitulated but the concession had come too late. An aroused citizenry soon forced the council members to vacate their offices, and a new council was chosen.[57]

Despite the numerous instances which demonstrate the power of popular pressure, it is apparent that often other factors proved decisive. In some instances, military assistance from anti-Lutheran forces proved more than adequate for maintaining the old order. Thus, when the Reformation movement gained a strong following in Schwaebish Gmuend, the city council resolutely tried to halt the growth of the new movement. In 1524 some representatives of the citizenry presented a written request for the appointment of a Lutheran minister, but the council informed the petitioners that the local priests had already been instructed to preach only the "pure Gospel."[58] Such responses proved unacceptable to the advocates of change, and pressure continued to build. Eventually, the Swabian League intervened militarily to maintain the position of the city council.[59]

Several years later, pressure for change had again become so intense that the city council could maintain itself only by getting military help from the Hapsburg Statthalter in Stuttgart.[60] Repeated appeals of external military assistance (coupled with a vigorous anti-Lutheran drive spearheaded by the city's Franciscans[61]) eventually allowed the council to break a popular movement.

In some instances, city councils avoided confrontation with the town populace by referring crucial issues to the citizenry. Thus, in 1529 the citizens of Biberach were asked to vote on the position the city should take relative to the protest of Speyer. A large majority voted for the Lutheran position; magistrates who opposed this action were forced out of office.[62] Similarly, when only 142 of 1076 enfranchised citizens of Esslingen voted against the introduction of Lutheranism, the city council moved to accommodate the demands of the majority.[63]

Sometimes the city council was slow to recognize the power of an aroused citizenry, as in Memmingen. Here the council at first opposed the growth of Lutheranism. In July 1523 when a group of citizens urged the city council to make concessions to Lutheranism, the council resisted. As pressure for a Reformation mounted, champions of the traditional position warned the council not to submit to the demands of the "common man."[64] but the opponents of change, including the burgermeister, found, themselves forced out of office.[65] Thus when the city council moved too slowly to implement the demands of the citizenry, a public demonstration in summer, 1524 again compelled the council to conform to popular pressure. Sweeping Lutheran practices were introduced early in 1525. The populace had scored a clear triumph. Shortly thereafter, in the turmoil of the Peasants War, the Swabian League intervened to restore traditional practices, but by late 1525 a Lutheran minister had again been installed.[66] External pressure and the defeat of the peasants had not deterred the citizens in their resolute drive to establish Lutheranism. Later, when the city had to take action relative to the Edict of Speyer, the city council referred the issue to the citizenry. When 751 of 812 voting citizens supported the Lutheran position, the council approved.[67]

It should be noted that although magisterial authorities were often compelled to carry out the wishes of the populace, the magistracy ordinarily still remained the channel through which citizens implemented their decisions. But the crucial factor in these instances is that the town councils or other authority figures were not the locus of decision-making; they were the instruments of the will of the populace, whether townsmen or peasants. Thus, the assumption that the response to the Reformation challenge may be expressed simply in terms of the "magisterial Reformation," one in which the political authorities determined what action was to be taken—must, in many instances, be rejected or modified. Frequently city councils or princes were forced to take action against their will; citizens, far from being passive, were often vigorous and decisive proponents of the new—or of the old—religion. Their motivations cannot be explained by any simple mono-causation. Economic, political, social and religious factors were usually so thoroughly intertwined that the role of the populace may not be viewed as only a struggle for economic justice, or political rights or religious freedom. In many instances, of course, the military might of a prince crushed popular agitation, yet often the will of the people maintained itself, and decided whether a region would become Protestant or remain Catholic. And once a decision had been made, the minority, whether Protestant or Catholic, further asserted independence from the authorities by often refusing to attend the established church services, by enduring persecution, or by emigrating. In any event, the populace may not be dismissed as being inconsequential in determining the course of the Reformation in Germany nor may the significance of either material or spiritual factors be ignored.

Notes

[1] J.K.F. Schlegel, *Kirchen-und Reformations-Geschichte* (Hanover: Helwing, 1829), II, 399.
[2] Cambridge University Press, 1958, p. 5.

³Hans Hillerbrand, *Men and Ideas in the Sixteenth Century* (Chicago: Rand McNally, 1969), p. 66.

⁴1964, p. 68.

⁵Karl-Heinz Klingenburg, Sibylle Badstubner, et al., *Deutsche Kunst und Literatur in der früehbuergerlichen Revolution* (Berlin: Henschelverlag, 1975), pp. 12, 13.

⁶Ibid., pp. 11-18.

⁷M.M. Smirin, *Die Volksreformation des Thomas Muentzer und der grosse Bauernkrieg* (Berlin, 1952).

⁸*Thomas Muentzer und seine Zeit* (Berlin, 1952), p. 109. See also Abraham Friesen, *Reformation and Utopia. (Wiesbaden, 1974).*

⁹Jerome Blum, et al., *The Emergence of the Modern World* (Boston: Little Brown, 1966), p. 119. See also Will Durant, *Reformation* (New York: Simon & Schuster, 1957), p. 393; Preserved Smith, *The Age of the Reformation* (New York: Henry Holt, 1920), p. 111; and Richard S. Dunn, *The Age of Religious Wars, 1559-1689* (New York: Norton, 1970), p. 6.

¹⁰*Luther and the Reformation* (New York: Russell and Russell, 1962), III, pp. 201-202.

¹¹George H. Williams, *The Radical Reformation* (Philadelphia: Westminster, 1962), p. 82.

¹²*Reichsstadt und Reformation* (Guetersloh: Gerd Mohn, 1962).

¹³"Der Bauernkrieg und das angebliche Ende der lutherischen Reformation als spontaner Volksbewegung." *Luther-Jahrbuch,* 1959, vol. XXVI (1959), pp. 109-134.

¹⁴"Der Laie als Richter im Glaubensstreit der Reformationszeit," pp. 31-54.

¹⁵"The Reformation in Nurnberg," in *The Social History of the Reformation,* ed. L.P. Buck and J.W. Zophy (Columbus, 1972).

¹⁶See Hella Brock, "Moglichkeiten emotional-gedanklicher Vertiefung von Einsichten in den deutschen Bauernkrieg durch Werke der Musik," in Max Steinmetz, ed., *Der Deutsche Bauernkrieg und Thomas Muentzer* (Leipzig: Karl-Marx-Universitat, 1976), 272-279.

¹⁷Edmund Hahn, "Die Reformationsbewegung in der Reichsstadt Rottweil," unpub. ms., 1926, p. 22.

¹⁸G. Rettig, "Bittschrift der vertriebenen Rottweiler an die Eidgenossen 1529," *Archiv des historischen Vereins des Kantons Bern,* Bd. XI (1896), p. 412.

¹⁹Ludwigsburg, Hauptstaatsarchiv, August 6, 1529 (Ferdinand to "den Ersamen, weisenn Burgermeister vnnd Rat der Statt Rotweill," B 203, Bu, 2).

²⁰Hahn, "Rottweil," pp. 44ff.

²¹Stuttgart, Hauptstaatsarchiv, B. 203, Rottweil, August 17, 1530.

²²Public demonstrations in 1527 disrupted Catholic and Lutheran services (Moriz von Rauch, *Johann Lachmann der Reformator Heilbronns* [Heilbronn: Rembold, 1923] p. 24). See also Moriz von Rauch, *Urkendenbuch der Stadt Heilbronn,* vierter Band (Stuttgart: Kohlhammer, 1922), for numerous documents illustrating the bitter struggle.

²³The chronicler notes that the installation of Lutheran ministers here was done "ohne die Zustimmung der Geistlichen der weltlichen Obrigkeit"; this was done by the "Volk," (Heide Stratenwerth, *Die Reformation in der Stadt Osnabrueck* (Wiesbaden, 1971), p. 70, 71.

²⁴Osnabruecker Geschichtsquellen, Bd. II. *Die niederdeutsche Bischofschronik* von Ertwin Erstman, fortgesetzt bis 1533 von Dietrich Lilie, hrg. von Fr. Runge (Osnabruck, 1894), p. 106.

²⁵Holscher, *Die Geschichte der Reformation in Goslar* (Hannover, 1902), p. 36.

²⁶"...es droht Aufruhr vom gemeinen Hausen," Goslar Stadtarchiv, Arch Nr. 2115, quoted in Holscher, op. cit., p. 36.

²⁷One of the six members of the small council notified Albrecht, Archbishop of Mainz, that "Bergknappen und der gemeine Mann [haben] den Rat genotigt, Amsdorff von Magdeburg herzurufen... noch bisher hat die Obrigkeit mit eigenem Willen keine Neuerung gestattet...," ibid.,

²⁸Heinrich Schrieber, *Die Reformation Luebecks* (Halle, 1902).

²⁹A contemporary chronicler has recorded the dramatic events: "Einige von den Burgern, die auf dem Rathaus waren, als sie sahen, dass der Ehrbare Rat nicht in Gottes Wort einwilligen wollte, riefen sie aus dem Fenster zu denen auf dem Markt: 'Wer bei Gottes Wort leben and sterben will, der hebe die Hand auf!' Da hob der Volkshaufen die Hand auf," quoted in *Die Reformation in Augenzeugenberichten,* hereausgegeben von Helmar Junghans (Duesseldorf: Karl Rauch, 1967), p. 385.

³⁰The council warned that such action would "zum ewigen Verderben dieser Stadt gereichen.... Als nun die Herren sahen, dass die Gemeinde so fest an dem ersten Artikel

[abolition of the mass] hielt und dass sie nichts erreichen konnten, gingen sie wieder zu dem Ratsstuhl.... Darauf gab der Ehrbare Rat zur Antwort: Weil es also nicht anders sein konnte" a Reformation would be introduced (ibid., pp. 386, 387).

[31]Walter Delius, *Die Reformatioinsgeschichte der Stadt Halle/Saale* (Berlin: Union Verlag, 1953), p. 58. The archbishop asserted that he would rather have a "Kleiner Christlicher gehorsamer rath als eyner vil personen und der alten religion tzuwidder."

[32]At the landtag in Kalbe (1541) Albrecht frankly admitted that the battle was lost: "Koennen doch Kaiser und Papst nicht wehren in diesen Landern, wie wollen wir's dann wehren? Darum handelt also, dass wir Geld Bekommen, wollen sie es ja so haben und lutherisch sein, wohlan, das mogen sie tun..." (ibid., p. 67).

[33]Rudolf Steinmetz, "Die Generalsuperintendenten von Hildesheim," *Zeitschrift der Gesellschaft fuer niedersachsiche Kirchengeschichte*, 1938, Jahrgang 43, p. 119.

[34]Konrad Preger, *Pankraz von Freyberg auf Hohenaschau* (Halle: Verein fuer Reformationsgeschichte, 1895), p. 29.

[35]Heinrich Schreiber, *Johannes Albrecht I, Herzog von Mecklenburg* (Halle: Verein fuer Reformationsgeschichte, 1899), p 33.

[36]Josef Ivo Hochle, *Geschichte der Reformation und Gegenreformation in der Stadt und Grafschaft Baden bis 1535* (Zurich: J.F. Kobold-Ludi, 1907), p. 7.

[37]Karl Ludwig Bender, "Die Reformation in Gengenbach," *Beitraege zur Badischen Kirchengeschichte*, Sammelband I, (Karlsruhe: Evang. Presserverband, 1962), p. 7.

[38]Stratenwerth, *Osnabrueck*, p. 109.

[39]Hans Rossler, *Geschichte und Strukturen der evangelischen Bewegung im Bistum Freising, 1520-1571* (Nuernberg: Verein fuer Bayerische Kirchengeschichte, 1966), pp. 116-128.

[40]Naujoks, *Obrigkeitsgedanke, Zunftverfassung und Reformation* (Stuttgart: Kohlheimer, 1958), p. 57. "...die groesste Stadte wir Strassburg, Augsburg and Nuernbert unter dem Druck der Bevolkerung lutherische Pradikanten Angenommen hatten...."

[41]Gustav Bossert, "Die Wiedeneinfuehrung der Messe in Frankfurt, 1535," *Archiv fuer Reformationsgeschichte*, XIII (1916), p. 150.

[42]In Hall "sein vil von der alten geschlechten, und auch sonst etlich von der statt hinaus zu sant Johans zur kirchen gange...." *Chronica zeit-unnd jarbuch vonn der statt Hall ursprung unnd was sich darinnen verloffen unnd wasz fur schlosser umb Hall gestanden*, durch M. Johnn Herolt zusammengetragen, in Geschichtsquellen der Stadt Hall, erster Band, bearbeitet von Christian Kolb (Stuttgart: Kohlhammer Verlag, 1894), p. 189.

[43]Karlheinz Blaschke, *Sachsen im Zeitalter der Reformation* (Guetersloh: Gerd Mohn, 1870), pp. 10, 11.

[44]Excerpts from the city records reflect some of the attitudes: "Veit Rosslin geht nach S [oflingen], weil er beim alten Glauben bleiben will. Da der Glaub frei sei, hoff er, man weerd ihn auch dabei lassen; er will auich in Zukunft nicht hie an die Predigt gehen, sondern bei dem Alten, wie es an ihn Kommen, bleiben," *Ulmische Reformationsakten von 1531 und 1532 in Wuerttembergische Vierteljahrshefte fur Landesgeschhichte*, neue Folge, IV. Jahrgang, 1894, p. 337. Another person interrogated gave a response which might well have reminded the authorities of a famous statement made ten years earlier in Worms: "Apollonia Schinerlerin: sie sei Gott und U.L. Fr. zu lieb hinaus und werd auf ihrem Glauben bleiben, es gefalle wem es wolle, sie sei Gott mehr schuldig dann einem Rat," ibid.

[45]The independent city of Reutlingen had been conquered by Duke Ulrich of Wuerttemberg and incorporated into his principality, but in 1519 the Swabian League expelled the duke from his territory. The Hapsburgs now assumed control of the duchy and set up their "Statthalter" in Stuttgart.

[46]Paul Schwarz, *600 Jahre Burgerschaftliche Selbsterwaltung der ehemaligen Reichsstadt* (Beutlingen, 1974), p. 93.

[47]Stuttgart, Staatsarchiv, Reichsstadt Reutlinger, Bu. 6, Jan., 11, 1524.

[48]Reutlingen, Stadtarchiv, Markteid 1525, Nr. 574/8, p. 2. The city authorities gave a graphic account of the event: "Da haben die am marktt die spies nidergelassen ain Ring gemacht vnd mitainander geredt man hab der gemaind allen in ire zunfthuse zusamen gebatten diwyl sie dann ietzo dyain so wollen sie die sach aldo handeln vnd nach dem burgermaister geschickt vnd im angezaigt das sich der prediger der kuntschaft hievorgemelt der prediger denn klein vnd gros Rat oder ain gantze gemaind auch verhorendenn er das Rain luttre wort gottes gepredigt...so werd sich ain Rat darin...halten wie sich gepur vnnd vf solhs haben sie nit wollen abtretten sonder

begert als auch beschehen das wir all zesamen schweren sollen by dem goswort zu beliben vnd das zuhandthaben" (Reutlingen, Stadtarchiv, Nr. 574/8, pp. 2, 3.

[49]Ibid., p. 2.

[50]Ferdinand decreed: . . ."das Ir Obbemelt Statt Reutlingen, und Inwoner derselben, auh den Prediger obangetzaigt nun hinfuran in allen sachen meidet,. .noch ainicherlay gemainschaft oder hanndlung...habet, noch teibet" (*Beylagen* in Christian F. Sattler, *Geschichte des Herzogthums Wurtemberg,* zweiter Theil [Tubingen: G.H. Reiss, 1770], pp. 237, 238.)

[51]Schwarz, *Reutlingen,* pp. 8-11.

[52]Naujoks, *Obrigkeitsgedanke,* p. 56.

[53]Lutheranism, the council feared, would give rise to "nichts anders dann Uffruren. . . ." (Ulm, Stadtarchiv, Ratsprotokolle, July 8, 1522).

[54]The council deplored the fact that the new teachings "im gemainen man wurtzelt und gewachsen, dass es mit gewalt ubel ze stilen sey," quoted in Naujoks, op. cit., p. 57.

[55]August Willburger, *Die Konstanzer Bischoefe____und die Glaubensspaltung* (Muenster: Aschendorffsche Buchdruckerei, 1927).

[56]Hans Platze ue Walter Schlesinger, *Geschichte Thueringens.* III. Bd. (Koeln: Bohlau Verlag, 1967), p 49.

[57]Koiditz, "Die Volksbewegung in Muehlhausen." The popular support of the early Reformation in Muehlausen is well demonstrated in this study, so that "die Reformation in Muehlausen war urspringlich eine echte Volksbewegung..." (p. 133).

[58]Naujoks, *Obrigkeitsgednke,* p. 61.

[59]Ibid., p. 64.

[60]Ibid., p. 71.

[61]Christoph Friedrich von Stalin, *Wirtembergische Geschichte,* vierter Theil (Stuttgart: J.G. Cotta'schen Buchhandlung, 1873), p. 247.

[62]Karl Weller u. Arnold Weller, *Wuerttembergische Geschichte im Sueddeutschen Raum* (Stuttgart: Konrad Theiss, 1972), p. 125. See also Albert Angele, ed., *Altbiberach um die Jahre der Reformation erlebt und fur die kommenden Generationen der Stadt beschrieben von den Zeitgenossen und edlen Bruddern Joachim I und Henrich VI von Pfummern* (Biberach, 1962).

[63]Ibid., p. 127; Naujoks, *Obrighkeitsgedanke,* p. 88.

[64]Wolfgant Schlenck, "Die Reichsstadt Memmingen und die Reformation," *Memminger Geschichtsblaetter,* (1968), p. 36; Memmingen, Stadtarchiv, Ratsprotokoll, 2. Februar 1524: "dieweyl denn ain rat selbst sag, er sey der gmaind nit gewaltig."

[65]Schlench, *Memminger Geschichtsblaetter, p. 38.*

[66]Ibid., p. 58.

[67]Ibid., pp. 64ff.

XVI
Class, Generation and Social Change: A Case in Salem, Massachusetts, 1636-1656

From the Latin poet Juvenal on through history we derive many of our ideas about the lower classes from satirists and elite-class observers. Colonial America is no exception, and we depend upon such writings as those of Sarah Kemble Knight and William Byrd for pictures of the illiterate subculture that was to become one of the factors in the development of the American character. As John Frye points out in this article there did exist a place of intersection for the dominant society and the emerging new popular society, this being the courtroom. Frye's brief study is set in Salem, Massachusetts, several decades before that community was to become embroiled in its mass-mania of demonic possession, slander and theocratic collapse. The seeds of dissension and class conflict had already sprouted by mid-century, however, and out of the petty wranglings and confused testimony, Frye constructs a case of counter-culture and generation gap, for the persons involved are not only illiterate farmers and tapsters, but rebellious scions of the bookish Puritan elite as well. In this article we are two centuries past Gutenburg, but it makes a fitting addition to a collection of essays on popular culture before printing because in 1647, Massachusetts had passed its "old deluder, Satan" school law, which meant, in New England, that literacy would become virtually universal by the next generation among men and women alike, and that, by the time of the American Revolution, we would be ready for a national society whose popular culture would increasingly be determined by the mass media as we understand them today.

John Frye has taught history and humanities at Triton College, River Grove, Illinois since 1970. He holds a Master's degree from Ohio State and a C. Phil. in African History from UCLA. The basic work for this paper was done under an NEH Summer Grant in 1975 at Northwestern University.

Class, Generation and Social Change: A Case in Salem, Massachusetts, 1636-1656

John Frye

In the 1950s Black musical styles became the rage among white middle class adolescents. Conservative moralists decried this phenomenon as degenerative. Their complaints were echoes of similar warnings heard 300 years earlier in Puritan Massachusetts—not specifically about Black music, of course, but about cultural changes in general. Massachusetts Bay Colony was pre-industrial and yet the common experience of opposition to youthful culture change by the Puritan elite of 1645 and conservatives of 1955 suggests that common issues of significance to the study of popular culture are present.

Puritan society in Massachusetts has been the object of intensive analysis. The Puritan elite has been analyzed and dissected from every conceivable perspective. Theology and politics, love and letters, poetry and prose, their illness and entertainments have received dozens, even hundreds, of studies. Economic life in the colony has an extensive literature. But the cultural life and values of the bulk of the population has, understandably, been neglected. In this paper "Puritan" will refer to the leadership of the Bay Colony and secondarily to church members in general. Most authorities agree that this is a rather small portion of the population, certainly less than half. A second group of persons to be discussed appear frequently in the court records on criminal charges or in civil suits, often both. Although I refer to this group as a class I do not mean to imply any rigorous sociological definition. They are simply a group of people who know each other. They are friends or enemies and most appear at the lower economic levels. The people discussed are either poor or they are propertyless sons of better-off farmers. It should be remembered though that the bulk of the Massachusetts Bay Colony population falls in neither of these categories. Most are neither members of this crime-prone class nor the Puritan class.

Most of the material following comes from the Essex court record dealing with Ipswich, one of several towns in Essex county. The population of this community was probably in the range of 700 to 800[1] Ipswich was chosen for economy of study, and although it differs from other Bay Colony towns it does not appear to be any more different from them than they are from one another. The county Court met in Ipswich nineteen times from 1641 to 1656.

In January 1651 Mark Symonds was fined 10 shillings "for one lie and 5s each for three other untruths, and 5s for railing."[2] He was also admonished for serving a warrant on Sunday and for "reproachful speeches against Mr. Samuell Symondes, the magistrate."[3] This case is not atypical in drawing in twelve or more witnesses and including what is in effect a mixture of criminal and civil issues. The twelve witnesses in this case unravel a long and complex relationship that reveals conflict within the community as well as values underlying the conflict. Again, typically, this case arose over an earlier one, regarding a certain hog which did or did not have a certain mark on its ear and belonged or did not belong to Robert Dutch or Goodman Cobean. In this case, however, lying is the charge.

The first lie Symonds was charged with was contradictory statements regarding the hog in question. Joseph Fowlar testified that on two different occasions Symonds had said that the mark was too small to be seen and then again that it could be clearly seen out to the street from a "parlor" window.[4] Fowlar then quoted Symonds as follows:

"Joseph Fowlar you thinke yt I prosecute against you in this matter about ye hogg, but I profess I doe not neither have I any hand in it."[5]

Richard Kimball, Sr. supported Fowlar's testimony.

The second lie involved the serving of a warrant on Daniel Rolfe. Not only did Symonds serve the warrant on Sunday, but as it turned out there was no name on the warrant and Rolfe only found out on his way to court.

The third allegation of a lie against Symonds came from John Kimball. He said that Symonds "after having prosecuted" Joseph Fowlar and John Broadstreet told Fowlar that he was not his accuser "and would go fourty miles to do him good."[6]

The fourth charge came from Thomas Whitbridge who alleged that Symonds had gone around the village claiming that Henry Kimball had paid him 5s 6d for two bullocks and a boy for plowing a field. If true this would have been an excessively high rate of pay.

Out of perspective this tedious list of trivial charges taxes the reader. In fact what is going on here is a vendetta. Fowlar, the Kimballs, Daniel Rolfe, Whitridge and John Broadstreet are all united by social ties of friendship or marriage. This episode is one of a long series involving these actors preceding and following this date. Here as elsewhere throughout the record individuals are using the Puritan court as a weapon in squabbles that have little to do with any real issue or rather the real issues have little to do with the court case. As the testimony attributed to Symonds makes clear, court was in fact seen by these people as a battlefield. Symonds prosecutes as a form of attack, just as one gets the feeling he is the victim of a concerted counterattack. Occasionally the Court recognizes that it is being used. In the conflict between Symonds and the Kimballs the Court had tried earlier to settle the conflict without success in November of 1650.[7] These interminable court struggles that drag on over years suggests that far from dominating or controlling the society at all levels, the Puritan courts served more as mediator or referee than arbitrator. Case after case the intra-community conflict continues suggesting a social level where Puritan control was unable or unwilling to go.

A second case of lying during this same court session of January 1651 will be instructive. The same John Broadstreet sued Joseph Muzy for slander. Muzy spread the rumor that Broadstreet had bastard children in "Road eyland [sic]."[8] Thomas Cott (related to the Kimballs above) testified that Muzy had made this allegation saying "he should know them [the bastard children] wherever he saw them for they had a natural mark and that was lowell ears like their father."[9] In extensive testimony it appeared that someone had said Broadstreet had "dealings" with maids at Rhode Island and that he owned bulls there with "dole" ears.[10] It is immaterial for our purposes whether Muzy misunderstood what was said or was purposely slandering Broadstreet. In testimony it was established that Muzy's rumor affected the relationship of Broadstreet and John Cross, an older prosperous local farmer. Witnesses testified that John Cross, recently deceased, had said, "he bore great love towards him [Broadstreet] so much that he could willingly have bestowed his daughter on him in marriage, and he had told him as much...until he heard a report raised by Joseph Muzie [sic]...."[11]

The view that these two cases represented the Puritan obsession with Christian morality and truth is incorrect. These two cases represent conflict within the community among persons most of whom are not church members. The questions involved are moral and legal, not Puritan. They are the same as would be raised in England or any agricultural pre-industrial society worldwide. The issue in these cases is not between the lower class and the Puritan government but within the lower class itself. That these cases appear in a Puritan court does not make them Puritan cases of morality. In these two instances the issue gives the appearance of congruence between the law and values of the dominant Puritans and this subordinant class. Other cases will show that this apparent congruence of values is misleading. What seems to be an expression of Puritan law is in fact conflict within a lower order, and a part of this conflict, perhaps not the most important part, we happen to see in the Puritan court record.

Values relating to sexuality have a wide literature in scholarship on Puritanism and an even wider popular mythology. A number of cases in the court record involve Sarah Turner.[12] Sarah reportedly threw water on Tobias Saunders "in a sporting way."[13] Taking the challenge, Saunders grabbed her, and a general melee ensued, spoiled as it were by the presence of persons who did not approve of this play which the Court described as "lascivious acts."[14] It was also reported that Sarah had dared Robert Tyler to kiss her as she could then prove that he had been eating her "Turnopps."[15]

John Bond was also cited in this same connection with indecent carriages with several women. He also was reported to have said that the magistrates were more "devils than men."[16] In 1648 Bond had been punished for similar offenses. He also had been involved in what seems to have been a training day riot and with two others had turned over a cannon. As part of the general disorder on this occasion Joseph Fowlar insulted "the Major" (probably John Endicott) and was later fined 40 shillings.[17] For Bond, this time, his father, John Bond, Sr. and Tobias Saunders (related by marriage to Daniel Rolfe) stood the court bond for John Jr.

Several things stand out in these examples regarding the subculture seen here emerging. First of all the connection of kinship and friendship among the crime-prone class is illustrated by Saunders standing bond and the riotous connection between John Bond and Joseph Fowlar. There are many examples throughout the record. Secondly the kind of "lascivious" act described here is not a rarity, and it is hardly the kind of behavior likely to start a licentious display, even a mild one, unless a number of people present share the same attitude toward sexual display as the instigator. It would be invaluable to know the incidence of reported crime versus unreported crime. This is unfortunately impossible. But to produce this kind of joking attitude toward sexuality there must have been a subculture to support it. It was unfortunate for Turner, Saunders and Bond in this case that there were others around who disapproved and reported the display. Thirdly, John Bond illustrates the antagonism toward authority that runs throughout this lower class element at Ipswich. It seems typical of subordinate group hostility toward superiors generally. This hostility runs the

range of political and religious authority. Thomas Scott was warned
to learn his catechism, and refusing to do so was fined. He
compounded his sin by associating with people who expressed
anabaptist views. In Massachusetts Bay anabaptism had the
character of being anti-establishment.

Puritan attitudes toward work and time have received much
comment in the literature. In one case five young men are
strenuously admonished by the Court for "going into the woods at
an unseasonable time of the night, and carrying fire and liquor with
them."[18] The five miscreants were Thomas Scott, Thomas Cooke (an
anabaptist), Joseph Fowlar and two relations of Scott's, John and
Thomas Kimball. The Court complained that their wives and others
had to go out and search for them. Clearly this is not the kind of
behavior sanctioned by Puritan values. Numerous court cases and
specific laws could be cited to illustrate the Puritan concern with
orderly and purposeful activity. The magistrates were concerned
with time and fined persons for making other people wait and on
occasion ordered people to "improve" their time.[19] In spite of the
near absence of clocks the Court divides time into units as small as a
quarter of an hour.[20] The group discussed here seem to have a much
more traditional peasant attitude toward time. Testimony by these
people never gives specific dates as the court carefully notes in its
records, but places events "during Michaelmass" or a "fortnight
before training." At this level the differences between the Puritan
concept of time and duty and the concepts of the lower class are more
readily perceived and understood. Puritan diversions and
entertainments could be based on a wealth, leisure and education
which were not the property of all others. The Puritan concept of
time would not likely have much impact on a group who rejected or
were indifferent to the theological basis of what appears to be the
Puritan concern with time.

These four court-related issues in Massachusetts Bay Colony
involved two different cultural systems: the dominant Puritan and a
subordinate class of people with a significantly different culture.
For the most part the four issues of lying, sexual attitudes, and time
and leisure do not concern questions we would see as judicial today.
The issues, however, can not be explained nor understood on the
basis of Puritans trying to enforce their culture on others. This
ignores the importance of the culture of the sub-group. As stringent
as Puritan enforcement sometimes was, there is no noticeable
diminution in the criminal activity of the lower group. The
friendship and kinship ties in the lower group apparently gave its
members sufficient reinforcement and support to perpetuate their
value system. In 1654 the court record shows that John Bond was

praised by a supporter for speaking in a "bold manner" against the magistrates.[21] Bond must have received much encouragement from his peers to continue the risky course he took against the Puritans. The perpetuation of this sub-culture in Puritan Massachusetts may be partly explained by the attitudes of the Puritans themselves who concluded from theological premises that human society could not be perfected and that evil would always be present. But there is another dimension to this Puritan attitude that will be helpful in understanding the position of the sub-culture.

The Puritan religious experience was a powerful and personal one resulting in sanctification. But sanctification was not inherited. The children of the sanctified needed their own passionate experience of salvation. Concern for their children dominates much Puritan writing. Children are weak, and lewd and evil persons served as bad models who would draw children away from the godly path.[22] Some Puritans were so distressed by the presence of ungodly people in Massachusetts that they advocated another migration, this time from New England to an even more remote place.[23] One Puritan warned of "idle and profane young men, servants, and other, with whome we must leave our children...."[24] Indeed Puritan fears seem well-founded not only in theology but in the vitality of the lower class culture in Ipswich and elsewhere in Massachusetts. In fact the dream of the founders of the Bay Colony of a godly civil state did die a quick death. In one sense in the cultural conflict between the Puritans and the sub-culture at Ipswich the Puritan culture died while the lower class culture continued. Many of those Colony residents with criminal records were younger sons and servants, the "profane young men" and lewd servants. Their values did, as the Puritans feared, outlast and triumph over the theological code of the godly.

Many of the young men mentioned above—Mark Symonds, Thomas Scott, the younger Kimballs—are sons of substantial members of the community; their fathers serve on juries, are church members, or hold other civic responsibilities. But in these cases and elsewhere we see them associated with a lower sort of people and they participate in rebellion, heresy and disrespectful activities. Some of the people noted here are the advance guard of the Puritan fear that their children will be led astray. Other issues are involved, economic and social questions which cannot be fully discussed here. But there is a cultural issue involved, a choice between differing value systems. The choice by a young man of loose sexual carriages or drinking or religious heresy may be symptomatic of other conflicts, but it is a moral choice that is not without significance in itself.

What relationship does all this have to the study of popular culture? One does not have far to look for examples of cultural change based on a youthful segment of society. The adoption of Black musical styles in the 1950s by a white middle class youth audience would be one of the easiest parallels. Others could be drawn. The problem of the "younger generation" surely precedes written history. But a larger question arises from the example of Ipswich outlined above and contemporary cultural changes based on mass culture. One suspects that an immature generation (culturally rather than physiologically defined) has greater acceptance of cultural change than a mature one. In stratified societies where different strata possess substantially different cultures the younger members of one group may be the opening wedge for cultural change by absorbing values, attitudes and beliefs from another stratum. Events in Ipswich and the Bay Colony as a whole allow for this interpretation. How much more true this may be for a culture with mass production and mass consumption of value rich entertainments such as our own. Such a hypothesis in no way vitiates the importance of other factors in culture change. It opens possibilities, however, for the interpretation of social changes which may stem from popular culture.

Notes

[1]Sidney Perley, *The History of Salem Massachusetts* (Salem, 1924), vol. II, p.176.

[2]Essex Institute, *Records and Files of the Quarterly Courts of Essex County Massachusetts Volume I, 1636-1656*. (Salem, 1911), p.225.

[3]Ibid., p.226.
[4]Ibid.
[5]Ibid.
[6]Ibid.
[7]Ibid., p.206.
[8]Ibid., p.210.
[9]Ibid.

[10]Ibiords and Files of the Quarterly Courts of Essex County Massachusetts Volume I, 1636-1656. (Salem, 1911), p.225.

[3]Ibid., p.226.
[4]Ibid.
[5]Ibid.
[6]Ibid.
[7]Ibid., p.206.
[8]Ibid., p.210.
[9]Ibid.
[10]Ibid., p.211.
[11]Ibid.
[12]Ibid., pp. 198-199.
[13]Ibid., p.198.
[14]Ibid.
[15]Ibid., 199.
[16]Ibid.

[17]Ibid., p.147.

[18]Ibid., pp.178-179.

[19]Samuel Sewall, *The History of Woburn, Middlesex County, Massachusetts* (Boston, 1868), p.51.

[20]Essex Institute, op. cit., p.26, 33.

[21]Ibid., p.368.

[22]Edmund Morgan, *The Puritan Family,* (New York, 1966), p.172.

[23]Ibid., p.170.

[24]Massachusetts Historical Society, *Collections,* (Fourth Series), Volume VII, pp.24-25.

Bibliographical Note

The primary source material for this study is drawn from: Essex Institute, *Records and Files of the Quarterly Courts of Essex County Massachusetts Volume I, 1636-1656.* (Salem, 1911); other sources used in preparation of the paper include: Massachusetts Historical Society, *Collections,* (Fourth Series), Volume VII; Sidney Perley, *The History of Salem, Massachusetts* (Salem, 1924),Volume II; Samuel Sewall, *The History of Woburn, Middlesex County, Massachusetts* (Boston, 1868); Edmund Morgan, *The Puritan Family* (New York, 1966).

XVII

Cement Lions and Cloth Elephants: Popular Arts of the Fante Asafo

In this essay the idea that some of the most illuminating inquiry into popular culture is at points of intersection between cultural traditions is clearly exemplified. Doran H. Ross' "Cement Lions and Cloth Elephants" includes intersections between a traditional folk society and an extended metropolitan system, between local hand production and mass-distributed manufactures, and between regional clusters of symbols and values and those of a superimposed alien system.

The Fante are a society of contemporary Ghana, civilized and sophisticated although still largely illiterate. Far from being remotely situated, they have been exposed to European influence since the Renaissance. At once preserving rich African traditions such as proverbial wisdom and adopting a wide variety of British structural and symbolic forms, this agrarian-fishing society has evolved a culture that is neither pure folk nor "mass," but is well-described as popular culture. Ross' original study focuses upon two popular art traditions of the Fante: cement shrines and cloth banners. Using methodology that draws upon the disciplines of the art historian, the ethnologist and the folklorist, Ross looks particularly at two icons, the indigenous elephant and the alien lion, and constructs for us a complex of art, social and political institutions, traditional wit and wisdom that exemplifies the creativity, energy and vivacity that can emerge with popular culture.

Doran H. Ross is an art historian with a concentration on Africa. He is author of several articles on the art of Africa and co-author with Herbert Cole of The Arts of Ghana.

Asafo shrine at Biriwa built in 1958.

Flag made for *asafo* company at Ekumfi Akra in 1976 illustrating the proverb: "Only the elephant can pull down the palm tree."

Cement Lions and Cloth Elephants: Popular Arts of the Fante Asafo

Doran H. Ross

Unicorns, griffins, angels and mermaids are not the traditional subject matter of African art. Nor are cannons, airplanes and warships. Still these images merge with such venerable African themes as wild animals, bush spirits and warriors in the popular arts of the Fante peoples of south-central Ghana. Brightly painted often life-sized shrine sculpture (fig. 1) and equally colorful appliqued flags (fig. 2) are the dominant art forms of the traditional Fante warrior groups. Though the technologies and much of the imagery are borrowed from European sources, their combination with indigenous motifs is uniquely Fante.[1]

The Fante number well over 600,000 and are one of several culturally and linguistically related groups known collectively as the Akan. Each of the twenty-one traditional Fante states is ruled by a paramount chief assisted by a council of elders and a hierarchy of divisional, town and village chiefs.[2] The economy is basically subsistence farming and fishing, but the larger towns have a growing middle class of merchants and civil servants. Although the Fante are among West Africa's best educated ethnic groups, a very large majority of the adult population is still illiterate. Christianity has made significant inroads in many areas, yet indigenous beliefs prosper alongside and often in conjunction with Western forms.

Coastal Fanteland has been exposed to European contact longer and more intensively than any other area of sub-Saharan Africa. Beginning with the Portuguese in 1471 a kaleidoscope of Dutch, English, French, Swedish, Danish and Brandenburg forces competed for gold and slaves. Between 1482 and 1828 a series of trading and slaving forts were built on the coast to support the various European interests. This contest for domination of the Gold Coast was not resolved until 1872 when Britain achieved sovereignty. It remained the sole colonial power until Ghanaian independence in 1957. Throughout this five hundred year history the European forts and their attendant garrisons exerted a profound influence on the traditional warrior groups (asafo) of the Fante.

Asafo is a pan-Akan military institution, but its development among the Fante is distinctive if for no other reason that its art. The original and primary function of *asafo* was, of course, defense of the state, but they also exercised considerable political influence, and indeed still do. Like many cultures throughout the world, the military counterbalances the power of the ruling elite. Although the *asafo* groups are ultimately subordinate to the chief, they are nevertheless closely involved in the selection of the chief, responsible for his installation, and necessary participants in required rituals to sustain the chief's rule. In some states they even have the power to remove the chief from office. Obviously the chief cannot rule successfully without the support of the *asafo*.[3]

Aside from military and political functions the *asafo* serve (or served) several other essential roles in Fante society. On the civic level they once operated as a kind of department of public works involved in road construction and sanitation projects. In the religious realm the *asafo* still are overseers and guardians of designated state gods and are responsible for the funeral arrangements of their members. They also continue to orchestrate at least one major festival annually and to provide community entertainment (drumming, singing and dancing) on other select occasions.

A traditional Fante state may have from two to fourteen or more *asafo* companies with as many as seven active companies in a single town. Each company is identified by a distinguishing number, name and location, e.g. Number 5 Company, Brofu-mba ("white man's children"), Cape Coast. The internal organization of *asafo* is not unlike their western military counterparts, and was probably influenced by them. Each company has its senior commanders (*supi* and *asafohen*), a variety of lesser officers, and designated flag carriers, hornblowers, drummers and priests or priestesses. Some companies also have women's groups headed by one or two female officers.

In the eighteenth and nineteenth centuries the Fante *asafo* were involved in numerous wars both among themselves and with surrounding Akan states. During the twentieth century the *asafo's* military role was replaced by the British and then Ghanaian governments; still the martial character of the companies persisted in numerous, often fatal, inter-company riots. The rivalries remain and *asafo* companies flourish today as highly competitive social and fraternal organizations maintaining many of their original civic and religious functions.

Any Fante town with two or more *asafo* companies is susceptible to inter-company rivalries. Perhaps oddly, art is often the cause of disputes. Each company has select colors, cloth patterns and emblems reserved for its exclusive use. Violation of the artistic prerogatives of one company by another is considered an act of aggression, for each jealously guards its artistic property. For the past one hundred years the colonial and Ghanaian governments have legislatively enforced these rights of exclusivity.

As in most Fante arts, *asafo* designs generally represent traditional proverbs or aphorisms, although historical and purely emblematic images are also common. The pairing of a visual image with a verbal proverb—the verbal-visual nexus of Akan art—is crucial to understanding *asafo* imagery. Among the Fante the oral presentation of proverbs is a well-developed art in itself. Although many of the world's cultures use proverbs, they seem to be more prevalent and important among the Fante and other Akan groups. As a society without written laws these proverbs help codify traditional customs concerning affairs of the Fante.[4] The number of proverbs currently in use probably totals several thousand, but only about two hundred fifty are used with consistency in *asafo* imagery. This somewhat narrowed corpus acts as a means of standardization and allows people from different locations to "read" each other's artistic messages. On the other hand, the highly developed system of metaphorical thought that permeates Akan intellectual life allows for an image-proverb to extend to other subjects and situations. For example, a common image on *asafo* shrines and flags is an elephant, either alone or interacting with something else. An isolated elephant commonly elicits the rather simple and obvious saying: "The elephant is the strongest animal in the bush," meaning that the *asafo* company displaying this image is the most powerful in town. The same message is expressed more elegantly in: "He who follows the elephant never gets wet from the dew on the bushes," i.e. the elephant clears the way. Other scenes are more complex. An elephant standing on an animal trap represents: "When elephant steps on trap, no more trap." In this case the animal stands for the owners of the image while the trap is a metaphor for a rival company. Alternately an image of an elephant on its back with a vulture standing next to it (fig. 3) illustrates: "The vulture is still afraid of the dead elephant." Here again the secondary figure of the vulture (which normally feeds on dead animals) is a rival and allegedly lesser company. In the same vein the very common image of an elephant with its trunk around a palm tree (fig. 2) expresses: "Only the elephant can uproot the palm tree." The palm is seen as the strongest tree in the forest, yet owners of this motif say the elephant is even stronger.

Still the elephant is not always viewed as dominant. If the pachyderm is an emblem of a rival company, the elephant and

Detail of 260 foot banner from Ekumfi Esaakyir made in 1974 and depicting the maxim: "Even the vulture is afraid of the dead elephant."

palm may represent: "Even the elephant is unable to pull down the palm tree." As a compromise to the two previous sayings for this image, a flag maker offered: "Since the elephant could not defeat the palm tree, he made friends with it." Some companies use the antelope to counter another company's elephant with the former standing on the back of the latter: "Though the elephant is the largest animal, the antelope [considered very wise and clever] rules the forest." Finally a man with his hand in the mouth of an elephant (fig. 4) depicts: "Though the elephant is a big animal, it does not have teeth to bite with." As should be clear from this series, many *asafo* images represent either real or imagined predatory relationships whose verbal-visual message constitutes a kind of fighting with art in a dialetic of bravura. Thus the principal theme of *asafo* iconography is generally the power and glory of one company expressed at the expense of another company.

Inter-company competition aside, the institution of *asafo* breeds none of the elitism characteristic of Fante royalty. While

Military shrine at Ekumfi Edumafa completed in 1974

chieftancy is aristocratic and limited to only one matrilineage, the patrilineal *asafo* is democratic and open to all. This distinction is visible in the arts. Royal regalia is constructed of precious materials, especially gold and exclusive hand woven textiles; *asafo* forms are made of readily available cement and commercially produced trade cloth.

The most prominent and enduring artistic expressions of *asafo* are their cement shrines (*posuban*).[5] These ostentatious, almost Disneyesque structures contrast vividly with the drab mud-walled, tin-roofed houses typical of the Fante. As of 1977 there were sixty-one monumental *posuban* in Fanteland. The earliest dates from 1883, but more than half have been erected since 1950, and several are currently under construction.[6] These military shrines have little connection with indigenous architecture; most are loosely patterned after the European forts that line the coast. The Fante themselves use "fort" and "castle" interchangeably with "posuban," "post" and "shrine" when referring to these monuments. Although the shrine is identified with the fort, most of the architectural details are somewhat ironically borrowed from Christian church building traditions on the coast. Rather than forts, in an interesting twist, five of the sixty-five *posuban* are modeled after heavily armed European warships (fig. 5).

Despite their flamboyant appearance, *posuban* serve several important functions: *asafo* meetings, funerals and festivals center on them (fig. 6). Company gods are located in or on the *posuban* and are ritually acknowledged at prescribed times throughout the year with offerings, blood sacrifices and prayers. The large majority of shrines lack sufficient interior space to accommodate human activities, but many companies use this restricted area for storing such regalia as drums, flags and uniforms. In addition to the above, *posuban* also serve as civic monuments. Common responses by the Fante to the question, "Why do you build *posuban*?" include: "It's important to the town," and "To show strangers."

Enhancing the architectural metaphor of *posuban* as fort, the single most common image found on them is cannons and/or cannon balls. Four monuments even have real cannons salvaged from the old European forts. Over half of the *posuban* have one or more images of past or present company leaders, usually dressed in a traditional amulet-laden warshirt (fig. 7). Unlike much *asafo* imagery, the cannons and company officers are straightforward representations and rarely have conventionalized verbal referents. A discussion of the sculptural program of one particularly rich *posuban* will help suggest the wide range of proverbial imagery found on these shrines.

"Man-of-war" *posuban* at Saraafa Aboano built in 1931.

Warship *posuban* of Number 6 Company, Anomabu, built in 1952 and photographed during annual Atranbir festival.

Asafo shrine from Gomoa Asikuma built ca. 1959 and displaying lion images and a figure of the company's senior officer.

The Fante town of Legu has two *asafo* companies (No. 1 and No. 2) and the intense rivalry between them is evident in the artistic one-upmanship that characterizes their shrine building. The monument of Number 2 Company (fig. 8) was officially "outdoored" or opened to the public on May 1, 1936, but most of the sculpture dates from the mid-1960s when the shrine was extensively remodeled. At the structure's front are two company leaders. The man on the horse was head of the company when the shrine was first built. This equestrian image, however, also represents a popular proverb: "If the horse is mad [crazy], the rider is not also mad," emphasizing the importance of strong leadership. Another named *asafohen* stands nearby holding a set of scales. Here again a proverb explains the meaning: "When you are going to fight, you must weigh your enemy." In other words, one must evaluate a situation before acting upon it. This idea of not underestimating your opponent is reiterated by the scales painted on the front with the Fante expression, "You must weigh war," underneath. Images of fishing canoes are also painted on the front and sides, emblematic of the town's main vocation.

Prominent on the four corners are nearly life-sized cement soldiers in World War II uniforms. Many Fante served in the Gold Coast Regiment, which fought in East Africa and Burma during the war. Upon their return European military uniforms joined the traditional warshirts as adornment for great warriors on the shrines. At the back of the *posuban* is a free-standing angel holding an open book. A concession to the company's Christian members, it is also representative of the eclectic Fante polytheism where "pagan" and Christian images are often found in the same shrine.

On one corner of the *posuban* behind a crouching soldier (fig. 9), a series of images illustrating five different proverbs is recessed in the wall. The clover leaf form at the top is "just decoration," but below it is a hand depicting the maxim, "Without the hand you cannot build," another aphorism stressing leadership. Underneath the hand is a two-headed winged "dragon" called alternately Funtum Yempa or *sasabonsam*. It is considered a clever all-powerful but evil bush spirit; "It can fly, it can dig in the ground, it can go anywhere." The *asafo* attach a rather long but conventionalized saying to this creature: "You think that this animal is going to do a bad thing. He thinks in secret that he is doing it. When you meet him he will have done it." Number 2 Company identifies with Funtum Yempa and is telling its rival that even if they anticipate No. 2's power, there is nothing that can be done to counter it. A second saying for the same image is more succinct: "Will you fly or will you vanish," i.e. whatever you do, you cannot

Posuban of Number 2 Company, Legu, built in 1936 and renovated in the mid 1960s.

Detail of Legu Number 2 Company shrine showing WW II soldier and series of proverbial motifs.

escape from No. 2.

The next image, a lizard, represents the proverb: "If the lizard has built the house, the mouse should not move in." This argues that rivals should not live off the fruits of Number 2 Company's labors. To the right of the lizard is a man with a bow and arrow aiming at a chameleon whose presence is implied but not represented. Its message is: "If you move too quickly you will be hit, if you move too slowly you will be hit." demonstrating that things should be done in the proper way at the proper speed. Finally at the bottom of this group are two men flanking a flag pole on a mound. The *asafo* say: "If all animals come out to show the flag [a euphemism for any *asafo* event], but the mouse is absent, then nobody is able to show the flag." This image emphasizes that everyone is important and that unity leads to success.

Returning to the front of the shrine, on the seond level is a woman seated in front of a *warri* board, a common West African game. The woman is head of the company's female contigent, and she is challenging Number 1 Company to beat her at the game. Competitive games like cards, draughts, and *warri* are frequently used by the *asafo* as a metaphor for war and to assert the prowess of one company over another. Two yellow and two green lions (the colors of No. 2) also adorn the upper level. Lions are the emblems of No. 2 while leopards represent No. 1. Number 2 Company says simply: "A dead lion is greater than a living leopard," suggesting that No. 2 at its worst is better than No. 1 at its best. Cement cannons and cannon balls and a sword with two blades are emblems of the company's military might, as are the vertically arranged dumbbell-shaped motifs. The latter show how cannon balls are made; the company claims, "If you take our weapons away, we can still make more." Lining the arches on the upper level is a plant called *brebia,* a common vine that covers many of Ghana's tallest trees. The *asafo* say they are like this vine and can conquer any problem.

At the top of the monument is an elephant with its trunk around a palm tree. At Legu the interpretation varies from those previously outlined: "If the elephant fells the palm, only the elephant can tap it for palm wine," another warning that one cannot take advantage of someone else's labors (cf. the lizard on the same shrine). The importance of palm wine, often called "war medicine" by the Fante, is reinforced by the palm wine pots on the four corners of the shrine.

In spite of the cement sculptures' shrine context, their subject matter is entirely secular. Most of the above sayings are not just *asafo* esoterica, but rather they are integral parts of everyday language. For example, "Will you fly or will you vanish," might be used to tell a child that he cannot escape his chores and responsibilities. "If the horse is mad, the rider is not also mad," demonstrates that others are not to be blamed for one's own fate. The image of a cock found on several shrines prompts a proverb often quoted in disputes over loans: "One does not buy a cock so it may crow in another's town."[7] The "portability" of the verbal messages associated with *asafo* arts extends the life of the sculptured forms. It increases the visibility of the imagery and makes it even more of a "popular" art.

An examination of the most common images on *asafo* shrines reveals diverse sources. Many motifs, however, are either a direct or indirect product of the British colonial presence. The creation of *posuban* in imitation of the European forts complete with cannons is the most obvious example. Warships and airplanes (fig. 10) occupy a similar position as instruments of military power along with European soldiers, naval officers, Native Authority Police and contemporary policemen. Other motifs are less obvious examples of British influence.

At first thought a lion, the third most common motif (found on 31 shrines), would seem to be an indigenous image (fig. 11). Yet the lion is principally a grassland feline and has always been rare in the heavily forested ecology of the Fante, and indeed of most Akan states. On the other hand the forest dwelling leopard (found on 16 shrines) is relatively common in the environment. This ecological fact is reflected in language. The Akan word for lion, *gyata,* is a loan word from the Mande, who live in the grasslands northwest of Ghana, while the word for leopard, *osebo,* is indigenous.[8] Understandably there are far fewer Akan proverbs about the lion than about the leopard, approximately one to four in Christaller's 1879 compendium of 3,600 proverbs.[9]

The lion and its relationship to the leopard in Fante art poses an intriguing problem. Lions are rare, if not nonexistent, in older Fante and Akan art forms such as *kuduo* and goldweights, while the leopard is probably the single most common mammal in both these object types.[10] Since the production of both *kuduo* and goldweights ceased around 1900 it would seem that the lion was a latecomer to the iconology of Fante art. Nevertheless today the lion is seen as superior to its spotted brother in the only two proverbs where they appear together: "A dead lion is greater than a living leopard"; and "Only a lion can drink from the palm wine pot of the leopard." Yet if the lion is a more potent power symbol than the leopard, why doesn't it occur in the older art forms? The answer lies in the nature of its relatively recent introduction.

It is clear that the British did not introduce the lion to the Fante,

Airplane on *posuban* at Tantum built in 1920.

Detail of lion, cannons, and *brebia* on shrine at Enyan Denkyira erected in 1950.

but it is equally certain that they were instrumental in popularizing its use. The Akan had a pronounced fascination with European heraldry and reproduced heraldic arms and compositional devices on indigenous chairs, combs, drums and other objects. The lion, of course, is by far the most popular common charge in European heraldry and is found on both the British and Dutch royal arms. These arms were ubiquitous symbols of European authority among the crowns' representatives in West Africa. Lions, however, were found in numerous other colonial contexts including the entryways to forts; military and naval banners, ships' figureheads; buttons on military uniforms; Victorian chairs; door knockers; ships' catheads; and numerous trade items. Without question the lion was the single most pervasive symbol of European power on the Gold Coast. Considering the Fante penchant for adopting European power symbols like forts and cannons, the popularity of the "European" lion is understandable.

The lion is not the only image borrowed from European heraldry. The unicorns on a *posuban* at Obohen (fig. 12) recall the unicorn on the British royal arms, but more significantly it was also on the crest of the Swanzy family, owners of one of the most prosperous trading companies on the coast. The unicorn was used as a trademark and could be found on most of the company's goods, e.g. stamped on cloth and embossed or engraved on brassware. Today the unicorn remains the symbol of the United Africa Company, commercial heir to F. & A. Swanzy Ltd.

Lions in various heraldic attitudes were also used as emblems by several West African commercial interests. In nonliterate societies like the Fante, heraldic crests and trademarks play an intensified role in establishing corporate identities. Company symbols adorned trading premises, identified their cargo ships and marked items sold by the company. Businesses were generally 'known by their symbols and were identified as "house of the lion," or "house of the unicorn" rather than by their more unmanageable (for the African) European names.[11]

Other relatively common heraldic images found on *asafo* shrines are less easily traceable to specific sources. Mermaids, found at Kormantine, Elmina and Saraafa Aboano (fig. 5) are widely dispersed images in West Africa and are conventionally called "Mammy Wata." Perhaps this motif was ultimately derived from figureheads of ships that plied coastal waters in earlier times.[12] The origin of the griffin at Lowtown, Saltpond, is unexplained. Still, so there is no confusion over its identity, the word "griffin" is modeled in relief below the image, though few can read it. The eagle is another suspect motif. They are relatively common on *posuban*,

(a or b) *Posuban* at Obohen constructed ca. 1945 with sculptures of unicorns added in the late 1960s.

however, though extremely rare in Fante proverbs and folklore. Significantly the eagle is the single most common bird in European heraldry and it is often found with multiple heads as are many Fante eagles. The various images of Funtum Yempa or *sasabonsam* are also suspiciously similar to certain heraldic monsters like the cockatrice, wyvern and griffin, although this may simply be an example of convergence.

The popularity of the elephant and palm tree motif was also probably enhanced by British colonialism. The British adopted the image of an elephant in profile standing in front of a palm as their symbol for the Gold Coast Colony. This emblem was repeated on mass-produced medals given to friendly chiefs and on messenger staffs identifying the official representatives of those chiefs. Perhaps more importantly the image is also found on British forts. At least one *asafo* shrine uses the British composition rather than the traditional Fante image of an elephant with its trunk wrapped around the palm and most *asafo* groups associate both scenes with the British.

Two other common *asafo* motifs are a product of European inputs—the padlock and the key and the clock. The symbolic use of locks and keys by the Fante was documented as early as 1602 when de Maress wrote, "Although they have but few Chests or Cupboards, yet they hang Keies at their Girdles because it makes a faire shew."[13] In the hands of Europeans, padlocks kept people alternately in or out of an area. They were instruments that brought either freedom or slavery, thus their power was very real. The *asafo* use representations of locks and keys to symbolically assert their own power in a town or state. They say: "We are the lock and key of the state, no one can move before we do, no decisions can be made without our consent." The chains found on several *posuban* are part of this same imagery.

Clocks are also power symbols related to behavior manipulation. Life in coastal towns was regulated in part by Western ideas of "doing things on time." Temporal intervals were marked by the raising of flags, firing of cannon and ringing of bells. It became clear to the Fante that the people who controlled time also controlled people. On *asafo* shrines nonfunctional clocks represent this same kind of power. The specific times at which they are permanently set vary from shrine to shrine. Several groups said their time marked either the start or finish of an important victory, therefore enhancing the identification with power.

Christianity provides one final class of colonial imputs to *asafo* arts. A figure of Jesus occurs on the two shrines at Apam in the not-too-Biblical pose of Christ blessing the *asafo* company. One or more angels are found on four different *posuban,* generally representing "God's messengers." The stereotypic Christian devil frequently merges with heraldic monsters and the traditional Funtum Yempa or *sasabonsam* in a fabulous multiheaded hybrid with wings, pointed tail, trident and horns, among other attributes. This is the all-seeing, all-powerful bush spirit previously discussed. Finally, in an isolated but startling example, a scene of Adam and Eve with the apple tree proclaims that Asafo Number 4 Company, Elmina is the "Wombir" (original) company of that town.[14]

British-inspired imagery tends to lack the rich proverbial referents associated with indigenous motifs. Still, these colonialisms were widely dispersed among the Fante. When translated from a colonial context to an *asafo posuban* they take on an iconic flavor that symbolically replicates the power of the British.

Still the importance of European politically oriented motifs should not be exaggerated. As humble an object as a glass bottle may inspire *asafo* designs. Purely ornamental images of clubs (as on playing cards) are found on a number of shrines and were borrowed from the contemporary brew called Club Beer. A stork on the *posuban* at Gomoa Tarkwa was copied from an embossed trademark on a bottle of Royal Stork Gin. At Gomoa Debiso a cement beer bottle stands next to a similar representation of a palm wine pot. Here a proverb explains the meaning: "Nothing in the world can conquer beer, but palm wine can conquer it," suggesting that traditional objects and values are superior to their modern replacements while at the same time arguing that the Debiso *asafo* company is superior to their more corrupt neighbors. Another common *asafo* motif shows a glass bottle with termites attacking it. The Fante says: "The termite can eat anything, except the bottle," i.e. everyone has his match.

Acculturated motifs aside, images with an entirely indigenous base are as much a part of Fante popular culture as those from external sources. Before examining a few more examples of the former, the second major art form of the Fanta *asafo* should be introduced. Flags (*franka*) are the portable, kinetic counterparts of the cement *posuban.* While there are only sixty-one monumental *posuban* in Fanteland, there may be as many as 3,000 *asafo* flags with an average per company somewhere between twenty to twenty-five flags.

The typical *asafo* flag is about four by six feet and is both machine and hand appliqued from common cotton trade cloth. The principal reason for the creation of a new flag is the installation of an *asafo* captain. The new officer must commission and pay for the new flag which then enters the collective property of the company. New motifs must be publically approved by the paramount chief of the state (fig. 13) and by the *tufohen* or general of the combined *asafo* companies to insure that the prerogatives of another company are not violated. New flags may also be made to replace old and tattered examples or to modernize dated motifs, for example, replacing a square-rigged man-of-war with a World War II destroyer. Old flags, regardless of condition, are retained to honor past events and deceased elders and to validate prized colors, cloths and emblems.

Flags are displayed at most major festivals, at the installation of new officers and at the funerals of company members. Methods of display vary. Most companies have a flagpole on or near their *posuban* from which one flag is flown. In some locations a series of flags is strung clothesline-style through the company area. But the principal means of display is by specially trained flag dancers in elaborately choreographed performances (fig. 14).

Flags, like many elements of the *posuban,* were ultimately borrowed from European traditions of military display; and, of course, flags were prominent on all the coastal forts. The colorful parade of regimental banners, naval designs and national flags that saturated the coast of Ghana through most of its five hundred year contact with Europe provided an impressive stimulus for flag production. Locally-made flags have a documented history of nearly three hundred years on the coast of Ghana.[15] Certainly the *asafo* tradition as we know it today was fully developed by 1859 as indicated in a letter written by the mayor of Cape Coast Castle:

When making their grand customs, each company, if it has no quarrel with any others, passes through the various quarters of the town with its original 'company flag,' but when there is a desire to convey defiance or insult, a company, in passing through the quarter inhabited by the company whom it is desired to annoy, will there display a flag having some device ostentatiously offensive.[16]

Contemporary flags display many of the same motifs found on military shrines. For example, the armed females in figures 15 and 16 both prompted the standardized saying: "If our women prepare for war, what will our men do?" Rather than portending a feminist resurrection, the *asafo* companies are telling their audiences that, if our women are so powerful and well-armed, just imagine how much more powerful our men will be. Again, *asafo* chauvinism is the reigning theme. The elephant with its trunk around a palm is also a common motif in both genres (fig. 2). In this example it is paired with a second proverb/image of a bird perched on the head of a man.

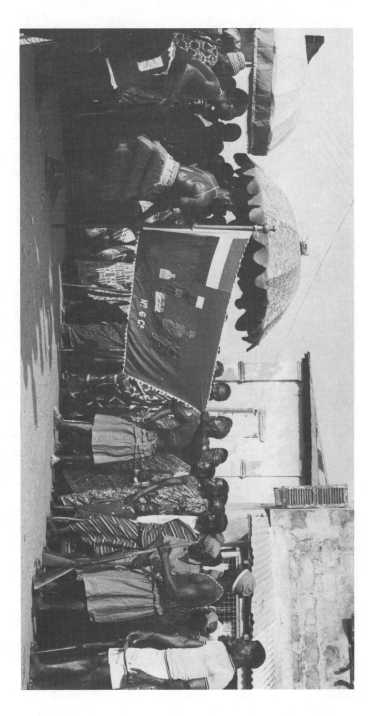

New flag of Anomabu Number 6 Company presented for approval to the paramount chief.

Flag dancer at Legu.

Detail of armed female warrior on shrine of Asafo Number 1 Company, Abeadze Dominase, outdoored in 1974 and representing the saying: "If our women prepare for war, what will our men do?"

Flag motif of Number 6 Company, Anomabu, illustrating same saying as fig. 15.

The Fante say: "If you see an unusual occurrence, something unusual must have initiated it." The unusual occurrence here is a bird on a man's head; the unusual cause for this is the elephant pulling down all the trees in the forest. This image reminds the *asafo* to look for the reasons behind the strange behavior of others. The man with the walking stick is telling the above story.

In addition to the smaller flags, appliqued banners up to three hundred feet long are found in many Fante towns. On select occasions these are either strung on tall poles or paraded in a snake-like procession through the town. At Ekumfi Esaakyir a 260 foot banner features thirty different motifs drawn from the same corpus of images found on the shrines and smaller flags., A few examples will suffice. The monkey moving from one tree to another (fig. 17) illustrates: "A monkey leaps only as far as it can reach," or as we say in the Western world, "Don't bite off more than you can chew." The house cat confronting four mice (fig. 18) elicits the expression: "The mouse can never put its hand into the sack that hangs around the neck of the cat." The cat naturally represents the owners of the flag and the mice stand for a rival company. The headless fish with a circle of flies (fig. 19) depicts: "Though flies eat any kind of fish, they will not touch the salted fish." The salted fish is the Esaakyir *asafo* which is not bothered by rival companies (flies).

Detail of Ekumfi Esaakyir banner depicting the proverb: "The monkey leaps only as far as it can reach."

Drawing from Ekumfi Esaakyir banner of the maxim: The mouse can never put its hand into the sack that hangs around the cat's neck.

Proverb from Ekumfi Esaakyir banner illustrating: "Though flies eat any kind of fish, they will not eat salted fish."

Although cement shrines and appliqued flags are the most visible art forms of the Fante *asafo,* they are by no means the only ones. Costuming, singing, drumming and dancing extend most of the same imagery into a mutually reinforcing theater of bravura. At the same time the serious, often militant imagery of *asafo* is tempered by expressions of many basic social values. Additionally there is a certain playfulness—a tongue-in-cheek social banter—in the subject matter that encourages group identification and comraderie, much like the songs and emblems of American college fraternities. *Asafo* arts are escalating in popularity and they will continue to evolve in an ongoing mix of the modern and the traditional. In many ways they are as much a catalyst for the continuing evolution of the institution as they are a product of that institution.

Notes

[1]The research on which this paper was based was conducted in Ghana during varying

periods of 1974-76 and 1978. All quotations not otherwise attributed were taken directly from translations of recorded interviews. The author would like to thank B.A. Firempong of the Institute of African Studies, University of Ghana, and Dr. Yaw Boateng for invaluable help in transcribing the tapes. Michael Emerson executed the drawings of the Esaakyir flag. Special thanks go to Dr. Herbert M. Cole, University of California, Santa Barbara, who provided essential insights into the workings of *asafo.*

²As in most of West Africa, reliable population statistics are unavailable. The figure provided here can only be considered an estimate. The situation is complicated by the fact that scholars disagree on exactly which states are Fante and which represent other Akan groups. The twenty-one states covered in the research are identifed as Fante because they exhibit the well-developed complex of *asafo* arts and attendant rituals that are generaly acknowledged to exist only among the Fante.

³The most complete discussion of the structure and function of Fante *asafo* is found in James Christensen, *Double Descent Among the Fante* (New Haven: Human Relations Area Files, 1954).

⁴An extended discussion of the role of proverbs in Fante society is provided by James Christensen, "The Role of Proverbs in Fante Culture," *Africa,* 28 (1958), 232-43. The importance of the verbal-visual nexus of Akan art is outlined in Herbert Cole and Doran Ross, *The Arts in Ghana* (Los Angeles: UCLA Museum of Cultural History, 1978), 9-12.

⁵The only previously published discussions of *asafo* arts are: Arthur ffoulkes, "The Company System in Cape Coast Castle," *Journal of the African Society,* 7 (1907/1908), 261-77; George Preston, "Perseus and Medusa in Africa: Military Art in Fanteland 1834-1972," *African Arts,* 8, No. 3 (1975), 36-41, 68-71; and Cole and Ross, pp. 186-207.

⁶The date for the earliest conclusively documented *posuban* was listed as 1888 in Cole and Ross, p. 187, fig. 365 for the shrine at Abandzi. This was based on interviews with the company elders. Subsequent research has uncovered an early photograph of this monument with the 1883 date clearly painted on the front.

⁷Christensen, "Role of Proverbs," p. 234.

⁸Ivor Wilks, "The Mande Loan Element in Twi," *Ghana Notes and Queries,* No. 4 (1962), 27.

⁹Johan Gottlieb Christaller, *A Collection of Three Thousand Six Hundred Tshi Proverbs* (Basel: Basel Evangelical Missionary Society, 1879). Christaller's work is entirely in the vernacular. A translation of 830 of these proverbs can be found in Robert Rattray, *Ashanti Proverbs* (Oxford: Clarendon Press, 1914).

¹⁰*Kuduo* are cast brass containers used for a variety of ritual purposes and for storing valuables. Goldweights are also cast of brass and are used as counterbalances in the weighing of gold. They are cast in an enormous range of figurative shapes representing most of the animals and plants important to the Akan as well as numerous genre scenes. The number of existing goldweights is several million and they form one of West Africa's most fascinating popular arts.

¹¹Frederick Pedler, *The Lion and the Unicorn in Africa* (London: Heinemann, 1974), 218-19.

¹²Jill Salmons, "Mammy Wata," *African Arts,* 10, No. 3 (1977), 13. Salmons' article elaborates on the role of Mammy Wata in the popular culture of southern Nigeria.

¹³Pieter de Marees, *A Description and Historical Declaration of the Golden Kingdom of Guinea,* in *Purchas His Pilgrims,* ed. Samuel Purchas (Glasgow: Maclehose, 1905), 171.

¹⁴The same artists who create *posuban* make similar images for a variety of contemporary Christian shrines. The militant subject matter in the sculpture of both make an instructive comparison. See Paul Breidenbach and Doran Ross, "The Holy Place: Twelve Apostles Healing Gardens," *African Arts,* 11, No. 4 (1978), 28-35.

¹⁵In 1693 Thomas Phillips visited an Akan general who had captured the Danish fort at Christiansborg and observed, "The flag he was flying was white with a black man painted in the middle brandishing a scymiter," Thomas Phillips, *Journal of a Voyage Made in the Hannibal of London, Ann. 1693, 1694, from England ... to Guinea,* in *Churchill's Collection of Voyages and Travels,* ed. Awnsham Churchill (London: n.p., 1752) vol. VI, 228.

¹⁶J. Mensah Sarbah, *Fanti Customary Laws* (London: William Clowes, 1897), 14.

Popular Culture Methodologies: A Bibliographic Afterword

Fred E.H. Schroeder

Before discussing methodology some remarks about the purposes of academic study of popular culture are necessary.

Underlying all academic study lies a simple cause—curiosity—and a simple end—the satisfaction of curiosity. These are simple, but not necessarily lacking in profoundness,for while curiosity may be a characteristic that we humans share with cats and monkeys, in human beings the range of curiosity is endless, and the objects of curiosity include such matters as why we behave as we do and what is the purpose and nature of human existence. Philosophers and theologians make a practice of addressing these questions directly; everyday humans ordinarily are confronted by them only in moments of crisis. For academic scholars in the humanities and social sciences, the profound philosophical questions probably underlie all studies as a "deep structure" but all too often are obscured by details, side-issues, and elaborate methodologies. Moreover, academic minds tend not to address the large questions wholly, but in parts that are closest to their own particular areas of curiosity.

The large question in popular culture is to ask: "What is the meaning and value of everyday life?" To put it another way, we are saying: today I ate a meal, read a newspaper, paid a sales tax, watched a television show—so what? who cares? For if these things mean nothing, if they are of no value, why then, it would appear that our own existence as human beings is without meaning or value. William Shakespeare projected this ordinary problem of making sense of one's life into the extraordinary life of Macbeth, who, after a period of participation in uncommon events such as we meet in history books, concluded that humans are no more than actors in a tale told by an idiot, full of sound and fury, and signifying nothing. If this is true of Macbeth's achievements and failures in international affairs and in controlling destiny, what of *our* commonplace yesterdays, todays and tomorrows?

Essentially, therefore, popular culture studies are not coolly objective, regardless of how academic their manner may be. They

319

are attempts to make meaning out of everyday existence. And overall, their method is to take the commonplace, the anonymous, the trivial, the everyday, and apply to them the same degree of serious attention that has been given to masterworks, to leaders and to great events. In this book the method has been applied to older and remote societies in a more-or-less conscious effort to show that just as the everyday live of people of the past signified something—if we look with care and sympathy against the backdrops of universal concerns and major trends—so our lives may have value too. Such, then, is the broadest method of popular culture study; and such is the major justification in answer to the challenges of *so what* and *who cares*.

Usually, however, when we inquire into "method" in a discipline we are not looking for such cosmic ideals. Rather we are looking for a critical, analytical approach, a rigorous framework for the research and presentation of findings. My own graduate training, for example, was in a relatively new area called American Studies. For two decades and more, American studies has been asking itself what is its "method." The exercise has been fruitless, but not necessarily useless. Theoretical disquisitions and methodological dogma can be useful starting points, so long as the quest for abstract perfection does not hinder action. Thus, my own view is that methodology should be regarded as existential and eclectic. By existential I mean that if curiosity presents a question, the "method" is in the doing, not in the talking about the doing: the question will imply some sort of means toward answering the question. For example, if the question is of the variety of "I wonder when," historical methods are implied; if the question is of the variety of "I wonder why," we are likely to be picking and choosing among several approaches that depend upon the rest of the question. Sometimes a psychological approach is indicated, as when we ask why people resisted a given religious movement. Most often, though, several methods must be drawn upon, and we may need an art historian's analytical tools, an anthropologist's functional explanations, a historian's evolutionary narrative, and so on. For these reasons, I ascribe to eclecticism.

Social scientists are more given to theorizing about methodology than are most other people. Partly, I suppose, this is due to the incredible complexity of human affairs, where social groups are made up of individuals who have unconscious as well as conscious lives, and where the network of influences from the environment, from outside groups and from historical traditions is infinitely variable. Regardless of the cause, it is the case that most of the methodological theories that relate to popular culture derive from the social sciences. Before alluding to some of these, and directing the reader to places where they can be examined more carefully, I would like to reemphasize my plea for eclecticism, because much of the concern about "method" in popular culture studies is "academic."

Academic, that is, in the sense of being impractically theoretical, as well as being a serious matter of scholarship and learning. In respect to the first sense of "academic" a great deal of discussion about method is directed toward finding *The Method,* a universally applicable philosopher's stone that is presumed to exist in the natural sciences. It doesn't. Further, concern about method is often defensive rhetoric rather than practical process. The rationalization behind this rhetoric seems to be that new fields of study are under attack from conventional disciplines, and that they can earn dignity in the world of scholarship by expounding high-flown theories in arcane tongues.

Nevertheless, methodology *is* a serious matter, especially for students and researchers who have encountered questions, problems and topics that suddenly or unexpectedly place them in unfamiliar or uncharted territory of popular culture. This can occur to persons who have been trained in the humanistic disciplines, where methodological emphasis has been placed almost exclusively upon methods of explaining *greatness, uniqueness* and *influentiality* rather than *popularity, typicality* and *reflexiveness.* The tools that equip one for dealing with Phidias, Virgil and Aquinas are not well-suited for grafitti, jokebooks and apocryphal legends. For these, the conventional critical tools work quickly, almost immediately dismissing the popular phenomenon as commonplace, trivial, shallow and mistaken. Such judgments may be valid enough, but they are unproductive. The fact that something does not measure up to the highest established standards of aesthetic or logical consistency, or that it is not the first, last, best or only of its class does not erase its existence, nor controvert its possible significance in human affairs. A book that was written to propose a method for dealing with popular literature in a manner that avoids the superficiality of elitist criticism is John Cawelti's *Adventure, Mystery, Romance. Formula Stories as Art and Popular Culture* (University of Chicago Press, 1976). This has been quite influential among students of popular culture, and may have some applicability to earlier popular literary arts. Readers of Cawelti would do well to look into David N. Feldman's counter-proposal, "Formalism and Popular Culture" (*Journal of Popular Culture,* IX:2 Fall 1975, pp. 384-402), in which he maintains that the techniques of Russian *Formalism* are equally valid for "elite" and for popular literature. The Feldman article appears in a special issue of the *Journal of Popular Culture* (IX:2) containing many methodological and theoretical articles. All of these tend to emphasize the modern media and none are specifically directed toward ancient or medieval cultures, but the article by Joseph Arpad, a folklorist, draws to some extent upon the theories of Claude Levi-Strauss and clearly shows relevance to pre-literate and non-literate societies. The brief article by Michael Real, a cultural anthropologist, was something of a preview of his book, *Mass-Mediated Culture* (Prentice-Hall, 1977). Throughout *Mass-Mediated Culture*, Real provides a variety of theories and methods drawn from cultural anthropology, from communications theory and from sociology. Two particularly lucid bibliographic and methodological articles on structuralism appeared in the 1978 bibliographic issue of *American Quarterly* (XXX:3, pp. 261-297): both John G. Blair's "Structuralism and the Humanities" and David Pace's "Structuralism and the Social Sciences" refer specifically to the analyses of popular culture by Roland Barthe, Vladimir Popp and others.

At this point, I may appear to be straying from the problems of applying specifically humanistic critical tools to popular arts. The overlap with social sciences is impossible to separate, and, of course, many recent practices in the humanities and arts have moved away from traditional methods of validating and evaluating elite cultural products. Nevertheless, the predominant critical techniques in the humanities are of limited value in analyzing popular phenomena. "New Critical" studies are almost useless for literature that does not aspire to individuality; biographical studies are virtually meaningless to anonymous or corporate productions. The same can be said of similar approaches to visual and plastic arts, but we might add that the current modes of abstract formal criticism, of identifying avant-garde new departures and of detailed analyses of creative geniuses are not very helpful to gaining understanding of mass-replicated and unconscious arts. Study of the performing arts shares many of the elitist and evaluative biases, but this is compounded by the fact that recording of actual performances was almost impossible until this century, and few popular performances were documented in writing or drawings. Methodologically, humanistic criticism and scholarship of the popular arts has been at its most comprehensive in historical approaches, that is, in the documentation and chronological ordering of the succession of movements, styles, technologies and fads in the various genres. Among these, the acknowledged history of American popular arts is Russel B. Nye's *The Unembarrassed Muse: The Popular Arts in America* (Dial, 1970). More germaine to the interests of this anthology is Peter Burke's *Popular Culture in Early Modern Europe* (New York University Press and Harper Torchbook, 1978). Burke, dealing with the period from about 1500-1800 found it necessary to invent a variety of methods of reconstruction from fragments, traditions, negative evidence and so on. The methodological chapters and the extensive bibliography are highly recommended.

Burke's book is the first reference that is directed at earlier and preliterate societies. The art historian Alan Gowans in a seminal article in the *Journal of Popular Culture* entitled "Popular Arts and the Historic Artifact: New Principles for Studying History in Art" (VII:2, Fall, 1973, 466-483) attacked the current critical schools as being irrelevant and dangerously twentieth-centric and provided a clear set of usable universal principles for looking at art with an historical eye. The term "popular culture" as a broadly inclusive generic is only about a decade old, and so some of the better methodological books are not indexed as such. George Kubler's *The Shape of Time. Remarks on the History of Things* (Yale University Press, 1962) is one of these. Starting with a cogent criticism of the limitations and distortions of contemporary art history methods, Kubler constructs a theory and method that is applicable to *all* man-made things, and that recognizes the multistranded complexity of human artifacts in the historical continuum.

Turning from methodologies that are outgrowths of the arts to those that have developed from the social sciences, it is worth noting that the social sciences are not so immobilized by deeply ingrained patterns of elitist thought. Still, when we are looking back into time (a thing that the humanities are superbly equipped to do) the social science methods that depend upon statistical data, sampling and probability are often inapplicable because of lack of evidence, or because they require interpretive and projective leaps that, while reasonable—or at least stimulating—are otherwise methodological masquerades of statistical approaches. This is said as a caution, however, not as an opposition; provocative studies of this sort are appearing with increasing frequency. *The Journal of Social History* contains many articles of this type. At present, the emphasis is on the eighteenth and nineteenth centuries in Europe and North America, but this appears to be more an accident of contributions than an exclusive limit set by editorial policy.

Another outgrowth of social sciences is in the behavioral fields of psychoanalysis and culture. Psychoanalysis, which presumes some degree of universality in human affairs, is at once applicable to high and low forms of expression, and to the past as well as to the present. Although sometimes carried to cultish extremes of overinterpretation, at other times it opens whole areas of popular life that have otherwise been ignored, such as we find in Lloyd DeMause's collection on *The History of Childhood* (Harper Torchbook, 1974). These are excellent examples of the problems and the possibilities of working from limited, fragmentary and covert sources. *The Journal of Social History,* incidentally, has also shown considerable interest in the history of childhood, as well as of the family and of sexual behavior. It should be noted that relatively few of these articles are tied to psychoanalytic theories. For a brilliant demonstration of the application of psychoanalysis to such a humanistic discipline as art history, Walter Abell's *The Collective Dream in Art* (Harvard University Press, 1957; Schocken Paperback 1966), is recommended. Subtitled "A Psycho-Historical Theory of Culture Based on Relations Between the Arts, Psychology and the Social Sciences," this book like Kubler's, is a strong warning against the tunnel-vision of separated disciplinary views of the past. Finally, a book that might elude students of popular culture because of its ostensible subject is Daniel F. McCall's *Africa in Time-Perspective: A Discussion of Historical Reconstruction from Unwritten Sources* (Oxford University Press, 1969). McCall is an anthropologist; the book is a statement of informed common sense, including not only such disciplines as archaeology and folklore, but ethno-botany and ethno-zoology as well. Many of McCall's examples are drawn from classical, medieval and Islamic history, and he is conscious of preliteracy throughout. In this, as with all the books and articles I have mentioned, it should go without saying that the bibliographies multiply this list of methodological resources by a large factor.

Readers of this essay will surely note some major omissions. It would be better to ascribe these to my personal ignorance than to oversight or intolerance. However, I have attempted to limit this list to works that are consciously dealing with popular culture and not with general social or aesthetic theories. I might also admit to some prejudices of a conservative sort. Undoubtedly, there is a tendency among students of popular culture to look for methodologies in various modern theoretical schools. Thus, one finds frequent references to such seminal theorists as Northrop Frye, Marshall McLuhan, Claude Levi-Straus, Carl Jung, Ernst Cassirer and others in books and articles on popular culture methodologies. It should be borne in mind, however, that a great deal of significant work is done along the more conventional lines of the disciplines.

Traditional historical methods are indicated when one is inquiring into causes of social events and cultural expression, or the evolution and development of certain phenomena. Similarly, literature and the visual arts have established traditions for the analysis of style, structure, theme and variation. In sociology and anthropology, various means of inquiring into the social function of cultural behaviors and artifacts are well established and presumed to be common knowledge. Oddly, the conventional methods are not so easily found out as modern "doctrinal" approaches. Often the conventional methods become second-nature to specialists in each discipline, who thereupon suppose that these ingrained methodologies are common sense; yet the very questions that each discipline regards as signficant and legitimate are only customary to the discipline, not universal to humanity. That is why the challenges of "so what" and "who cares" are reasonable and justifiable. Our purposes and methods are not necessarily patently clear.

Ultimately, methodology is a means to an end, and the end must be more important than the means. True, there is intellectual delight in exercising a new methodology, in carrying an argument beyond the edge of convention, in dazzling our colleagues with brilliant command of a multitude of disciplines, in building an unassailable case of fact or theory; but if all is spent on a question "that is so derivative as to become unintelligible, the same thing may be said for all of us, that we do not admire what we do not understand." The commonplaces that are the stuff of popular culture are as Marianne Moore said of the raw stuff of poetry: "These things are important not because a high-sounding interpretation can be put upon them but because they are useful."